Planning and Organizing Standards-Based Differentiated Instruction

Second Edition

Planning and Organizing Standards-Based Differentiated Instruction

Second Edition

Carolyn Chapman

Rita King

CORWIN

A SAGE Company

CORWIN
A SAGE Company

FOR INFORMATION:

Corwin

A SAGE Company

2455 Teller Road

Thousand Oaks, California 91320

(800) 233-9936

www.corwin.com

SAGE Publications Ltd.

1 Oliver's Yard

55 City Road

London EC1Y 1SP

United Kingdom

SAGE Publications India Pvt. Ltd.

B 1/I 1 Mohan Cooperative Industrial Area

Mathura Road, New Delhi 110 044

India

SAGE Publications Asia-Pacific Pte. Ltd.

3 Church Street

#10-04 Samsung Hub

Singapore 049483

Printed in the United States of America

A catalog record of this book is available from the Library of Congress.

ISBN: 978-1-4522-9959-4

This book is printed on acid-free paper.

SFI label applies to text stock

Acquisitions Editor: Jessica Allan

Editorial Assistant: Cesar Reyes

Production Editor: Libby Larson

Copy Editor: Megan Granger

Typesetter: C&M Digitals (P) Ltd.

Proofreader: Dennis W. Webb

Indexer: Judy Hunt

Cover Designer: Candice Harman

13 14 15 16 17 10 9 8 7 6 5 4 3 2 1

Contents

Acknowledgments

Thank you to Jim Chapman, Carolyn's husband, for his ceaseless support, encouragement and ideas to keep us on track. Thank you to General Lee, Rita's golden retriever for his patience. We appreciate our families, friends, and colleagues who inspired and urged us on through the highs and lows of our endeavors.

A special thank you to Dr. James L. Herman, Tennessee's representative to the Partnership for Assessment of Readiness for College and Career (PARCC) and a trainer in the Common Core State Standards (CCSS). Dr. Herman endorsed our initial ideas for this guide and confirmed our belief that teachers must differentiate to teach the standards to all students.

We extend our gratitude to everyone at Corwin. Jessica Allan, the senior acquisitions editor, believed in our preliminary objectives, added to them and supported us throughout this project. Meg Granger, the copy editor, spent endless hours interpreting our notes and using her knowledge and skills to put it all together. We deeply appreciate the extraordinary expertise of Libby Larson, senior project editor. Her extensive organizational skills and attention to details guided the final stages of our book.

Thank you to educators who use our books as guides to differentiate instruction. Through the years they validated our strategies and activities as practical tools and techniques. Their encouraging and inspiring words gave us the impetus to create this resource for classroom teachers.

About the Authors

 **Carolyn Chapman** (on the left in photo) continues her life's goal as an international professional developer, leading conference keynoter, and well-known author to make a difference in the minds and hearts of educators and learners. She supports educators in their process of change for today's students. She has taught in kindergarten to college classrooms. Her interactive, practical, energetic, motivating presentations provide professional development opportunities that focus on challenging the mind to ensure success for learners of all ages.

Carolyn walks her walk and talks her talk to make a difference in the journey of learning in today's classrooms. She inspires educators to put excitement and quality in effective instruction. She is renowned for her expertise in many areas, including differentiated instruction, formative assessment, reading and writing strategies, multiple intelligences, and brain-compatible learning.

Carolyn has authored and coauthored many best-selling educational publications. The books include:

Differentiated Assessment Strategies: One Tool Doesn't Fit All, Differentiated Instructional Strategies for Reading in the Content Areas, Differentiated Instructional Strategies for Writing in the Content Areas, Differentiated Instructional Strategies: One Size Doesn't Fit All, Test Success in the Brain-Compatible Classroom, Multiple Assessments for Multiple Intelligences, Multiple Intelligences Through Centers and Projects, If the Shoe Fits . . . How to Develop Multiple Intelligences in the Classroom, Activities for the Differentiated Classroom and *Motivating Students: 25 Strategies to Light the Fire of Engagement.* Each publication demonstrates Carolyn's desire and determination to have an effective impact for educators and students. She may be contacted at cjchapman52@gmail.com.

Rita King (on the right in the photo above) is an international trainer, consultant, author, and keynote speaker. She served as the principal and director of the teacher-training program at Middle Tennessee State University's laboratory school and taught courses for the elementary and leadership departments. Rita has extensive experience as a teacher, administrator, and professional consultant and trainer in PreK–12 classrooms. The state of Tennessee recognized her as an Exemplary Educator.

Rita is coauthor, with Carolyn Chapman, of the following second-edition bestsellers: *Test Success in the Brain-Compatible Classroom, Differentiated Instructional Strategies for Reading in the Content Areas, Differentiated Instructional Strategies for Writing in the Content Areas, Differentiated Assessment Strategies: One Tool Doesn't Fit All,* and *Differentiated Management Strategies: Work Smarter, Not Harder.*

Rita's professional training and consulting sessions give educators innovative, engaging activities to develop students as self-directed, independent learners. Participants enjoy her dynamic presentations and practical strategies, which can be implemented immediately to improve instruction.

Rita's areas of expertise include differentiated instructional strategies, assessment, classroom management, and working with traditional or Common Core State Standards. She may be reached through King Learning Associates, Inc. at www.kinglearningassociates.com, by phone at (615) 848-8439, or via e-mail at kingrs@bellsouth.net.

1

Introduction

Oh, the many hats we wear daily as educators! We assume many roles to meet the unique needs of our students. We know that one hat does not fit everyone, because each individual comes to each learning segment with a unique bank of prior knowledge and experiences. We consider the learner's needs and choose the most appropriate style for each activity or event. In daily instruction, we wear a variety of hats. We need them to be appropriate, so we search for the right one!

Hats are worn for specific jobs and special occasions. For example, educators wear uniform hats as they carry out federal, state, and local curriculum mandates to address standards and learners' needs. These established guidelines provide a framework for expectations and responsibilities in each grade level. It is important for educators to become familiar with the uniform hats and have them accessible at all times to fulfill the requirements.

Differentiated instruction challenges educators to wear numerous hats daily as they adapt to the learners' unique needs. Most teachers have a large collection of comfortable hats, or favorite instructional approaches. Often the most comfortable instructional hat does not coordinate with a student's strengths or preferred learning styles. When this occurs, the teacher must wear an uncomfortable hat to reach the learner.

Responsive educators go to great lengths to find the right hat for the student to learn each standard. For example, when a struggling student is a visual learner and visual/spatial approaches are the teacher's weakness, the teacher needs to put on a glitzy hat and plan visual strategies for the learner.

Your authors have had extensive careers in teaching and administration. In recent years, we have worked internationally with districts and schools as professional developers, trainers, and consultants. We know teachers have limited time, resources, and energy to expend on designing differentiated instructional strategies and activities to teach each standard.

In this resource, we provide approaches, techniques, and ideas that are practical, cost free, and easy to implement or adapt in all grade levels to meet the learners' diverse needs.

■ STANDARDS-BASED INSTRUCTION

As we write this second edition, a majority of states have volunteered to adopt national or Common Core State Standards (CCSS). The impetus for this initiative was a major study identifying the standards students need for success in college and career (Conley, 2003). Some organizations and states are questioning the value of CCSS. We know this debate will continue into the future. We also realize that expectations or mandated standards will continue to be used as the benchmarks for learning and the framework for curriculum development. We believe that standards provide a blueprint for planning and teaching.

Teaching the Standards

Standards are the expectations or learning goals for each grade level, with precise criteria for mastery. The knowledge, concepts, and skills are defined and provide the "what" for instruction. Teachers have the privilege of guiding students to master each standard. They accomplish this feat by selecting the appropriate content material, choosing the best strategies, and identifying the most effective assessment tools for an individual or specific group of students.

The following information is presented as a practical guide to teaching the standards.

> *Know the standards.* Keep a list of the standards nearby while planning and teaching. Study the lists often so you know the instructional expectations. Familiarity with the standards makes it easier to strategically place them in daily instruction.

> *Chunk the standards.* Teach more than one standard in a lesson segment if they work together to make the lesson relevant and challenging. This step is similar to finding two jigsaw pieces that fit together perfectly.

> *Post the standard(s).* Post the standard(s) to address during instruction in a designated space so you and the students understand the lesson's goal(s).

> *Continually assess the learner's mastery level of the standard.* Monitor the learner's knowledge-base level in relation to his or her mastery of the standard. Plan interventions, grade level, and enrichment assignments as needed through active learning experiences.

> *Provide immediate feedback, if possible.* Give specific feedback with suggestions for improvement. Teach students how to use self-assessment strategies, checklists, and answer keys to accelerate the feedback process.

Use novel ways to teach the standards. Use motivating and intriguing learning experiences. Plan lessons with personally relevant tasks that give students control of their learning to enhance memory and recall of the standard.

Spiral the standards. Revisit the standards. Have you thoroughly taught a standard and realized later that the students did not remember it? Often, information is learned for a short time and forgotten. Spiral the standards using computer games, quick quizzes, station activities, and other activities as needed throughout the year. Remember the familiar adage, "If you don't use it, you lose it."

Provide personally meaningful application experiences with the standard. Apply the standard with examples from the students' daily lives. Often, students appear to understand a standard but fail in applying it later. This occurs because the learners did not have opportunities to reach the level of automaticity in using it. Plan application experiences that relate to the individuals' daily lives. Students must have personal experiences with the standard to take ownership of it.

The following chart, Figure 1.1, lists restrictions placed on teachers by mandates related to standards. It also emphasizes the autonomy teachers have to address standards using their professional expertise and judgment in creating productive learning experiences every day.

Figure 1.1 Empowering Autonomy

Standards mandate teachers to . . .	Standards empower teachers to . . .
Use standardized tests	Assess before, during, and after learning
Set expectations for each learner to perform at the mastery level on each standard	Plan differentiated instruction with motivating and customized strategies for each learner
Provide opportunities for students to model their thinking	Select a particular topic or unit to teach the standard(s)
Equip each learner with skills for critical/analytical thinking and problem-solving techniques	Use flexible grouping for optimal learning
Prepare each student to be successful in the world of work or college	Provide opportunities for students to model their thinking

As we continue the teaching and learning journey, using more innovative and productive practices, we must remember that our schools have become more effective each decade. Educators and invested entities continue to work diligently toward excellence so every learner will be successful. Hopefully, the recently formulated standards initiative will move us one more step in that direction.

■ USING DIFFERENTIATED INSTRUCTION

In the flagship book of our series, Gregory and Chapman (2012, p. x) provide the following explanation for differentiation: *Differentiation is a philosophy that enables teachers to plan strategically to reach the needs of diverse learners in classrooms today to achieve targeted standards.* To carry out this belief, teachers differentiate instruction to meet the individual's needs. Each lesson is based on the learner's assessment data related to the identified standard. Differentiated strategies, the "how" of instruction, are selected to deliver customized assignments and activities. This is a challenging and rewarding task.

The differentiation movement is making educators more aware of the need to reach the diverse needs of the classroom population. This idea has been discussed for centuries, but today, more than ever, educators are more successful in meeting this goal. They are improving because they have more assessment tools, instructional techniques, models, strategies, and resources. We have more multidimensional classrooms today. But with so many standards to address and personalized tasks occurring simultaneously, teachers need well-planned differentiated strategies to be successful.

■ WHAT ARE DIFFERENTIATED INSTRUCTIONAL STRATEGIES?

Differentiated instructional strategies are used to carry out the philosophy of differentiation. Teachers are expected to organize and customize instruction to provide the very best learning opportunities to address the targeted standard(s) for the student. Routines and rules are carefully selected or written to meet the learner's changing needs.

Teachers taking the first steps into differentiated instruction need to begin with small steps, choosing one or two strategies or activities to implement. Teachers currently using differentiated techniques can adapt the ideas to tweak their skills, reaffirm their beliefs in present approaches, add novel strategies, or put a new twist on old ways of doing things. After the target standard(s) are identified, use the checklists, charts, outlines, activities, and suggestions in this book to plan and organize differentiated instruction.

The keys to successful implementation of differentiated instructional strategies include the following:

- Selecting the standard(s) to teach
- Maintaining a comfortable, stimulating learning environment that instills in each student a desire to learn and improve
- Assessing students' individual needs before, during, and after learning

- Using assessment data to plan strategically with the most beneficial models, techniques, and strategies
- Selecting and organizing instructional activities for the total group, individuals, partners, and small groups

TEACHER JUDGMENT: CHOOSING THE APPROPRIATE HAT FOR THE OCCASION ■

Teacher judgment is a key to selecting the appropriate hat to wear for each instructional event. For example, after analyzing the assessment data, the teacher decides how to use the results.

Here are some questions to address for student productivity.

- What is the best strategy to use so this individual learns the identified standard, skill, or concept?
- Do I assume the role of a facilitator or teacher?
- Does the student need to work independently or with a partner?
- Will I need to rewind or fast-forward the curriculum for this student?
- Do I need to continue with grade-level instruction for this learning segment?

Effective instructional decisions are based on the teacher's ability to select the standard and the content information to reach and teach each learner. Selection, organization, and pacing of instruction for the student's uniqueness are determined by many factors, including the learner's . . .

Knowledge base	Cultural background	Learning styles
Strengths and needs	Special adaptations	Preferences
Cognitive ability	Personality	Interests
Social needs	Emotional factors	Self-concept

ANALYZING SELF AND PURPOSE OF DIFFERENTIATING ■

Take time for a self-assessment before making critical decisions relating to differentiation. Identify aspects of instruction you currently use to meet the unique needs of learners and areas to improve. The following checklists will assist you with these self-analysis tasks. Each individual changes with their personal attitude, background, and experience. Identify your stage of buy-in for standard-based differential instruction.

Complete the activity below to see how ready you are to implement differentiation strategies for the standards. Use this form often to reassess your growth.

Y = *YES! I do this!* N = *NEED! I need to improve.*

To differentiate, a teacher needs to do the following:

_____ 1. Know the standards and the students

_____ 2. Teach with knowledge, passion, and "with-it-ness"

_____ 3. Use assessment data to guide planning for students' diverse needs

_____ 4. Give students more control of learning to make the information their own

_____ 5. Customize instruction using the most effective resources

_____ 6. Establish flexible grouping for engaging intervention

_____ 7. Provide choice

_____ 8. Strategically plan targeted interventions

_____ 9. Plan enriching, problem-solving opportunities

_____ 10. Create an optimal learning environment

Figure 1.2 Stages of Differentiation Buy-In

Introduction. 1

Stages	Implementation Thoughts and Reactions to Buy-In
Stage 1: Not interested *I don't need a new hat.* [Complete denial]	☐ My old hat is very comfortable. ☐ I don't have the time or energy to try anything new. ☐ This new style will soon pass.
Stage 2: Discovering *Trying on the new hat.* [Investigation]	☐ I'll just try it on to see how it fits. ☐ I may keep wearing my old hat. ☐ Others like this style, but do I need it?
Stage 3: Wearing the hat *This hat works on certain occasions.* [Buy-in]	☐ I am using it more often. ☐ I am feeling confidence. ☐ I wear it for specific occasions and times.
Stage 4: Favorite hat *This is my best hat!* [Preferred approach]	☐ I wear it as one of my most comfortable hats. ☐ I wear it with pride and encourage others to wear it. ☐ It works for teaching and learning in my classroom.

TEACHING STYLE ANALYSIS ◼

Your personal presentation style is reflected in daily teaching. Some students are more comfortable in quiet rooms, while others need the buzz of active engagement. Some students may respond positively to your style, while others may be uncomfortable in your established environment. It's important to be sure learners are productive with your style. Knowing each individual is crucial. For example, learning will ultimately suffer if a student thrives on movement but is never allowed to get the wiggles out. Analyze your teaching traits by identifying your personal learning styles, personality traits, multiple intelligences, and tolerance levels. Select strategies to support your comfort levels in these areas.

Use the following Likert scale as an informal self-analysis of your teaching preferences. Your approaches may fall between the two extremes. Use the results to become a more effective educator.

Teacher Centered		Student Centered
Teacher directed	⟷	Facilitator
Enforces strict rules	⟷	Self-directed learners
Unaware of personal needs	⟷	Meets personal needs
Delegates responsibilities	⟷	Shares responsibilities
Subject/task focus	⟷	Focus on learning

OUR GOALS IN WRITING THIS BOOK ◼

We wrote this book to assist teachers with the complex task of teaching the standards through differentiated instruction. We know the body of knowledge related to differentiated instruction continues to grow as researchers share information about how the brain learns. Brain imaging is not available to schools, so we have to take the findings of brain specialists to identify the best practices for individual learners.

Our beliefs for effective teaching and learning are based on the latest research that guides our work. We designed this guide to assist effective differentiating teachers by . . .

- Emphasizing the importance of strategically selecting the standard(s) and organizing instruction for each learning segment
- Providing techniques, tips, and strategies to design and maintain an organized, productive learning environment
- Presenting models as blueprints for planning and organizing differentiated instruction
- Providing techniques and ideas to incorporate flexible grouping strategies for targeted interventions and customized instruction
- Adding a treasure trove of instructional strategies for differentiated instruction
- Assisting in the process of gathering and managing assessment data before, during, and after learning to guide instruction

- Providing planning tools and suggestions to use strategically to teach the targeted standards

We encourage readers to adapt our ideas and suggestions to implement standard-based differentiated instruction. Choose the right hat at the right time, and "Put on the Ritz" to give each student optimal learning opportunities.

■ READY FOR THE CHANGE!

As you become comfortable with the idea of teaching standards through differentiation, use the following chart, Figure 1.3, to examine your readiness to implement the changes:

Figure 1.3 Reactions to Change	
Introduction. 2	
Teacher Position	**Reactions and Actions Toward Change**
Holding back	☐ You are fearful of the new idea. ☐ You think, "I don't believe this could ever be for me." ☐ You do not perceive differentiation as a valuable use of your time. It would not be worth the time and energy you need to put into it. ☐ You are required to teach using a mandated program or method. The changes needed to differentiate are out of your control.
Ready to move forward	☐ Obtain support from colleagues or other educators who believe in the value of differentiation. ☐ Examine and appreciate your beliefs and opinions. ☐ Confront your fears and barriers to change. ☐ Explore and learn about new possibilities. ☐ Keep in mind that change comes gradually. Begin to change and adjust the instructional techniques and strategies in your comfort zone. ☐ Ask yourself questions similar to the following: 　○ Which strategies and activities do I want to keep? 　○ What is the easiest adjustment or change I can make to move forward?

Self-Analysis of Progress in Establishing a Differentiated Instruction Classroom

Periodically assess yourself as a teacher in establishing a differentiated classroom. Use the following implementation checklist (Figure 1.4) to mark and identify the components you currently use. Highlight areas to improve. Analyze the results to identify your implementation phase and set goals for improvement.

Figure 1.4 Phases for Implementation

Phase 1	Phase 2	Phase 3
☐ Teach students and standards with the most effective resources and materials.	☐ Create work zones for student-focused activities using centers, stations, and labs.	☐ Assess before, during, and after the learning using informal and formal tools.
☐ Teach with varied instructional strategies around the learners' modalities, styles, and intelligences.	☐ Give choice for students to show what they know.	☐ Use data effectively to plan for individual needs.
☐ Realize that people learn differently.	☐ Realize that assessment drives curriculum.	☐ Adjust assignments strategically.
☐ Employ effective assessment tools during and after the learning.	☐ Provide student-focused activities.	☐ Use flexible grouping by moving students as needed.
☐ Survey students.	☐ Provide opportunities for student to model learining.	☐ Grade using a blending of grade-level assessments and materials on knowledge level.
☐ Create a brain-compatible climate.	☐ Use flexible grouping, including TAPS.	☐ Implement the models for effective planning.

☐ Establish rituals and routines.	☐ Survey students to discover interests, habits, and knowledge base.	☐ Plan using
		   ○ Agendas
		   ○ Choice boards
		   ○ Cubing activities

☐ Use novelty to challenge learners.	☐ Incorporate leveled computer programs.	☐ Level activities for centers and independent activities.
☐ Provide critical and creative thinking opportunities.	☐ Use a variety of graphic organizers.	☐ Working smarter, not harder!
☐ Be an effective questioner.		☐ Students are more responsible for their learning.
☐ Group by students' interests and ability.		

Where are you in implementing differentiated instruction?

Phase 1   Phase 2   Phase 3

◄───►

■ A PREVIEW OF THE BOOK

Each strategy, technique, and guideline was carefully selected and narrowed to five-star summary statements. The goal is to give our readers star power to work smarter, not harder.

Below is a chapter-by-chapter description to present the overview of the major topics explored in the upcoming chapters in this resource. The overview may be used to plan professional learning opportunities for individuals or groups. Each session can be planned by an assessment of the group's desires and needs.

At the end of each chapter, probing questions, suggestions, and activities are provided to use as a guide to lead sessions for a professional learning community (PLC) book study.

Introduction

A standards-based classroom uses differentiated instruction to teach, and to learn the needed information based on the gathered formative assessment data. This chapter introduces the book, as well as information about CCSS and differentiated instruction. The strategies, techniques, and tips presented throughout the resource can be easily adapted to teach standards, outcomes, and benchmarks in all grade levels.

Differentiated Learning Environment

The environment plays a vital role in what and how much students learn. Classroom goals are met by establishing an accepting affective environment and a productive physical climate. This chapter explores ways to improve the classroom environment to increase student learning. Both the physical and emotional climate of the room are important to the community of learners who call it home. In this section, educators will learn to put on their chef's hat to cook up a recipe for affective and cognitive success.

Differentiated Formative Assessment

Teachers need to compile the data to draw academic conclusions. Because of the differentiated and standard movement, teachers are assessing before, during, and after learning. Assessment reveals what a learner knows and doesn't know. It provides valuable insight into student needs and assists teachers in planning well-rounded and meaningful lessons.

Both informal and formal assessments provide teachers with the needed information to plan strategically. Teachers often assess students with formal assessment tools. This takes hours of preparation and administration. Some informal tools such as response cards or signals can provide the immediate information needed. This chapter is designed to help teachers assess their students in meaningful ways.

Differentiated Instructional Strategies

This chapter discusses many varied instructional strategies for meeting the unique needs of the learners. Activities are presented to engage learners before, during, and after learning. Choice boards, cubing activities, intriguing graphic organizers, centers, and stations are presented, with suggestions for customized planning. Teachers who can select the perfect strategy to teach the standards and engage all learners will have a classroom of students who are focused and motivated to learn.

Flexible Grouping Strategies

A teacher continually assesses the students' work to identify areas for improvement. The strategies presented in this chapter can guide instructional decisions needed in the Response to Intervention steps for Tiers I, II, and III, because the grouping techniques are tailored to a learner's identified need. The information in this chapter answers the following questions when planning: How will students be grouped to learn? Does the individual need to work with a partner on a specific skill? Should the learner work alone while the rest of the class receives additional instruction in an area they have mastered? Does an identified group need an intervention or tutoring session?

When a teacher remembers to keep group flexible and add variety to the grouping strategies, students stay engaged in learning. This chapter explores various flexible grouping strategies and discusses how to use them in the classroom while managing multiple activities occurring simultaneously.

Planning With Differentiated Models

When preparing to plan a unit of study or a special activity, teachers can don their thinking hats! By choosing the best planning framework for instruction, goals of the lesson will be met in an engaging way and students will learn. We present twelve planning models to teach the standards in a differentiated classroom.

Teachers are challenged to fill in the gaps for students who do not have the proper background to learn the identified standards. Learners who know the information must be challenged. This chapter will help teachers identify the model to choose for planning to meet each learner's identified needs so everyone learns every day.

Planning for Standards With Differentiated Instruction

Once teachers have the tools and elements necessary to create a differentiated environment in their classrooms, they need to identify a standard, assess it, and strategically plan differentiated instruction. This chapter provides checklists and simplified grids for recording data to help teachers plan for each learner's identified needs and strengths. Administrators or colleagues may use the classroom observation tool to design improvement plans. The teacher may also use it, as a self-analysis tool and to set professional development goals.

■   UNDERSTANDING THE BOOK FORMAT

The following format is used with each model and strategy to provide information for practical application to teach the standards in differentiated classrooms:

What is _____?	A working definition and description of the model or strategy is outlined.
What are the instructional benefits?	A rationale is presented for using the model, tool, or strategy to meet the diverse needs of students.
Implementing standards using _____	What is the relevance of the standard(s)? This links the standard with the model, tool, or strategy. Recommended key steps for implementing the model or strategy are listed.
Demystifying	The simplified definitions, analogies, metaphors, and suggested dialogue in this section can be used to explain the model or strategy to students, parents, or colleagues.
Five-star tips	Suggested techniques and approaches are presented, with advice and points for immediate implementation.
Examples	The sample situations and scenarios provide practical ideas for application of the models and strategies.

Next, an overview of the PLC philosophy is presented. The information is designed to provide a deeper understanding of collaborative studies and their value in guiding the faculty and staff through this resource for standards-based differentiation.

This section includes self-reflective questions or statements to direct to personal thinking and application after the reading. Activities are listed for planning a Professional Learning Community (PLC) study for this resource.

Figure 1.5   Overview of a PLC

What Is a PLC Study?

A PLC study is a long-term academic learning process to examine, investigate, and explore a targeted area of need for personal growth. The study group can consist of everyone in the school or a small team of teachers, administrators, and/or staff members who are stakeholders in the students' success. Each study session is designed to focus on improving teaching and learning on a chosen topic related to a need.

What Are the Educational Benefits of a PLC Study?

- When selecting the topic and the book resource of the study, teaching and learning is always in the spotlight.
- The members use consensus to identify the topic and a resource.
- Purposeful professional development and training is designed with specific goals, a set time frame, and agendas for each session.
- Each member is expected to attend all sessions.
- The group works collaboratively to meet the goals. The study must be a valuable use of time, a growing experience for each participant, and have a lasting academic impact on teaching and learning.
- Participants engage in professional development opportunities, including reading, brainstorming, sharing, and discussing. They continually seek new ways to grow in knowledge to improve student learning.

Administrator's Role

- Guide the faculty and staff to create a vision for each learner's success.
- Select schoolwide goals and objectives to focus on the strengths and needs of the participants.
- Obtain staff input with surveys on the topics and book choices for professional study. Read the book choice or selection.
- Provide opportunities for the participants to be involved in study-related applications during the session and in the classroom.
- Be an actively engaged participant in the study to learn and provide needed support schoolwide. Visit classrooms periodically to observe results of the study in action. Showcase success in sharing celebrations.

Teacher's Role

- Be an active member in the topic and book selection process for the PLC study.
- Commit and buy in to the study by joining peers in sessions to read, discuss, question, find answers, share, and debate issues.
- Emphasize the value of learning in lessons and daily routines. Realize that each participant is an expert and team member. Respect and value each contribution.
- Refer to the different ways individuals learn. Continue to ask yourself, "How can I use what I am learning and grow professionally."

**Five-Star
Tips for Establishing a PLC Study**

1. Identify the needs of the staff with regard to the topic of interests or area for improvement. Give team members a voice in selecting the topics. Discuss and prioritize the suggestions. Come to consensus on the topic, goals, and purposes.

2. Select the book, article collection, websites, video series, and/or other resources to use during the study.

3. Develop a timeline for the study.

4. Ask each group member to commit to being present and accountable.

5. Establish team roles.

     a. Select a leader to conduct the meetings.

     b. Assign a participant from the administrative level to be a team member.

     c. Share responsibilities so each person makes a valuable contribution.

Examples of PLC Studies in Action

Example A: Book Study Team

The team agrees to study a book of interest. A meeting calendar is distributed with scheduled reading assignments. Each member signs the schedule after the recorder or team leader outlines the meeting dates. The goals are set as the group identifies what everyone wants to gain from the study. Readings and discussions are valuable uses of time because the team is learning together. Individual members can apply the new ideas and techniques in their various job roles.

> The most powerful strategy for improving teaching and learning is to create the collaborative culture and collective responsibility of a PLC.
>
> —DuFour, Rick, & Mattos (2013)

Example B: A Video Series Study

A video series is carefully chosen for the study topic. Short segments are shown. Participants discuss important aspects of the scenes and reflect on ways they can apply the new ideas in planning and instruction.

Example C: Personal Taping Series

Each team member videotapes a portion of his or her teaching. Individuals sign up for a night of stardom to lead the group and show the video contribution. Before the video is shown, the star teacher provides an introduction to highlight important scenes. Each clip is shown and discussed. Viewers adapt the learned information and share application ideas to improve their teaching.

Figure 1.6   Personal Reflections for an Independent Study

1. What are the mandates for using standards in your country, state, district, or school? How do they impact your role as an educator?

2. How do you use differentiated instruction to meet the students' diverse needs?

3. Read the chart (Figure 1.4) on page 9 and select the phase of implementation with differentiation that describes your teaching. What steps will you take to move to the next phase and improve instruction?

4. Preview the books and tab sections that address your areas of interest or needs.

5. What do you want to learn while reading and studying this book with your colleagues?

Figure 1.7   Five Activities for the PLC Study

1. Introduction: Assess your implementation status
   a. Complete the self assessment on page 6.
   b. Write your individual needs, as identified on the survey. Include other related areas for improvement.
   c. Use your list of identified needs to set your personal improvement goals for the PLC study.

2. Define terms
   a. Prepare for the activity by identifying important vocabulary words from the list on page 5. Write each word on an index card. Spread the completed cards on a table or in an accessible area.
   b. Form partner teams. One partner selects a word card and obtains a sheet of copy paper.
   c. Partners write the term in an artistic way on the paper and add a definition of the term using their own terminology.
   d. Add brainstorm ideas for using the term in the classroom.

3. Find your phase of implementation of differentiated instruction
   a. Find a pondering partner.
   b. Share your phase of differentiated instruction implementation results from page 9.
   c. Discuss highlights of effective strategies and techniques implemented in your classroom.
   d. Discuss your levels of implementation as indicated on the Likert scale.
   e. Share your next steps for improving or maintaining an optimal learning environment.

4. Standards
   a. Discuss recent mandates related to standards. Include the authors' statements related to common core implementation.
   b. Review the chart (Figure 1.1) on page 3. Emphasize the autonomy teachers possess in making major decisions related to standards.
   c. Discuss the many ways your school maintains a focus on teaching the standards.

(Continued)

(Continued)

5. Set goals for the PLC study
    a. Form groups of 4 to 5 participants, and have each team identify a recorder.
    b. Ask individuals in the groups to share their personal goals for the study. The recorder lists the goals.
    c. Each group prioritizes the list.
    d. Each recorder lists one or two goals from the group to create a class list.
    e. The class identifies goals for the study by coming to consensus on the most important items on the compiled list.

2

Differentiated Learning Environment

IN A STANDARDS-BASED DIFFERENTIATED CLASSROOM, ALL ASPECTS OF THE environment are designed to provide each student with positive, productive, nourishing learning experiences. The affective and physical environments are consciously established and maintained. Like a chef, a teacher needs to prepare the right recipe for the appropriate situation.

The affective realm includes the student's attitude toward learning and feelings about personal relationships with peers and the teacher. A positive classroom environment feeds the brain's ability to receive, process, and apply information. The physical realm includes the arrangement of desks, furniture, books, and materials. The appearance of posted information and displays has a major impact on the learner's perception of the physical environment. The main ingredient of the instructional recipe is the identified standard(s) addressed. Visible posting of the standard makes students and the teacher focus on the purpose of the teaching and learning. This is like a cook keeping the recipe in sight to use as a guide.

Any standards-based classroom can be designed as a comfortable, inviting place to learn. This was evident to us in a visit to a small, but cozy, high school classroom. We asked students why they were so anxious to get to this class. They said, "We hurry because we like our teacher. We feel at home." This teacher established an extremely positive climate for learning in one of the smallest classrooms we have visited.

An inviting and comfortable learning culture supports the unique needs of each student and fosters personal and academic success. Finding the right recipe to manage the complexities of the learning environment in the differentiated classroom is a key to success.

■ ESTABLISHING THE AFFECTIVE ENVIRONMENT

The affective environment is the tone or climate for learning. The classroom needs to be a safe, inviting place that gives students a sense of home when they enter the room. The teacher must monitor the classroom to be sure it is safe, comfortable, and risk free. Students need to feel honored and encouraged to try new things. When all individuals feel that others support and genuinely care about their success, the climate is ideal. Intentionally create warm, inspiring surroundings so students think, "I know I am going to be accepted, comfortable, and able to learn here." Strategically plan all aspects of the classroom to create, develop, and maintain positive attitudes for learning. Remember, an affective environment produces feelings associated with learning that are often recalled by students for a lifetime.

Present Evidence of Your Expectations

Learners usually want to live up to the teacher's expectations, particularly when they feel the teacher cares about them. In the play *My Fair Lady*, Professor Higgins demonstrates the lasting impact of personal investment and high expectations. He transforms a coarse-speaking girl of the streets into a lady with beauty and formal grace. The professor verbalizes and demonstrates his expectations for her success while guiding the transformation. Likewise, students need to know that you see their potential and hear your encouraging words.

> Treat people as if they were what they ought to be, and you help them become what they are capable of being.
>
> —Johann Von Goethe

Present evidence of your expectations:

- Display phrases, sayings, and rules to support and encourage learners.
- Show interest in each individual's personal life and outside achievements. Be an active listener!
- Verbalize high, achievable academic goals for the class and for individuals.
- Display personal goal statements for standards that students can use or adapt.
- Use verbal and visual reminders.

Establish Rules and Routines

To create a safe learning environment, establish manageable rules and basic routines. Provide opportunities for students or groups to assist in developing these guidelines, and they will be more likely to follow them. Include your expectations in the rules for successful differentiated instruction. Be sure the rules are written in positive terms and posted so each student understands the behavior you want to observe.

Guidelines for introducing rules and routines:

- Display the rule or routine in a visual format and explain its purpose.
- State and model each step or procedure.
- Call on students to role-play, demonstrate, and restate it.
- Establish consistent consequences for breaking rules.
- Review the rules and routines periodically during the first few days of implementation.

Model Expectations for Rules and Routines

Rules and routines must be in place in differentiated classrooms. It is crucial to emphasize and demonstrate your expectations of proper behavior. Provide students opportunities to role-play or create simulations to practice each new rule or routine after introducing it. Also give them opportunities to ask questions and express concerns. Yes, this takes time, but it saves time in the long run, because students will internalize the new expectations. Students have fewer questions and feel more confident while engaging in activities when they know and understand the guidelines.

The experiences and personalities of some students make them natural followers and pleasers, while others tend to break rules to test boundaries. Whatever the cause, give extra guidance to individuals who have difficulty following these expectations.

Be Consistent and Persistent in Enforcing Rules and Routines

Students want to know what to expect. They need rules and routines written in language they understand. Avoid changing a rule or consequence unless it is absolutely necessary.

- Practice rules and routines until they are understood and established.
- Carry out consequences immediately following infractions.
- Be consistent with identified consequences. Failure to "follow through" creates uncertainty and deteriorates respect students have for the teacher.
- Be persistent in applying the rules to all learners in all situations.
- Explicitly state your expectation for students to follow rules and routines the first time. Do not give second chances as options.

Note: Students often receive second chances in their homes and in after-school activities. It may take them a while to conform to the "first-time" expectation. When students receive second chances, they do not perceive the teacher as being consistent and persistent. Second chances tell learners it is okay to ignore the rule or routine the first time. Consider what could happen if students formed the habit of waiting for a second chance and you said, *"Stop! Don't cross the street! A car is coming!"*

- Explain why quick responses are important and how they save time for learning. Use banners, posters, and other visuals to challenge students with the "first-time" expectation. Examples: *Say it one time! Save time—do it right the first time!*

Make Manners Mandatory

Manners are an essential part of establishing an environment where all learners feel honored and respected. Remember, for some students, the classroom is the only environment where they learn how to use manners and extend common courtesies.

- Introduce the concept of manners by explaining that the first syllable, *man-*, is derived from a Latin word meaning "hand." People who show their manners are reaching out a hand to others to assist and show their respect. Let students know you expect them to be kind, courteous, and helpful every day to create a special learning team.
- Make it clear that negative comments and "put-downs" about classmates are not tolerated. Guide students in a brainstorming session to create a list of common negative statements or "put-downs." Lead a discussion about how these statements make the receiver feel. Post this reminder: *If you can't say something kind or nice about someone, don't say anything.*
- Explain the importance of using positive comments in making everyone comfortable as they learn. Guide the class through a brainstorming session to gather a list of "put-ups," or praise statements. Display these positive words and phrases on a poster or chart. Encourage students to add to the list throughout the year. Some examples: *Way to go! You deserve a pat on the back. You can do it!*
- Discuss the importance of interpersonal relationships in a differentiated classroom. Emphasize the value of respect and cooperation. Post a list of words and phrases that reflect the manners you expect, such as "thank you" and "excuse me."
- Earn the respect of students. Expect them to respect you and others.

Realize That Body Language Speaks—and Make It Speak for You

Body language is a valuable management tool. Quiet, unobtrusive movements replace verbal comments and actions that interrupt learning. Use it to give individual and group feedback. Be aware of its effectiveness when groups and individuals are engaged in thinking.

Facial Language

Facial expressions are a universal language. Seasoned teachers rely on them as management tools. Use facial expressions to set the tone for learning as students enter the room and throughout the day. Collect a variety of expressions that are comfortable for you and practice them in front of the mirror to be sure they send the right message.

Here are a few examples:

- Wink = pleased; happy; approval
- Frown = disappointment; disapproval; sadness
- Arching or raising eyebrows = surprise; disbelief; caution
- Turning head side to side = disapproval; warning
- Smile = approval; praise

Facial language can be learned through the observation of family members, actors, colleagues, and friends. Practice the "Don't even think about it!" look. As soon as the learner or group responds appropriately, replace that look of displeasure with the "I am proud of you!" expression.

Hand Language

Use hand language to support and strengthen verbal and facial language.

- Thumbs up = approval; Good job!
- Palm toward the student = Wait! Stop!
- Make a heart symbol with index fingers and thumbs = I like that!
- Move the index finger forward and back toward you = Come here.
- Form a circle with a finger and thumb = Okay; Great!

Know your students and be aware of their body language. Familiarize them with the quiet signals they need to recognize and respond to in various situations. Identify specific signals for struggling students.

Positioning Language: Be on the Move!

In a differentiated classroom, the teacher is on the move, meeting individual and small-group needs. Strategically plan and assess your moves with and among students.

- Face the majority of the class when working with individuals or groups.
- Vary the length of time you remain in one location.
- Teach students how to work independently and in small groups while you monitor and assist others.
- Continuously vary your walking pattern.
- Analyze your movement with a video recording or ask someone to record your patterns of movement on a classroom map.

Use positioning as a management strategy. Students who struggle or need special attention may require frequent teacher proximity. Off-task students usually return to work when the teacher simply moves in their direction. Proximity combined with body language provides quiet feedback.

- Place yourself on eye level with the learner while assisting and coaching.
- Position yourself so you and the student have the same view of an object, book, or paper you are reviewing or discussing.

- Stand in front of the student and above his or her eye level when giving a strong directive or correction for disruptive behavior.
- Avoid placing yourself in a dangerous position directly behind or above a student without announcing or indicating your presence.
- Position yourself at a distance when a student is addressing the class. Move to the opposite side of the room, if possible. A learner usually addresses comments in the teacher's direction during class presentations. When the teacher stands at a distance, a student speaks louder, making it easier for everyone to hear.

Make Words Work

Your statements set the tone. Negative comments create emotional barriers to learning, so screen and control your thoughts before speaking. Create a mental file of humorous techniques and positive words and phrases to replace unnecessary, negative comments.

Use Humor

When students list the characteristics of effective teachers, they seldom fail to emphasize a sense of humor. Laughter leads to positive feelings about the experience and cements learning.

In his explanation of how the brain learns, David Sousa (2011, p. 68) outlines the benefits of using humor to enhance learning:

- More oxygen enters the bloodstream and fuels the brain.
- An endorphin surge increases enjoyment and attention.
- The experience creates a positive climate, bonding, and community spirit.
- Retention increases because the emotions are involved.
- Mental health is improved as stress is relieved and attitudes improve.

Here are a few effective ways you can inject a bit of humor into your lessons.

> The wheels of creativity can be greased with humor.
>
> —Goleman, Kaufman, and Ray (1993)

- Introduce a segment of learning with a joke that relates to the study.
- Use a cartoon related to the topic.
- Offer students opportunities to use humor in activities and assignments.
- Use humorous examples as a memory technique.
- Smile and be a happy person.

Eliminate SCARcastic Humor and Remarks

Sarcasm is defined as "cutting of the flesh" because it leaves emotional scars. Recipients and classmates often laugh at sarcastic comments, but they seldom forget the remarks or the way the words made them feel. In social gatherings and reunions years later, they recall the comments and talk about the pain and agony that lingers. Refer to this type of humor as "*SCARcasm*" to emphasize its negative impact.

Pressures to teach many standards and skills in a little time can lead teachers to use sarcastic remarks when frustrated with a learner who is not meeting expectations or maintaining the pace of instruction. SCARcastic remarks frequently create barriers to learning. Become consciously aware of statements such as the following:

- You are this age and you don't know how to _____?
- Let me just show you ONE more time.
- The answer is the same now as it was the last time you asked.
- Your brother was good at math.
- I don't know why this is so hard for you.

When you realize you are becoming frustrated, remind yourself to replace negative thoughts and comments with encouraging statements similar to these:

- Let's talk about the problems you have right and see what you need to do.
- This one is correct, so tell me how you did it.
- Now tell me what you do next.
- Because you understand _____, you will be able to _____.
- Let me show you how to "zap this gap!"

Use Positive Praise Statements

- You've got it!
- I knew I would see your best work on _____.
- You will be successful because _____.
- I can't wait to see you _____.
- I am proud of you each time I see _____.

Give verbal rewards in specific terms to reinforce expectations. Students who receive praise often repeat their actions simply to please the teacher or to re-create the feelings that come with success.

Realize the Impact of Vicarious Learning

In differentiated classrooms, students often learn indirectly or vicariously by hearing and seeing the teacher interact with others. For example, if the teacher reminds one student to place a dollar sign in front of her answers in money problems, the students who overhear this statement may check their work to see if they have dollar signs in place.

Make only positive comments or reminders in public. If a statement is intimidating or embarrassing, students who overhear it will have negative reactions when they see the teacher coming their way. If negative comments are necessary, make them in private.

Answer questions with positive statements and praise. This makes other students eager to add comments and ask questions.

Establish Open Communication

When students are comfortable talking to the adults in their lives, they are more equipped to take risks and fail. Only when they are open to failure will they learn. It is important for the students to feel that they can talk to the teacher about both positive and negative issues.

Honor Student Contributions

Be approachable so students can make statements or ask questions comfortably. Praise them for coming to you or for making contributions. When you need uninterrupted time, tell students so they won't be confused or hurt if you have to turn them away.

Use the following suggestions to demonstrate that you are approachable:

- Smile.
- Be attentive and project the "I care about you" attitude.
- Make comments to encourage creative and critical thinking.
- Correct with dignity and respect.
- Expect and praise concentration, hard work, and persistence.

Listen With Intent

Listen actively. Be aware of your expectations as a listener. Honor the individual who is talking.

- Use direct eye contact with the student who is speaking. Avoid multitasking.
- Be an active listener by nodding when appropriate, asking clarifying questions when necessary, and showing that you care about what is being said.
- Establish open communication, and stay neutral.
- If you do not agree with a student, respect the student's opinion by remaining neutral. Avoid saying, "I disagree." Instead, respond with, "I hear what you are saying" or "I value your thinking."
- Provide opportunities for students to participate in open discussions. With teacher guidance, they will learn valuable lessons in respecting the views of others and in forming their own opinions.
- Avoid expecting incorrect answers from low-ability students. Listen carefully, because they may be right.
- Students who are expected to know the answers should feel comfortable in raising their hands to say, "I do not know this." Honor them for speaking up.
- Avoid making judgment calls with inappropriate remarks.

Build Rapport

Rapport is a genuine, caring, and harmonious relationship or emotional bond that exists between the teacher, students, and classmates. A learner who likes and respects the teacher usually wants to please and eagerly responds to praise.

In a positive differentiated classroom environment, students know they are honored and valued as members of the learning community. They feel that the teacher appreciates their unique strengths and weaknesses and has their best interests in mind when making instructional decisions.

Learners who have good relationships with everyone in the class usually feel confident and comfortable. They are more likely to ask questions and to explore new ways of thinking when the teacher

- responds to their moods.
- recognizes important episodes in their personal lives.
- treats their errors as teaching opportunities rather than mistakes.
- accepts new and unique ways of processing information.
- celebrates each success.

Be "With It"

Students perceive a "with-it" teacher as someone who knows and understands their world. Use "with-it-ness" to build rapport with students and to respect their uniqueness.

1. Survey students often to know their current fads, interests, and favorite things. Remember, student interests are forever changing, so stay "with it."

2. Watch their favorite television shows, and become familiar with their computer games and music choices.

3. If possible, avoid burdening students with homework on special occasions associated with the school. They need to enjoy the social events and feel relaxed as they support school-sponsored activities.

4. Let students know you are interested in their personal lives. Have conversations about their extracurricular activities, such as ballgames, concerts, or other events.

   Examples:
   o You have on my favorite shirt today.
   o You must be proud of your sister's _____.
   o I heard you had a good game last night! Tell me about it.
   o The teacher in your after-school class said you _____.
   o We will use your favorite song during our study of _____.

5. Continually gather information to increase "with-it-ness."
   o Identify what motivates, informs, and inspires your students so you have a better understanding of their backgrounds and value systems.
   o Make a connection with your students—if they know you truly care about and support them, they will work hard to please you.
   o Create opportunities for students to connect things and happenings in their world to content and skills for higher retention.

6. Remember: "With-it-ness" demonstrates understanding and caring about what is important in the learners' lives.

Give Extra Attention

Identify students who need extra attention. Maintain open communication with learners and their parents so you know when someone is dealing with death, illness, divorce, poverty, physical handicaps, or other emotional problems. Sensitive and shy students often need opportunities to develop interpersonal skills and self-confidence. Let other teachers, administrators, and the support staff know when a student needs more time and attention. Roles such as the following provide opportunities for individuals to engage in more social interactions:

- Delivering messages
- Leading routine activities
- Collecting and dispensing materials
- Working with a partner to organize materials and supplies
- Tutoring or reading to classmates or younger students

Celebrate Success

Celebrate the success of a student, a small group, or the class. Challenge individuals and groups to create their own celebration activity.
Examples:

High-fives	Chants	Banners
Songs	Pennants	Posters
Cheers	Raps	Signs

WOW Your Students

How often do you enjoy hearing your students say, "I can't wait to see what you are going to do next," or "I don't want to go to my next class. May I stay with you?" One way to create these reactions is to give your students a "WOW" every day. According to Stephen Barkley (2005), a WOW learning experience accomplishes the following:

- Provides novelty.
- Creates positive emotions.
- Notifies the brain that something new and exciting is happening.
- Primes the pump for learning!
- Motivates students to have the desire to learn.*

Using Novelty

The brain responds to anything new or different. Use novelty to gain attention, enhance instruction, and intrigue learners. Design appealing and different activities to make each learning experience a pleasant, memorable event and to keep students guessing about what might happen next.

---

*Reprinted with permission from Performance Learning Systems, Inc.©, an educational services company located in Allentown, Pennsylvania, U.S.A. and on the World Wide Web at www.plsweb.com. Copyright © 2005 Performance Learning Systems, Inc. All rights reserved.

Interesting and exciting activities enhance retention because they create a memory hook or emotion connected to the information.

Use the following ideas to add novelty to your environment:

- Greet students at the door dressed as a person or character in the lesson.
- Play a musical snippet, when it is least expected, to support instruction.
- End the lesson with a snack to reinforce a standard, skill, or concept.
- Sprinkle confetti in the center of each group when the task is completed.
- Vary the exit strategies to celebrate the day's learning or to entice students to come back tomorrow.

Foster Self-Efficacy

Self-efficacy is the "I believe in me" feeling. At home and in school, students need to feel they are great and getting greater every day. Take advantage of any opportunity to provide support and build confidence so your students know they will succeed.

> Few things help an individual more than to place responsibility upon him, and to let him know that you trust him.
>
> —Booker T. Washington

Develop a Sense of Ownership

Periodically ask your students, "What do we need to do to make our classroom a better place to learn?" Give students a sense of ownership in the teaching and learning process by sharing responsibilities in preparing, organizing, and maintaining the environment during routines and activities. Assigned roles benefit students, especially those who need more confidence, feelings of success, and belonging. The tasks also create opportunities for students to know one another informally as they work together.

Students can share responsibility by

- Labeling displays, materials, and artifacts.
- Preparing bulletin boards and centers.
- Designing games, puzzles, and activities for learning zones.
- Collecting artifacts, models, and pictures to support instruction.
- Organizing materials and furniture for an activity and cleaning up after tasks are completed.

As students assume roles that lead to success, they develop pride and internal commitment to class goals. Struggling students, who often feel ostracized, need a sense of ownership and belonging to fuel their desire to learn.

Guide students to develop their ability to reason and become responsible for their own actions and learning. Explain that it takes time to think. Teach learners to do the following:

- Identify the error or incorrect action
- Describe the error in their own words

- Tell "how and why" the action occurred
- Describe the steps needed to correct or improve the mistake or inappropriate action
- State or write a personal improvement plan

When students have a personal sense of ownership, they are more likely to reason through their academic and social actions. Independent thinking serves as a skill throughout their lives.

Give Choices

Consider the many choices most students have in their daily activities before and after school. It makes little sense to strip them of this ability once they are inside the classroom. Providing choices fosters buy-in to instruction and develops independent thinkers. Give learners options to demonstrate what they know about the identified standards.

Remember to consider the students' ages, characteristics, and preferences in designing choice activities. Provide options in seating arrangements, seating types, working teams, and activities.

Teach Resiliency

Struggling students often experience negative feelings and depression while striving to learn. They need to know how to bring themselves out of negative mental states that are often associated with failure and disappointment. This ability is crucial in all aspects of an individual's life.

Remind students that

- everyone faces obstacles.
- mistakes and failures are learning opportunities.
- it is brave to admit when they need help.
- they can use their strengths to strengthen their weaknesses.
- victory over failure calls for celebration!

Introduce students, especially struggling learners, to techniques they can use to become resilient. Give real-world examples of triumphs over adversity.

- Read materials students can relate to for self-encouragement, and discuss the lessons they present.
- Share personal stories of triumph over disaster found in newspapers and magazines. Examples: Professional basketball star Michael Jordan was eliminated in his high school basketball team tryouts. Patricia Polacco, a nonreader, became a famous author.
- Share sayings and jingles students can use after their failures and disappointments.

Examples:

If at first you don't succeed, try, try again.

When life gives you lemons, make lemonade.

You only fail if you don't get up the last time you fall.

- Play or sing songs with upbeat lyrics.
- Have students identify their personal support sources, including classmates, friends, teachers, parents, grandparents, and other adults.

Teach Stress-Reducing Strategies

All students need to know how to relieve stress at school and in their daily activities. Students who are identified as being at risk or struggling, academically or personally, need to know how to apply these techniques independently as needed.

Discuss the value of good stress and the negative impact of bad stress. Introduce stress-reducing activities. See the examples in Figure 2.1.

Figure 2.1 Dealing With Stress

Stress Reducers	
Physical Exercises • Jumping jacks • Running in place • Toe touches and reaching for the sky • Arm windmills • Shoulder shrugs and stretches	***Relaxation Exercises*** • Take a deep breath and exhale slowly. • Tense and relax specific muscles repeatedly. • Lie down. Listen to soothing music with eyes closed. • Stare at an object in a distant point. • Imagine a pen slowly drawing an outline around your body. Remove all other thoughts.
Mental Exercises • Take a mental mini-vacation to your favorite place. • Visualize and concentrate on your favorite person, pet, or scene for 2 or 3 minutes. • Use games and brain teasers. • Complete word games such as crosswords and acrostics. • Play number games such as Sudoku.	***Rest Spot*** • Reserve a space that is used only for relaxation as a reward. • Use a beanbag, a rug, or a lounge chair. • Encourage students to go to the Rest Spot when they need to relax or regain self-control. • Use the Rest Spot to work alone or to think.

Motivate the Unmotivated

Unmotivated students often are unchallenged and not interested in the standard, so they are bored and frustrated. Learners need support, encouragement, role models, high expectations, and engaging learning experiences.

Find ways to unlock unmotivated minds. Thoroughly investigate various aspects of the learner, including academic, social, and emotional needs. Consider the individual's abilities, home life, and previous academic experiences.

Teachers usually become aware of unmotivated learners through informal observation. The following behaviors can be identified during classroom activities:

- Slouching in the seat with arms folded
- Avoiding eye contact
- Talking back with negative statements

Examples:

I am not going to work on _____.

This is too hard.

I can't do this!

You can't make me _____.

- Lowering his or her head
- Being slow in following directions and in contributing to discussions

Use the following ideas to motivate the unmotivated:

- Offer the learner a choice of activities engaging his or her strengths and interests in challenging and intriguing ways.
- Show the student how the information relates to his or her world to understand the personal value and purpose of the standard or information.
- Identify next steps for the learner's needs. Present instruction and activities in small chunks within his or her level of success.
- Respect and honor every student as a valuable team member and contributor to the learning community. Each learner must feel accepted as an individual by classmates and adults.
- Find ways for the student to contribute to the class. Praise the smallest success.

MANAGING THE PHYSICAL ENVIRONMENT ■

The physical environment includes the classroom furniture, displays, storage areas, lighting, and temperature. It consists of all peripheries—everything within the learners' visual range. The design of the physical environment for productive learning has positive impact on each student.

Managing Students' Personal Space

Each student needs personal space in the classroom. Teach students to respect items belonging to classmates, such as coats, bags, extra books, and supplies.

- Provide each student with designated personal space.
- Allow students to personalize their spaces with their names, drawings, stickers, and special objects.
- Ask students who share spaces with individuals from other classes to remove their personal items daily.
- Store student work in personalized portfolios, cubbies, lockers, notebooks, folders, or boxes.
- Establish rules that require respect for personal items and space.

Designate Common/Group Work Areas

Explain how and when common meeting areas are used. Identify spaces for class meetings, independent conferences, small-group discussions, presentations, and learning celebrations.

Provide work areas for student conferences, partner tasks, and small-group work. Identify locations for students to work together or engage in conversations by grouping chairs or desks together, sitting or standing in discussion huddles, or gathering around a table.

Designate Display Spaces

Establish areas for groups and individuals to display their work. Display progress summaries, timelines, flowcharts, drawings, booklets, flyers, and exhibits.

Use the following idea to rotate displays of student work: Post work related to the current study inside the classroom. When a unit is complete, move the display to an area in the hall outside the classroom. Refer to these visuals to reinforce and review previously taught information. Now the room is ready for student artifacts and displays related to the next topic of study.

Students can display their work on . . .			
walls	window shades	bulletin boards	desks
doors	clotheslines	file cabinets	tables
cork boards	chart stands	chairs	posts
hallways	cabinet doors	window sills	ribbons

Managing Student Materials

Some teachers use organizers, files, and lists so they know where everything is located. They don't waste valuable time looking for things. Other teachers do not need neat, organized surroundings. Students have a tendency to conform to the personal organizational style of the adult in the room. Here are some suggestions to assist with organizing materials:

- Provide a space or home for everything. Teach students to keep books, materials, equipment, and personal items in the identified area. Post the well-known phrase, "A place for everything and everything in its place."
- Color-code each item to match its home or space.
- Organize materials by categories.
- Teach students to clean up. Use reminders such as, "If I mess up, I clean up."
- Discard materials that are no longer needed.

Use attractive containers in centers, stations, zones, and labs:

Sealable plastic bags	Storage tubs with lids	Crates/boxes
Bags with handles	Buckets/baskets	Folders/envelopes

Managing Your Piles and Files

Many teachers spend valuable time looking for things. Survey your classroom. Ask yourself if your piles and files appear as clutter to students, parents, administrators, and visitors. Perceptions are often more important than reality. If individuals see you as being disorganized, they may connect this with ineffectiveness. Teachers are natural pack rats. If you fit this description, make your clutter appear organized. You do not want an assistant or substitute to open your closet and say, "I won't be able to find one thing in this mess!"

Managing Tips for Pack Rats

Teachers who differentiate instruction usually have more activities and materials than traditional educators. The following suggestions are for pack rats. Use these tips to organize or to appear organized:

- Honor your personal organizational style. If you need visible stacks of paper, use a cubby storage unit.
- Purchase inexpensive containers that are the same size, shape, color, and design. Place your teaching materials in the color-coded containers, and label them.
- Designate an accessible area for students to obtain community materials and supplies.
- Identify a personal space for items that are "off limits" to students.
- Assign a learner to assist with organization of materials and supplies.

Managing Student Papers

Students need clear directions and guidelines for placement of completed assignments, paperwork, and products. Create routines and rituals so students easily assume this responsibility.

Examples:

- Use "in/out" baskets, trays, folders, or containers. Display them in the same place daily. Avoid using the teacher's desk as an "in/out" station.
- Designate an area for materials needed for the day's or week's assignments. At the end of the day, remove extra items. Gather materials for the next day in one place for easy access.
- Color-code folders by subject or assignment level. Consistently use color-coding for independent assignments and center activities.
- Assign a student as a materials manager or assistant.
- Designate areas with answer sheets and unique writing implements for students to check their own papers. Direct students to place their completed work in a

basket   display area   booklet   portfolio   notebook   file

Organizational Tips for Sharing a Classroom With Another Adult

Teachers who work together in differentiated classrooms or inclusion situations must work cooperatively to create a positive learning environment. The way they honor and respect each other as they share the room, materials, and responsibilities is evident to students.

Teachers who share a classroom or a work area with a colleague need to consider each individual's organizational style. Be aware of the other person's natural tendencies, and avoid overpowering or undervaluing these characteristics. Remember, creative individuals often are less organized. Usually, analytical thinkers are organizers, so they may have communication barriers with pile-gathering thinkers.

Communicate your organizational needs to adults who work with you. Discuss the physical space and ways to honor personal organizational styles.

If more than one class shares one classroom with different teachers, divide the display areas into assigned sections for each class. Provide places for students to display work when it is completed. This develops a print-rich environment. If space is available, rotate the displayed work of each class throughout the year.

Managing Noise Levels

In differentiated classrooms, groups and individuals simultaneously engage in various activities. Use the following ideas to reduce noise levels and the amount of movement during active engagement. (Also see Figure 2.2.)

- Provide supply carts or containers near student work areas for groups to share extra pencils, paper, crayons, markers, sticky notes, scissors, glue, and assignment materials.

- Create clear walkways to easily assist each learner. Provide easy passages for students, too.
- Designate quiet zones and places for louder voices in other activities.
- Establish, teach, and practice movement during transitions, such as how to efficiently move to and from partner or small-group assignments.
- Discuss appropriate voice levels for different kinds of activities. Display a poster with each noise level identified and explanations of each one. Teach students to identify the appropriate noise level before beginning individual and group activities. A sign with the voice level displayed may be placed in stations or work areas.

Figure 2.2 Noise Monitor

Voice Level	What Does It Mean?	When Is It Used?
0	No talking	When taking tests When receiving directions During independent work time While someone is presenting or speaking to the class During lecturettes During announcements
1	Whisper	When others are concentrating on their work When sharing ideas or responses with a partner
2	Low voice	When working with a partner or small group When engaging in activities with a classmate
3	Talking voice	When there is no danger of interrupting the thinking of other people
4	Speaking voice	For projecting your voice to be heard by everyone When giving directions to the group When sharing with the group When responding to someone from a distance
5	Loud voice	While playing outside During gym activities During games During celebrations

Managing Time

Consider the value of time in each learning experience. Be aware of wasted or lost time. For example, plan activities for students or groups who finish work early. Develop routines and rituals that are easily repeated by students. Teach the class that time is a valuable resource to use wisely. See Figure 2.3.

Figure 2.3 Dealing With Time

Time Killers	Time Savers
Repeating directions and expectations	• Train students to listen the first time • Give one or two directions at a time • Call on one or two students to repeat the directions • Role-play or create simulations • Give a visual or verbal signal to let students know they need to listen to directions
Passing out papers	• Establish a routine with designated distributors • Color-code baskets or small tubs for groups or individuals to obtain papers or materials • Give the papers to three or four students to distribute • Arrange papers in seating order
Collecting papers	• Provide privacy by asking students to fold their papers and place their name on the outside • Designate a container for papers • Idenitify a "materials" person • Collect work as students exit the room

Managing Class Time

Emphasize the value of time in lessons, activities, and transitions. Establish and teach routines. A key to managing class time is to use clear, concise directions that students can state and understand.

- Have focus and sponge activities ready to use as needed for interruptions and difficult moments.
- Turn routines and responsibilities over to students whenever possible.
- Establish procedures to distribute or obtain materials.
- Have supplies and resources easily accessible for each activity.
- Save time by designing quality assignments based on assessment data gathered before, during, and after learning.

Figure 2.4   Time Management

Time Waster	Time Saver
Repeating yourself	1. Privately record your teaching and listen for repetition. 2. Identify patterns and become aware of when it is happening. 3. Make a list and check off completed items. 4. Do not procrastinate! Complete the task while it is fresh in your mind. 5. Ask an observer to note your repetitions.
Communicating	1. Use emails, text messages, notes, or the phone selectively. 2. Create forms and checklists to send to parents routinely. 3. Cluster messages for a specific response time. 4. Be prepared with an agenda before conferences. 5. Identify effect devices and tools for home/school communications.
Getting off task	1. Become aware of what pulls you off task. 2. Make a checklist of tasks and prioritize it. Check each item as completed. 3. Use agendas, lists, a PowerPoint presentation, or an outline. 4. Do not let bird-walking questions and comments pull you from the lesson's flow. Address those after completing the task. 5. Tell students to hand you notes with questions that are unrelated to the study.
Looking for lost items	1. Everything needs a place. Return each item to its home after using it. 2. Keep supplies and materials near your work space. If you have more than one work area, place supplies such as pens, notepads, paper, stapler, and paper clips in each one. 3. Create your own filing system. 4. Ask yourself, "Where did I have it last?" 5. Gather needed instructional materials and supplies early so last-minute searches are avoided.
Correcting papers	1. Establish a way for students to correct many of their own papers. This needs to be done promptly to provide feedback and immediate intervention. 2. Only correct necessary assignments. Remember that every paper does not require a grade. Some work is designed for practice. 3. Grade the work immediately instead of letting it pile up. 4. Have students keep corrected papers in a folder or portfolio. They can use them to talk about what they are learning or need next. 5. Involve students in some peer editing and sharing.

Time Waster	Time Saver
Becoming overwhelmed	1. Prioritize! Accomplish one thing and then move to the next. 2. Set a deadline. Complete one segment and celebrate! 3. Take a break. When you return, it may not be as overwhelming. 4. Complete the most difficult task first. Relax your mind. Then move to the easier ones. 5. Obtain assistance from someone else. Delegate and share the responsibility for work.
Having a full calendar	1. Realize how much you can do! 2. Do not take on more responsibilities than you can handle. 3. Prioritize. 4. Keep an appointment calendar with you at all times. 5. Complete scheduled tasks before taking on another responsibility.
Procrastinating	1. Remember, do not put off tasks you can do today. 2. Set a new goal when one is reached. 3. Get the most dreaded items out of the way first. 4. Celebrate and move to the next task or assignment. 5. Place deadlines on segments of the task.
Not delegating to others	1. Share responsibilities. 2. Form committees with members to help. 3. Delegate! 4. Use the talents of other people. 5. Friends, coworkers, and parents are usually eager to assist, especially if they know students benefit.
Unorganized materials	1. Everything has a place or a home where it belongs. Teach students to return items to their "homes." 2. Place color-coded labels on the place where the material is stored with the same color on the material. 3. Organize things by categories. 4. Teach students to clean up. Post reminders such as, "If you mess up, you clean up." 5. Discard materials that are no longer needed.
Collecting and distributing papers	1. Use portfolios, folders, or containers. Display them in the same place daily but not on the teacher's desk. 2. Find a place for the materials needed for the day's or week's assignments. At the end of the day, remove extra items. Gather materials for the next day and make them accessible.

(Continued)

(Continued)

Time Waster	Time Saver
	3. Color-code folders by subjects or levels of tiered assignments. Keep them in the same location. Use the same colors for independent assignments or center activities. 4. Assign a student to be a materials manager. 5. Designate areas for answer sheets so students can check their own papers.
Not able to concentrate	1. Practice active listening. Focus all your attention on the individual talking so you hear what he or she says. 2. Probe with questions and restating for more details and clarification. 3. Restate the learning. 4. When confused or stressed, take a break and come back to it. 5. Unclutter your mind, reduce tension, and then listen.
Classroom movement	1. Be visible. Keep moving among students. 2. Never form a walking pattern. 3. Stand on the opposite side of the room when a student is speaking. Students usually focus on the teacher when talking or presenting to the group. 4. Use nonverbals to get messages across and send signals. 5. Place yourself at eye level and on the same side of the paper, book, or artifact so the students view you as a helper. In this position you see the information from the same view as the student.
Controlling offtask behaviors	1. Use student names in context. 2. Use positive remarks: "I like the way. . . ." 3. Keep a calm voice in upsetting circumstances. 4. Use voice inflection while presenting content to show your passion. 5. Omit sarcasm. (See the "SCARcasm" section on page 22)
Stressing out!	1. Take a deep breath. 2. Walk away for a minute. 3. Pat yourself on the back for reaching so many students! 4. Name the many ways you reached students today! 5. Don't sweat the small stuff!

Time Waster	Time Saver
Fearing change	1. Look for support by finding colleagues or someone who is a believer in differentiation. 2. Examine your beliefs and opinions. 3. Confront your fears and barriers related to change. 4. Explore and learn about new ways to reach individual learners. 5. Remember that change often comes gradually. Identify the strategies and activities you currently use and want to keep. Start changing by implementing the segments or ideas that are the easiest and most comfortable for you.

Figure 2.5 Eleven Time Savers to Ensure Success

1. Familiarize yourself with the standards.
2. Vary your instructional strategies and activities.
3. Create a productive learning climate.
4. Exhibit "with-it-ness."
5. Provide a wide variety of material and resources.
6. Learn the students' likes, dislikes, strengths, and weaknesses.
7. Assess before, during, and after learning.
8. Adjust assignments when necessary.
9. Plan student-focused opportunities.
10. Use flexible grouping designs.
11. Realize that change is gradual.

Managing Personal Time

- Be a list maker, and prioritize items. Check or mark through completed tasks on the list. Place activities, due dates, appointments, and other important events on a personal electronic device or a calendar. Avoid crowding too many expectations or overlapping tasks in one time frame.

- Meet time guidelines and due dates by recording the deadline warning a few days prior to the event's date.
- If asked for a commitment, respond with, "I'll get back to you." This response gives you time to check your calendar. Be sure the commitment period is a valuable use of your time.
- Arrive at school early to prepare for the day and organize your thoughts.
- Schedule time for planning and time for you.

■ SETTING THE TONE

The way you present yourself and your expectations has a major impact on the way students respond to you. Make each student feel excited about being a unique member of your class every day with every action and comment you make.

Earn your students' respect. Show that you know your subject and the standards. Let them see and feel your passion. Make it clear why they need to listen to you and how you will listen to them. Demonstrate that you truly care for each individual. Show your genuine interest in each student's success in school and in life. State your desire for each individual to be a happy, productive citizen in class and in life. Be dedicated to helping every student learn the subject, standards, and skills they need. Be sure they leave each day knowing they will enjoy learning with you tomorrow.

Entering and Preparing for Class

When you are prepared, learners realize they are important to you. Arrive early and think through the day's activities for teaching and learning. Gather the necessary supplies before your students arrive. Plan well to make each moment of learning a worthwhile experience.

Greeting Students

Observe how students enter a room. Do they joke and laugh or avoid social interactions? These behaviors can be relevant for learning. The entrance style of individuals of any age provides valuable information. Make mental notes as you meet and greet students at the door.

Your presence and personal exchanges with students as they enter the classroom set the tone for learning. This time can be used to interact with students who have unique needs. Here are some greetings that make entrances more inviting for learners:

- Call each individual by name.
- Notice and comment on changes such as new clothes or a different hairstyle.
- Share a welcoming handshake or noncontact high-five.
- Use a kind, personal comment or question to show you are excited about seeing each individual.
- Smile!

Remember the value of informal, social interactions. Give students opportunities to say "hello" and socialize before class formally begins. During this time, they can gather materials or supplies and prepare for the day.

Jump-Start Each Day of Learning

Jump-start the learners' day using a variety of strategies and approaches. Most students need to begin the year with structured activities. When they become accustomed to routines, select activities to encourage creativity, stimulate higher-order thinking, or showcase talents and interests.

Place a focus or bell-ringer challenge in the same place each day. After students meet, greet, and check for needed class materials, they begin the assignment.

Bell-Ringer Activities

- Go on a scavenger hunt to find _____ in the text.
- Work the brain challenge activity.
- Write three things you recall from yesterday's lesson or standard.
- Share, discuss, and check your homework with a partner.
- Make a list of important facts from yesterday's learning.

Plan activities that create an initial routine to begin the day and promote order. Select or design each activity with the students' individual needs in mind. For example, in the following activity, each student has a specific role that develops communication skills, increases confidence, and develops responsibility.

Example:

Select five students to serve as the news team.

- First student—local or school news
- Second student—state news
- Third student—national news
- Fourth student—weather report
- Fifth student—makes announcements

Since all students are engaged as members of the news team or audience, the teacher has time to conference with students, prepare the lunch count, take the roll, or prepare for the first lesson.

Calling the Roll

Calling the roll consumes valuable time. After the first few days, when the roll is finalized, use another quick, efficient method to check attendance. Use procedures similar to the following to save class time.

Example A: Clothesline Rolls

Share classroom management responsibilities with students. Adapt the following procedure to your grade level:

1. Hang a clothesline. Place a container for the clothespins nearby.

2. Place the students' names on clothespins. Provide time for the class to personalize their clothespins with miniature drawings that symbolize them, such as representations of their hobbies, interests, or pets.

3. Tell students to find their clothespin on the line and place it in the container when they enter the room.

4. Record absentees by taking names from the remaining clothespins.

5. Assign one student to place all pins on the line for the following day.

Example B: Chart Rolls

Write the name of each student in bright colors and various fonts around the outer edges of a chart or poster. Ask students to place a clothespin or colorful clip on or next to their names when they arrive. Keep the clothespins or clips in a box that is easy to access.

Example C: Check-In

Display a grid with students' names listed on the left-hand side and dates listed on the top row. When students enter the room, each individual places a checkmark beside his or her name under the appropriate date.

Example D: Learning Students' Names

1. Guide students through steps to personalize a name tent. Provide a wide-tipped dark marker and an index card for each learner. Give students directions similar to the following:
   a. Fold the index card in half to create a name tent.
   b. Write the name you want to be called in large, colorful letters on each side of the card.
   c. Draw symbols representing your hobbies and interests on each side of the name tent.

2. Designate one or two students to distribute the name tents each day.

3. Observe the name tents at empty seats to record absences.

4. Use these cards during class to call on individuals.

Example E: Name Tags

Prepare name tags for students to use during the first few weeks. Learners pick up and return them to a designated area. Provide time for students to personalize the name tags with bright colors, designs, and symbols.

Managing Lesson Closures and Classroom Exits

Planned, structured procedures create organized closures and exits. In differentiated classrooms, students often are working in small groups or as individuals when it is time to bring closure to the lesson. Maintain a focus on learning as students complete activities or prepare to exit the classroom. Practice the selected procedure or routine.

Wrap-Ups

Wrap-ups are closures for lessons and activities. Avoid interrupting students during their tasks and related discussions. Use a signal to notify students that they have a designated amount of time to wrap up or bring activities to a close. This lets them know you value their work and conversations. Use another signal to end the activity.

Example A: Sharing "Aha" Moments of the Day

Students write an important fact or concept learned. This "aha" is shared with a partner or small group. Call on some individuals to share the "aha" with the class.

Example B: Ticket Out the Door

Tell students to write on a sticky note one to three facts learned. Ask them to place their notes on the door as they exit.

Example C: Exit Statements

End each learning session on a high note using a statement similar to the following:

- I am proud of the things you learned today.
- I like the way you worked together to learn.
- You won't believe what we are going to do tomorrow!

Perceptions of Organized Chaos

A differentiated classroom may appear to be in a state of chaos to individuals who are accustomed to traditional classroom settings. Often, the teacher is serving as a learning facilitator who is monitoring, guiding thinking, assisting, assessing, modeling, observing, encouraging, and questioning small groups and individuals. Visitors may enter the room and say, "Where is your teacher?"

Differentiated classrooms have multidimensional environments because . . .

- Students simultaneously engage in various activities.
- The noise level is higher with constructive, busy noise.
- Students move from one area to another as they work on individual, partner, or small-group tasks.
- Conversations related to various tasks may be heard from students working in different areas of the room.
- Individuals and small groups are engaged using easily accessible manipulatives, materials, books, reference tools, and computers.

■ SELECT YOUR HATS FOR THE ENVIRONMENT

As stated previously, differentiated classrooms are multidimensional, complex places. Use the following chart to identify the hats you may need to manage the many aspects of your classroom. Adapt and add to our suggestions as you prepare the optimal learning environment for your students. See Figure 2.6.

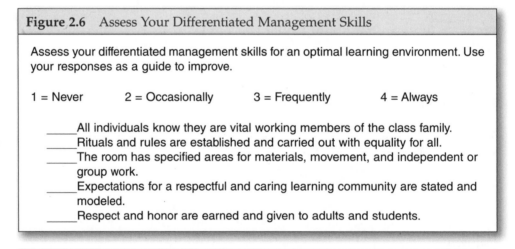

Figure 2.6 Assess Your Differentiated Management Skills

Assess your differentiated management skills for an optimal learning environment. Use your responses as a guide to improve.

| 1 = Never | 2 = Occasionally | 3 = Frequently | 4 = Always |

_____All individuals know they are vital working members of the class family.
_____Rituals and rules are established and carried out with equality for all.
_____The room has specified areas for materials, movement, and independent or group work.
_____Expectations for a respectful and caring learning community are stated and modeled.
_____Respect and honor are earned and given to adults and students.

■ CONCLUSION

Be consciously aware of the learning environment every day. Design and maintain an optimal climate for the success of each individual. When wearing the chef's hat, you are responsible for creating a safe, comfortable place where students are free to take risks. Use the right ingredients so each student is nourished and enjoys the experience. Keep this hat handy as you evaluate, manage, and re-create your classroom environment.

Figure 2.7 Personal Reflections for Establishing a Learning Environment

1. Are your classroom rules and expectations written in positive terms? If not, how can you accomplish this task? How will you be more consistent and persistent with your established rules?

2. Identify your verbal or body language strengths and weaknesses when delivering instruction and while interacting with students. Set personal improvement goals.

3. List ways to use humor effectively during instruction or to build rapport with students. Remember, always avoid "SCARcastic" humor.

4. Identify how and when your stress impacts your students. How do you reduce the learners' anxiety and stress?

5. What time wasters take away from teaching and learning? How can you use this identified time more productively?

Figure 2.8 Five Activities for the Professional Learning Community Study (PLC)

1. Think! Pair! Share!

What are the characteristics of a productive differentiated learning environment?

   a. Tell individuals to brainstorm a personal response list using words or phrases to answer the question presented above. Participants record their responses on a sticky note.
   b. Form partner teams to read the responses.
   c. Call on the partner teams to share their response highlights with the total group. Compile a class list.

2. Jigsaw

   a. Divide participants to create four-member groups.
   b. Have each participant fold a sheet of paper into four sections and number each section on both sides to create eight boxes.
   c. Ask each group to count off to eight. Individuals will receive two numbers.
   d. Assign the two topics that correspond with the individual's two numbers from the following list.

1. Make rules work	5. Build rapport
2. Make body language speak	6. WOW your students
3. Make words work	7. Foster self-efficacy
4. Establish open communication	8. Motivate the unmotivated

   e. Tell each participant to read the information for the two topics and take summarizing notes in the corresponding numbered sections on the paper. Encourage readers to add helpful tips to share with the total group.

(Continued)

(Continued)

   f. Ask individuals to take turns giving a summary of each assigned topic. Other members listen, take notes on their grid sheets, discuss each topic summary, and identify important facts.

   g. Call on each group for a jigsaw summary of their topics. Encourage other participants to use their books to highlight the showcased ideas and take notes during each summary presentation.

3. Physical Environment Carousel

   a. Divide participants into interest groups, and give each team a sheet of chart paper.

   b. Ask the groups to identify the most important aspect of managing an optimal physical environment. Each group writes the identified need across the top of the large sheet of paper. Post the charts around the room.

   c. Move each group to a chart. Ask them to brainstorm and add implementation management tips to the chart until they are signaled to stop.

Bell-Ringer Ideas	Closure Ideas

   d. Tell the groups to move to the next chart and add management tips. Continue with the same procedure to complete the charts as time allows.

   e. Following the final signal, each group takes a chart, organizes the entries, and presents the most valuable tips to the total group.

   f. Post the charts for viewing in a faculty workroom or professional development space.

4. Bell Ringers and Closures

   a. Give each group a large sheet of chart paper.

   b. Assign a recorder to draw a T-chart for brainstorming.

   c. Call on a volunteer in each group to compile the ideas. Copy and distribute the list.

5. Time Wasters

   a. Brainstorm a class list of time wasters.

   b. Form partner teams, and then choose one time waster from the list.

   c. Partners find a comfortable place to work on the assignment.

   d. Each team writes the chosen time waster heading and the brainstorm prescriptions and alternatives for using the time wisely. They add questions or concerns related to the problem.

   e. Provide class-sharing time. Have someone in each group compile the prescriptions for time wasters. Copy and distribute them to each participant.

3

Differentiated Formative Assessment

FORMATIVE ASSESSMENT IS AN ESSENTIAL, ONGOING PROCESS IN A differentiated classroom. Put on your detective hat and compile evidence of student needs in given situations. Observations often provide the needed information. Use a blend of informal and formal formative assessment tools to gather data before, during, and after learning to identify individual strengths and needs. Like a detective, compile all the information for the report. Some cases require deeper investigations, such as fingerprinting and DNA analysis, to gather needed data. It may be necessary to go deeper into the learner's mind to discover what is known and lacking in relation to the standard. Use the analyzed results to customize instructional plans for the targeted students.

Preassessment is a prerequisite for differentiation. You must know how to select and administer the most appropriate assessment tools. Managing assessment is a complex task, but remember that each learner benefits from personalized instruction.

■ FORMATIVE ASSESSMENT BEFORE LEARNING: PREASSESSMENT

What Is Preassessment?

Preassessment is administered with a formal or informal assessment tool to pinpoint the learner's knowledge related to an upcoming standard, skill, topic, or concept. The data are analyzed to identify the student's background knowledge, prior experiences, abilities, interests, and attitudes in relation to the new learning.

The most useful preassessment data are gathered 1 to 2 weeks before planning. This gives you ample time to analyze each learner's knowledge base, customize the strategies and activities, and gather the resources and materials for the upcoming study. A close examination is crucial because the results are used to strategically plan each lesson for individuals in a differentiated classroom. When students' strengths and weaknesses are addressed in an instructional design, you are working smarter, not harder.

What Are the Instructional Benefits of Using Preassessment?

- An effective preassessment reveals the student's knowledge base related to the upcoming standard(s), topic, or skill. It identifies the entry point for instruction.
- Preassessment data pinpoint the learner's knowledge on standards, concepts, and objectives.
- The results divulge the learner's specific needs for reteaching, grade-level instruction, or enrichment.
- Informed grouping decisions can be made when a preassessment reveals a wide range of understanding in the class.
- Preassessment results guide the selection and design of the most appropriate instructional strategies to accommodate the identified individual and group needs.

Implementing the Standards Using Preassessment

- Identify the standard(s) to review or introduce in the upcoming unit. Design the preassessment to reveal the learner's prior knowledge in relation to the standard(s).
- When preparing the preassessment tool, chunk the standards that can be addressed simultaneously.
- Use the preassessment session as a promo or hook to spark interest for the upcoming standards, topics, or skills.
- Develop a repertoire of formal and informal preassessment tools to coordinate with the standard and the learner's instructional needs.
- If an informal assessment unveils needed information, use it instead of a time-consuming, formal assessment.

Demystifying Preassessment

Introduce the term *preassessment* to students by discussing lessons needed to learn a sport. Here is a metaphor you can adapt for the word's debut:

The coach preassesses each person's skills to plan the practice session. Individuals who routinely play the game begin with more advanced skills and information. Individuals playing for the first time begin with the basic skills.

Explain that you use preassessments in the same way to identify each student's knowledge of an upcoming standard. Remind students to honor the strengths of others and to respect their weaknesses. Emphasize the importance of doing their best and being honest on each preassessment. Explain that the information helps you plan and organize lessons to reinforce their strengths or to zap their gaps in learning.

★ ★ ★ ★ ★

Five-Star
Tips for Preassessment

1. Explain to students how preassessment data guide planning for their unique needs. Emphasize the value of the results so they will provide their best responses for the assessments. Make upbeat, positive comments so students do not become stressed about the "test." Remember, negative thoughts interfere with thinking.

2. Preassess an upcoming topic. Provide ample time to use the gathered data to plan for learners' specific needs.

3. Introduce and demonstrate a preassessment tool the first two or three times it is administered, or until students know how to use it.

4. Use a variety of formal and informal preassessment tools. When students know how to use a tool independently, add it to your assessment tool kit to gather data in future sessions.

5. Engage students in data analysis and planning.

Preassessment Examples

Example A: Using a Teacher-Made Pretest

Develop a pretest similar to the following to discover what students know about an upcoming topic or standard.

- List facts you know about _____.
- What experiences have you had with _____?
- Illustrate _____.
- Write one or two paragraphs that describe _____.
- List facts you would use to teach someone about _____.
- How does learning about _____ make you feel?

Gather the data and analyze the information to plan differentiated instruction for the upcoming standard. Use the same test as a posttest. This process often unveils the learner's attitude as well as background knowledge.

Example B: Color-Coding the Facts

Provide a list of key content facts such as the major characters, events, steps, and places from the upcoming unit or topic. Ask students to color-code each entry based on their level of understanding.

Green dot: *I know it!*

Black dot: *I know a little about it.*

Blue dot: *I don't know anything about it.*

Example C: Getting in Shape

Announce the next unit using an exciting advertisement such as a jingle or ad. Explain to students that this preassessment activity actively engages them in self-assessment and lets them help you plan instruction for the upcoming standard or skill by "Getting in Shape."

1. Display large outlines of the following shapes with the descriptor key similar to the following on a wall.

   Circle: *I know a lot about it.*

   Square: *I know a little about it.*

   Triangle: *I don't know anything about it.*

2. Make a list of the most important facts in the upcoming unit.

3. State a fact from the list.

4. Tell students to stand in front of the shape that represents their knowledge of each fact as it is read.

5. Gather data to plan the new study by using a chart similar to the following to record where students stand. Students may number the facts on a card and record a response for each one by drawing the selected shape.

Figure 3.1 Shape Up!			
Fact	**Circle** **I know a lot about it!**	**Square** **I know a little about it!**	**Triangle** **I don't know anything about it.**
1.			
2.			
3.			

FORMATIVE ASSESSMENT DURING THE LEARNING: ONGOING ■

What Is Ongoing Assessment?

Ongoing or continuous assessment is essential in the differentiated classroom. The teacher observes and monitors individuals as they engage in activities and classwork to adjust or customize instruction as needed. Students also monitor themselves during learning with self-assessment tools designed to help them examine their own work. Students know how and when to obtain assistance when a problem or gap in learning occurs. They develop the ability to their own progress and use praise statements as self-affirmations.

What Are the Instructional Benefits of Ongoing Assessments?

- Constant assessment keeps the teacher abreast of progress, misunderstandings, "aha" moments, and mastery.
- Students receive assistance as soon as a need is identified. This immediate response for intervention keeps individuals from falling behind, becoming frustrated with a task, or losing valuable learning time.
- By gathering and recording the appropriate data, the assessor can see patterns and customize future assignments accordingly.
- Ongoing data analysis assists in diagnosing flexible groupings, as well as adjusting assignments and tasks to best serve individual needs.
- When ongoing assessment is used effectively, learners are not bored or frustrated with the information or skills, because lessons are personalized. The teacher and students do not have to wait for summative assessment results.

Implementing Standards Using Ongoing Assessment

- Assess using an array of teacher- and student-focused tools to obtain data efficiently.
- Act promptly on your findings. Remember to adjust assignments for individuals as the need arises.
- Move the learner to the most effective grouping design to zap gaps or enrich learning using TAPS (total group, alone, partner, or small group).
- Establish ways for students to self-assess, clarify misunderstandings, model, make corrections, and set new goals as they work.
- Examine the assessment data to create and tailor the individualized plans so each student is adequately challenged on his or her level of success.

Demystifying Ongoing Assessment

Explain the importance of the teacher and each student using assessment during learning to "zap the gaps" or extend learning. Emphasize the importance of asking for assistance when they do not understand a step or a part of the assignment while they are working. Let them know how and when to ask for help to keep them on their learning tracks.

Compare ongoing assessment to the work of an artist. As work progresses with the painting, the artist pauses to study the texture, color, and design. Adjustments are made as needed.

Five-Star
Tips for Using Ongoing Assessment

1. Explain ongoing assessment with the teacher and student roles for "zapping gaps" during learning.

2. Introduce and model each assessment tool used during learning.

3. Use the brain-jamming activity (Example A below) to introduce metacognitive strategies and ways to model thinking while learning. Verbalize the inside thinking that accompanies each assessment tool.

4. Give corrective feedback or praise. Teach students to see each mistake or misunderstanding as an opportunity to learn.

5. Be prepared to intervene and adjust plans, assignments, and activities for groups or individuals.

Note: If an observation checklist is the assessment tool, show the form to the student and explain its use. This removes apprehension the learner may have during an assessment. For example, when a teacher is observing and using a checklist, the student often thinks, "Why is the teacher watching me and taking notes?" or "Will the notes be sent to my parents?" A simple explanation helps the learner feel like a partner in the learning process, as it removes the negative messages.

Examples of Ongoing Assessment

Example A: Brain Jamming

During the reading of a text segment, the student ponders specific questions to conduct a personal brain probe. The responses are used as an internal check of comprehension, to identify needs, to connect to new learning, and to prompt self-praise.

Examples:

What was the author saying?

Do I need help to understand this process or section?

How can I remember the important facts?

Example B: Project Partner

Assign long-term individual projects to several students. At the beginning of the assignment, each student receives a project packet that includes a timeline with designated dates for parts of the project to be completed. Periodically, each student meets with the project partner to discuss the segments completed, the problems encountered, and the light bulb moments that occur during the project process. In each conference, the students share information and strategies. They fill out an individual or partner checklist and comment page to record findings from each session. The partner interaction emphasizes the project process.

Example C: Card Responses

Students are in the middle of a unit of study. Feedback is needed to see if learners understand the information presented in two to four categories. A class set of response cards is created with the categories listed on each side of the cards.

The teacher asks a question or makes a statement related to one of the categories. After a thinking period of about 10 seconds, the students pinch the appropriate category to answer the question or correspond to the statement. The teacher says, "1 . . . 2 . . . 3 . . . show me!" Each student holds the card for the teacher to see. This informal, game-like assessment shows what has been learned by each individual and the category that requires review or reteaching.

Sample cards:

- Prime/Composite
- Invertebrate/Vertebrate
- Fiction/Nonfiction
- Add/Subtract/Multiply/Divide

■ FORMATIVE ASSESSMENT AFTER LEARNING: SUMMATIVE

What Is Assessment After Learning?

Assessment after learning identifies standards and concepts mastered by each student following a segment or unit of study. Typically, informal assessments are used to identify needs for review or reteaching, while formal assessments are administered when a grade is needed. In each assessment approach, the results are analyzed to see if each learner reached the goals or objectives. New plans are tailored to provide the next steps for learning.

What Are the Instructional Benefits of Using Assessment After Learning?

- Assessments administered after learning reveal specific, individual needs in relation to a standard.
- The results determine the learner's knowledge level and guide planning for the upcoming study.
- The data become a direct guide for the student and teacher to identify problem areas and recognize progress.
- When the formative assessment reveals that more than one student had similar errors, the teacher can group these learners and correct their errors and revise the instructional strategy or materials.
- The results can be compared to previous assessment performances to monitor progress over time. The teacher can use the information to discuss the learner's strengths and needs in student and parent conferences.

Implementing Standards Using Summative Assessment

- Design or select summative evaluations that make it easy to identify what a student learned or did not learn during the study.
- Compile and examine the formative assessment data to pinpoint individual and group strengths and weaknesses.
- Use the analyzed data to make informed instructional plans. For example, a student who fails to master a standard is assigned customized activities for review and practice.
- Administer questions and evaluations in different forms to give students opportunities to show what they learned. Teach learners to review their notes and the text after the assessment to identify the most important facts or skills to remember.
- Whenever possible, involve students in the data analysis and show them how to set new goals for learning.

Demystifying Assessment After Learning

Explain the importance of using assessment after learning to uncover needs that can be addressed in the new plans. Use a lecturette such as the following to compare the summative assessment to a championship skating event:

> *The trainer and the skater analyze each aspect of the performance to identify skills that need improvement before the next competition. The judges' low marks indicate areas where more instruction and/or practice is needed before the next event.*

Five-Star Tips for Using Assessment After Learning

1. Choose the summative evaluation that will most clearly reveal what students learned during the study.

2. Use a combination of assessment formats such as teacher-made tests, portfolio conferences, presentations, multiple-choice tests, open-ended questions, manipulative tasks, games, and graphic organizers. Obtain a broad picture of the student's strengths and needs by viewing the learner's work from a variety of assessments.

3. Provide students with self-assessment tools, including questioning techniques, to use in assignments and activities. This develops self-directed, independent learners.

4. Engage students in peer and small-group assessments after learning to identify accurate answers, correct their errors, and set new goals.

5. Analyze assessment results to adapt instruction for an immediate intervention or design plans for future lessons.

Examples of Formative Assessment After Learning

Example A: Draw What You Know!

Draw the life cycle of the butterfly on the chart paper provided. Write the name of each stage with two to three descriptive sentences next to the picture.

Example B: Create What You Know!

Use the manipulatives to create a model of an atom. Use scrap paper to label each component. Ask your study buddy or a classmate to use the diagram provided to check your work.

Example C: Explain What You Know! Portfolio Partners

Partners find a comfortable meeting area to sit with their portfolios and a checklist of completed activities and assignments. They examine each portfolio, discussing what they learned, including their thinking processes, areas of growth, and needs. Partners take turns sharing and listening. After both students share, they mark the checklist and record comments in their own portfolios as evidence of this meaningful learning event.

Assess Your Use of Formal and Informal Formative Assessment Tools

List the formative assessment tools you are currently using before, during, and after learning. Label each tool as informal (I) or formal (F).

Figure 3.2 Assessment Tool Analysis

Tools Used Label as Follows:		
I = Informal		F = Formal
Before	During	After

Figure 3.3 Assessment Tool Gala

Time	Assessment Tools	Verbal Responses
Preassessment tools	☐ Squaring off: Four corners Body signals ☐ Stand up, sit down ☐ Thumb it ☐ Web search ☐ Blog ☐ Wikis ☐ Pretest ☐ Journal ☐ KWL Chart	I know . . . I want to learn . . . I do not know . . . I know some about . . . To improve I need to . . . I need . . . I like . . . I do not like . . . I am afraid of . . . I look forward to . . . I hope I get to learn . . .
Time	**Examples of Tools**	**Examples of Verbal Responses**
During assessment tools	☐ Checkpoint tests ☐ Word or fact wall ☐ Check and correct	I am learning . . . I am confused about . . . I want to learn . . .

	Body Signals	This activity is easy for me because . . .
	☐ Fist of 5	This is hard because . . .
	☐ Reach for the top	I need . . .
	☐ Arm gauge	I have learned . . .
	☐ Speedometer arm	I have a question about . . .
	☐ Observation	I like . . .
	☐ Anecdotal records	I do not like . . .
	☐ Portfolio gathering	I hope I . . .
	☐ Write it to show it	I need to change the way I am doing . . .
	☐ Wipe-off boards, write and show answer	It will help if I can . . .
	☐ Talk the thinking	I understand . . .
	☐ Show the process	I will explain . . .
	☐ Show with a manipulative	I know . . .
	☐ Link it to previous learning	I do not know . . .
	☐ Notes	My least favorite part is . . .
	☐ Journal	My favorite part is . . .
	☐ Learning log	I need to tell you . . .
		I need to explain . . .
	Response Cards	Why am I doing this?
	☐ + or −	How can I use this later?
	☐ Yes or no	
	☐ A B C D	
	☐ Face the fact: happy, so-so, sad	
Post-assessment tools	☐ Portfolios	I was successful because . . .
	☐ Wraparound reflection	I can improve by . . .
	☐ Posttest	Now I know . . .
	☐ Conversation circle	I will use this to . . .
	☐ Rotation reflections	Next I need to . . .
	☐ Paper pass	I am still questioning . . .
	☐ Partner or small-group sharing	I learned . . .
	☐ Carousel	My favorite part was . . .
	☐ Teach it to someone	This was my least favorite.
	☐ Whip-around responses	I liked . . .
	☐ eportfolio	I did not like . . .
	☐ Talking topic	Next time I need . . .
	☐ Grand finale celebration	My biggest "aha's" were . . .
	☐ Blank page at the end of test:	I need to learn more about . . .
	☐ "Tell me what you know about this subject that was not examined in this test."	
	☐ Center response logs	
	Graphic Organizers	
	☐ Donut	
	☐ Wheel	
	☐ Flowchart	
	☐ Ladder	
	☐ Hand	
	☐ Star	

■ SELF-ASSESSMENT

What Is Self-Assessment?

Self-assessment occurs when individual students analyze their own work. They identify what they know, what they don't know, and what they need to learn next. Using self-assessment formative tools before, during, and after learning, students find and correct their own mistakes in daily work, projects, tests, activities, and homework. It takes time for students to find and correct their mistakes, but it is one of the most beneficial experiences you can provide during standard-based instruction. Guide students to realize they need to link prior experiences to the new standard. Provide time for reflection to accomplish this feat.

What Are the Instructional Benefits of Using Self-Assessment?

- Students develop a sense of ownership and control over their personal progress when they know how to use assessment tools to analyze their own work and use the results for self-improvement.
- Learners receive immediate feedback while checking their work. When students identify mistakes and make corrections immediately, they are more likely to stay focused and motivated.
- Reward for "a job well done" is immediate during self-assessment. Learners gain a sense of pride as they confirm correct answers.
- Self-assessment frees the teacher from extra paperwork and provides more time for instruction. Learners work harder, and the teacher works smarter!
- Students learn to appreciate their strengths and accept their weaknesses, value progress, and view mistakes as hurdles in their learning tasks.

Implementing Standards Using Self-Assessment

- Introduce the term *self-assessment*. Explain the value of using self-assessment to improve with a standard. Discuss the fact that adults may not be available to check work.
- Teach students to model their step-by-step thinking processes with self-talk and other techniques they can use while identifying the accurate responses and correcting mistakes.
- Guide students through a practice session using each assessment tool. Model, model, model the self-assessment cycle until the expectations are understood and established.
- Create a list of personal affirmations for students to use, such as, "I am great and getting greater" and "Wow! I learned a lot this time!"

- Teach students to recognize their correct responses and successes. Emphasize the value of always improving through self-assessment by identifying needs, monitoring progress, and setting new goals.

Demystifying Self-Assessment

Introduce the term *self-assessment* as a way for an individual to look at his or her own needs to improve. Explain the value of using self-assessment for improvement by giving examples from the students' world outside the classroom.

Example:

An individual who swims the 200-meter butterfly stroke in 2 minutes and 45 seconds assesses her ability during and after the session. The swimmer may decide to work on correct form, pacing, breathing techniques, or the turnaround speed at the end of each lap to improve her time. Specific goals are set for the next practice session.

Explain that each time mistakes are corrected the learner is growing and improving. Share facts and stories about individuals who continually moved toward their potential. For example, as a boy, Benjamin Franklin analyzed his improvement every day and recorded his thoughts and goals in a journal.

★ ★ ★ ★ ★

Five-Star
Tips for Self-Assessment

1. Demonstrate strategies for students to check over their work before turning it in for a grade. For example, when students complete a math problem, show them step-by-step procedures to review the work.

2. Model each assessment tool until students have a full understanding of it. When students know how to use it independently, assign the tool in a self-assessment activity.

3. Designate a specific area as a Self-Check Zone or Feedback Station, where students check their work. Provide an answer key and a colored pencil or pen for checking. Post directions so students know where to place checked, corrected papers.

4. Encourage students to self-assess assignments and activities completed in learning zones, centers, and stations. Keep small pieces of paper available for students to assess their likes, dislikes, understandings, and misunderstandings.

5. Remember, students need to check their own work as soon as possible after completing an assignment. When learners know how to find errors and make corrections, each self-assessment experience becomes a valuable instructional activity.

Examples of Self-Assessment Tools

Example A: Students Learning From Mistakes

Use self-assessment procedures similar to the following to give immediate feedback:

1. Provide time for students to check their papers after a written assignment.

2. Post rules for self-checking similar to the following:
   - Pencils are not allowed during checking time.
   - Use the green pen to check your work.
   - Each green mark represents an area of needed growth.
   - Draw a green line through the incorrect answer or step.
   - Follow the rules so you will not lose your self-checking privilege.

3. Call on a student to announce and explain correct answers when time permits.

4. Use the self-assessment process to provide feedback.

5. Designate an area for completed work.

Example B: Self-Assessment Prompts

Teach students to monitor their own progress. Present prompts similar to the following to coordinate with standards:

Before

- My current level is _____.
- To improve, I need to _____.
- I need the following tools and materials: _____, _____.
- I need help with these new words: _____, _____.
- I need more information about _____.

During

- I am learning _____.
- I mastered _____. Now I need _____.
- This activity is (easy/difficult) for me because I _____.
- I need to change the way I am _____.
- I am learning _____.
- I need help with _____.
- I mastered _____.

After

- I was successful because I _____.
- I can improve by _____.
- I completed _____ today. To improve tomorrow, I need to _____.
- I correctly answered _____ on this lesson because I knew how to _____.
- I read _____ pages and learned _____.

Example C: Self-Assessment Rubric

Adapt the following self-assessment rubric for students to use in all activities and assignments.

Figure 3.4 Self-Assessment Rubric	
4 Star learner	• I always do my best. • I use everything I know to learn more. • I can share what I know to teach others.
3 Polishing my learning skills	• I can work alone with little assistance. • I can find needed resources. • I check my own work.
2 Ready to believe in me	• I am learning to think about how I learn. • I can work with others. • I know more than I thought I knew.
1 At the beginning	• The teacher reminds me to stay on task. • It is hard to get started on assignments. • Classmates tell me to listen and work. • I need to learn how to be a good team member.
My self-assessment level on this rubric is _____ because _____.	

■ INFORMAL FORMATIVE ASSESSMENT

What Is Informal Formative Assessment?

Informal formative assessment provides a quick but useful analysis of the learners' knowledge and skills for planning instruction and for self-improvement. The results are not used as a grade, because the analysis is subjective. Each informal tool is presented in an intriguing and challenging way. It requires each student in the class or group to provide an individual, observable answer to a question, prompt, or quiz. The teacher observes the responses. When a general need or learning gap is noted, an intervention with an immediate fix is implemented to keep the learner on track. When the results reveal a specific need that cannot be met directly, it is recorded for a future intervention through planning.

What Are the Instructional Benefits of Using Informal Formative Assessment?

Informal formative assessment provides the following:

- A quick view of group progress and individual needs
- A frequent and continuous procedure to gather needed data in less time than formal assessments
- A process for collecting data with minimal preparation and no recorded grades
- Novel and challenging ways to collect data.
- Various tools to engage test-phobic students so they show what they know without being hindered by fear

Implementing Standards Using Informal Formative Assessment

- Develop a collection trove of informal formative assessment tools so the appropriate one can be selected as needed.
- Model each informal formative tool and technique until students can use it with little or no teacher guidance.
- Analyze the results and use the findings in planning instruction for the diverse needs of learners.
- Create a nonthreatening environment and encourage students to be honest in their responses. Explain how their levels of understanding are used to plan their customized assignments and activities.
- Infuse the following guidelines throughout your explanation of informal formative assessment:
  - ○ It is important to know what you know and what you do not know so you can learn more.

   o Answer truthfully without checking other classmates' responses so the teacher will have accurate information to plan the most beneficial activities and assignments for you to learn the standard(s).

   o Enjoy the assessment activity, but realize the importance of it.

   o Use informal assessments to check your knowledge before, during, and after learning.

   o Remember, you move from the lowest to the top level with knowledge and experience.

Demystifying Informal Formative Assessment

Introduce informal formative assessments as quick, easy tools to obtain an overall view of what students have learned. Explain that these informal assessment tools are selected so the results can be used to plan for individuals and groups. Compare formal and informal formative assessments. Help students understand that the results are not used to determine a grade. Most formal assessments take more time and are used for grades.

Explain the importance of being honest with responses on informal formative assessments so the "right" activities and assignments are used to meet the students' diverse needs.

★ ★ ★ ★ ★

**Five-Star
Tips for Using Informal Formative Assessments**

1. Use a variety of informal response tools to teach students how to analyze their knowledge level in relation to the standard.

2. Engage students in informal assessments using body movements to show what they know. Use directions that are as simple as in the following:

   • Stand up if you know a lot about _____.
   • Lean over on your desk if you know some things about _____.
   • Stay in your seat if you do not know anything about _____.

3. Move forward with instruction when informal responses indicate that students know the information.

4. Observe reactions and facial expressions for valuable feedback. Pleasant expressions reflect understanding. Proud gestures indicate confidence.

5. Be alert and aware of student reactions to informal formative assessments, such as hesitation and reluctance to respond to questions or prompts. When students look to classmates for answers, they need more instruction. When a few students require more instruction or practice, address their needs in a small group with a targeted intervention.

Figure 3.5 Informal Assessment Tools

Bodily/Kinesthetic	Visual/Spatial	Verbal/Linguistic
Make a motion! • Create a signal • Use a hand signal • Use a nonverbal reaction • Wave a mini flag or sign	***Show it!*** • Use response cards • Respond on individual dry-erase boards • Use color-coded signals such as Popsicle sticks, signs, or disks • Create a specific design • Design a model	***Respond orally*** • Use a short answer • Give your point of view • Record your answer • Tell a friend • Brainstorm responses
Act it out! • Be a human replica • Simulate • Demonstrate • Use a manipulative • Use a prop	***Draw it!*** • A picture • A mural • A mini poster • A symbol • A caricature	***Report it!*** • To the teacher • To a peer • On a web page • In a video • On a blog
Show feelings/emotions • With a body signal • Likert arm • Thumb it • Using facial expressions • Role-play • Response cards • Miming	***Create it!*** • A replica • A display • A mini poster • A timeline • A diorama	***Write it*** • As a journal entry • On a chart • As notes • In a list • In a different genre • On an epage

RESPONSE CARDS ■

What Is a Response Card?

A response card is an informal formative assessment tool that allows teachers to check for understanding, knowledge, interests, and feelings before, during, or after a lesson. The cards may be used with an individual, partners, or a group.

Each student receives an identical set of cards with response options written on each side of the card in a multiple-choice format. When the teacher asks a question that requires a response, each learner holds up the card and indicates the correct answer by grasping or pinching the answer with a thumb on one side of the card and a forefinger on the opposite side of the card, pointing to the answer on both sides. For instance, when practicing multiple-choice responses, each student receives a card with A B C D written in the same place on the front and back of the card. When a question is posed, students study the possible answers posted and draw their conclusions before answering. Each student selects the answer to the question by pointing to it or by pinching the selection and holding the card up for the teacher to view. The teacher observes the action of the individual's fingers. Levels of confidence and insecurity with responses are usually evident.

What Are the Instructional Benefits of Using Response Cards?

- Often, when a teacher asks a question or seeks a response, one student responds. Classmates do not have to think or make an effort. This supports passive learning behaviors. When response cards are used, *all* students are actively engaged, because each individual is accountable for answering every question.
- An individual's knowledge can be gauged with a glance.
- The teacher has an opportunity to call on a student who responds correctly and follow it with a brief discussion. It is easy to take advantage of the teaching moment when several wrong answers are evident on one item. Elaboration is unnecessary and boredom is avoided when everyone responds with the correct answer.
- A quick mental or written note identifies learners for reteaching or review in an intervention with a small group or the total class.
- Response cards are easy to design for all grade levels and subject areas.

Implementing Standards Using Response Cards

- Decide where and when to use response cards for assessment. If the response card activity is the best way to assess a skill, ask the following:
  - What is the card design?
  - When will it be used?
  - Who will use it?
  - How will the results be recorded?
- Decide who will make the response cards:
  - The teacher makes the set.
  - Each student makes a card. Provide clear directions with a sample the first time students design the card.

○ Set up a response-card production center. As students finish tasks, they enter the production center to design the assessment cards using facts learned in assignments or activities.

- Explain the purpose of the informal formative assessment with concise, clear directions for using response cards.
- Design response cards to use as needed before, during, or after learning with the total class, small group, or partners.
- Collect data from the responses by making mental or written notes for future planning.
- Teach students how to create response cards from their assignments. Provide opportunities for the cards to be used as self-assessment tools in learning zones or review sessions.

Demystifying Response Cards

Tell students that response or answer cards are designed for them to show what they know in assessment activities and games.

The response card has a list of several answers to a question in a multiple-choice format. The possible answers are written on each side of the card. One answer is the best response. Select the correct answer, and show it by pinching the answer on each side of the card.

Explain to students how their responses assist you in selecting activities and assignments.

Five-Star
Tips for Making Response Cards

1. Use 3 × 5-inch or 5 × 8-inch index cards or tag board. Use cards that are big enough to write the answer choices in large print. It is time-consuming and expensive to laminate cards, so make three or four extra cards as replacements for lost or damaged ones.

2. Use bold markers with wide tips to make responses easy to see across the room. Colors that work best are black, purple, blue, brown, and green. Avoid yellow, red, orange, pink, and lighter shades. Use markers that will not bleed through the card.

3. Place multiple-choice items on the card in a vertical list using large, bold print. Turn the card over and write the same entries in the same position as entries on the front of the card. When the learner uses these duo response cards with the lists of possible answers on the front and back, the teacher and the student view the revealed response at the same time.

4. The first time students make a response card, show them how to hold it up to a light or window to be sure they write each word on the back in exactly the same place as the matching word on the front. This makes it easy for the student to grasp or pinch the selected response on each side of the card.

5. If you plan to add entries to the same card later, leave adequate space. For example, if the group studies two countries, write them on the response card and leave space to add additional countries later. Collect the response cards in a clear storage bag, folder, envelope, or small file box.

Five-Star
Tips for Using Response Cards

1. Identify options for storing, distributing, and collecting response cards that fit your classroom situation. Use the following distribution ideas:

   - Hand each student a card for the lesson as he or she enters the class. Have students return the cards on their way out.
   - Place cards in a basket so students can pick them up.
   - Place the cards in several locations around the room for easy accessibility: in the center of a cluster of desks or on a shelf, table, or cart.
   - If each student keeps a personal set of response cards, consider the following storage ideas:
     - Manila envelope
     - Clear storage bags
     - Notebook (Punch a hole in the upper left side of each card.)
     - Folder
     - Desk clip

2. Provide the lead-in question or statement. Direct students to hold the cards close in front of them to study the options. This is their thinking time. Give a signal for students to reveal their answers, such as saying, "1, 2, 3 . . . show me!"

3. Observe how students approach their answers. If someone is not answering honestly, guesses, or looks on a classmate's card, record the insecure action as an assessment!

4. Look closely at the students' reactions, because they reflect feelings about what they know. Call on a learner who responds correctly and quickly to explain his or her answer.

5. Use the following chart to guide observations as students select their response card answers.

Figure 3.6   Response Card Observation

Observation	Revelations and Reactions
The learner quickly indicates the correct answer without looking around for assistance.	This indicates confidence with the answer. Call on this student for the answer and an explanation.
The student points to an answer and then checks with classmates to see if the answer is correct.	This learner needs to use confidence builders such as: *Yes! I've got it!* *Give me a high-five!* *I have the right answer!* *I am so proud of me!* Do not tell this student to keep his or her eyes on his or her own card. Use the student's action as part of the data to plan confidence-building instruction.

(Continued)

(Continued)

Observation	Revelations and Reactions
The student waits and then looks at the answers of classmates before responding.	This action implies that the student does not know the answer and needs to learn more about this piece of information. Reteaching may be required. Remember to avoid saying, "Turn around!" because the action is a valuable part of the assessment.

Examples of Response Cards in Action

Example A: Ready Response to Reinforce a Concept or Skill

The teacher greets students at the door with premade response cards. Each student receives a card for use at a point in the lesson. When it is time for responses, the card is ready and accessible, so no time is wasted in distribution. Students drop them in a basket as they exit the classroom. The teacher stores the cards for the next lesson.

Example B: Turning Confusion Into a Light Bulb Moment

The class is confused about the difference between two or three categories presented during instruction. Students quickly form four-member teams. One person in each group tears a piece of paper into four equal parts. One section is dealt to each member. The teacher gives directions for making a response card using the confusing terms. Once all cards are complete, the teacher provides a question. Each group discusses the question and comes to consensus on the correct response before pinching the correct answer on the cards. When a signal is given, individuals raise the cards for the teacher to view and praise each light bulb moment. The teacher continues to give questions and provide discussion time. Students drop their response cards in a receptacle as they leave the room.

Example C: Partner Response Cards

Place response cards in a center for partners to use as a game for review or reinforcement. Partners face each other. The teaching partner reads questions while the other student responds. Answers are checked using a key. Students swap roles so each one has an opportunity to be the teacher as they play the assessment game.

SIGNAL RESPONSES   ■

What Is a Signal Response?

Students use a signal such as a raised hand or an action sign to respond to a question. This is a quick, informal formative way to assess the learner's knowledge, feelings, attitudes, and interests.

What Are the Instructional Benefits of Signal Responses?

- A signal is a quick, nonthreatening assessment tool for the differentiated classroom.
- The teacher gathers needed data in a brief period of time.
- No student materials are required.
- Students actively engage in the assessment and have fun with the game format.
- The assessment strategy can be used before, during, and after learning.

Implementing Standards Using Signal Responses

- Select a signal to reveal the information needed for planning. Be sure the action is easy for students to learn.
- Demonstrate use of the signal.
- Use the same signal often so it becomes a routine response for the group. Avoid using one signal as the "only" response. When one signal is used too often, it can become a mundane procedure. The learner thinks, "Here we go again!" and stops taking the response seriously. When the student is comfortable using a signal response, introduce a new one. Select or design new signals to add novelty to the informal assessment strategies.
- Remember to use signals to check attitudes, feelings, interests, understanding, and knowledge.
- Use signals to assess understanding before, during, and after the lesson:

  Before: Use a signal response a week or two before the information is taught to reveal the students' attitudes, interests, and knowledge base related to an upcoming standard, skill, concept, or fact.

  During: Present questions during learning to identify students who need specific segments adjusted or revamped in an intervention. Responses also uncover the students' comfort level, confusion, understanding, or need for more explanation.

  After: Use signals after learning to identify the students' immediate needs and information to address in plans for the next learning experience. Use the responses to reveal the students' strengths, interests, and overall understanding.

Demystifying Signal Responses

Tell students they will use signal responses throughout their lives. Give them examples, such as the peace sign, raising a hand, and nodding or shaking their heads to indicate yes or no. Explain that the sender and the receiver must understand the meaning attached to the signal.

Explain how signals will be used to give you information for planning lessons and activities. Introduce signal responses by asking students to use the "thumb-up" signal to indicate their knowledge of a sport, historical event, or vacation site.

Thumb up: *I know a lot!*

Thumb to the side: *I know something.*

Thumb down: *I don't know anything about it.*

★ ★ ★ ★ ★

Five-Star
Tips for Using Signal Responses

1. Assess with a signal response a week or two before teaching a standard so you can use the data to develop plans for individual students. Also use signal responses during and after learning.
2. Teach the signal, its purpose, and its meaning. Explain how the information will be used.
3. Use the quickest, easiest signals to reveal the students' knowledge.
4. Build the learner's repertoire of signal responses. After a signal is learned, use it strategically for an individual student, a small group, or the total class.
5. Use signal responses as one part of the data when making curriculum decisions!

Examples of Effective Response Signals

Example A: Telling Hands

When you have 5 minutes before or after a lesson, preassess for an upcoming lesson. Use a list of vocabulary words, concepts, or facts for the next identified standard. Demonstrate the following "Telling Hands" activity as a preassessment.

Hands reach up forming a Y: *YES! I know it.*

Hands touch high over the head forming an O: *Oh, I know a little about it.*

Hands over the ears: *I have never heard this.*

Option:

Announce "Stand and Deliver" time! Each student who responds with the "YES! I know it" signal becomes a "Stand and Deliver" captain. Divide the other students into small groups. Assign one captain to each group to share knowledge about the topic and to lead a related discussion.

Example B: Body Language

Use the following signal responses to assess vocabulary words, concepts, or facts:

Reach for the sky: *I can do it.*

Hands on waist: *I can do some of it.*

Hands on knees: *I need help.*

Example C: Signal and Shout (A Review for a Test)

At the end of a unit, the teacher and/or students develop fill-in-the-blank statements as a review for a test.

Tell students to point to their brains when they know the answer. Read one statement. Provide thinking time by waiting for individual signals, and then ring a bell. Students who know the answer shout it in unison. Students who do not know the answer write the statement and correct response as a study note. The steps are repeated.

■ STAND AND SHOW!

What Is Stand and Show?

Stand and Show is an informal assessment tool designed for students to indicate their knowledge level in relation to a standard, topic, or skill. Words, phrases, or numbers are posted to indicate varying levels of understanding, such as the following:

I know a lot!	I know a little!	I don't have a clue!
Professional	Amateur	Rookie
3	2	1

The place the student chooses to stand identifies the learner's knowledge level. Stand and Show can identify the learners' interests or feelings about an upcoming unit topic. This is a valuable informal assessment tool to use before, during, and after learning to identify progress.

What Are the Instructional Benefits of Stand and Show?

- Post colorful, novel signs to present the various levels of background knowledge.
- When students stand and show their level of knowledge, the teacher has a clear view of where each individual stands and the overall positions taken by the whole group. The names of students on each level are recorded to plan strategies and activities.
- The novelty added to assessment generates positive attitudes toward learning.
- Explain the major benefits of Stand and Show. Each student stands in the area that matches his or her knowledge level.
- Use Stand and Show with several topics or skills. Students see and appreciate how knowledge levels are diverse and constantly changing.

Implementing Standards Using Stand and Show

When Stand and Show is identified as an assessment tool to gather the needed information, consider the space and time allotted.

Decide how the learners on each level will express themselves after they take their positions. Some options include the following:
   o Each class member presents opinions or reasons for taking this position or stand, showing respect for peer choices.

o Have each group conduct a brainstorming session to identify the important facts they know about the topic and display them on a graffiti-style poster.

o Lead a class discussion of the information by calling on volunteers from each position.

o Make a list of students in their selected positions so you can design the instructional plan to meet their diverse needs.

o Use the same informal tool until the class understands how it works. Vary the level terms and format for novelty.

Demystifying Stand and Show

Tell students they will stand in specific places to show the level of what they know, believe in, or find interesting in relation to a topic, skill, or standard. Emphasize that some students will stand in different areas each time, because the place chosen is determined by each person's current knowledge base and experiences. Explain how a student's position helps your future planning for personal needs in an upcoming study.

★ ★ ★ ★ ★

**Five-Star
Tips for Stand and Show**

1. Identify the purpose of the Stand-and-Show assessment activity.
   Examples:

   To assess the learner's knowledge base   To express feelings

   To state a belief   To give an opinion

2. Establish areas with ample spacing to avoid overcrowding.

3. Give explicit directions before learners move to their positions.

4. Ask students to select and write their Stand-and-Show position before moving to the designated area. Tell students to discuss the reasons they selected the position after everyone is in place.

5. Establish a system for student movement that fits the activity and the arrangement of your classroom.

Examples of Stand and Show

Figure 3.7 Stand and Show at Work

Activity	How does it look?	How does it work?
Four corners or squaring off!	Label four classroom corners or areas to indicate levels of understanding and knowledge. Example | I do not know.	I know a little.
I know a lot!	I am an expert!		• The teacher names the topic, standard, skill, or concept. • Students go to the area that matches their knowledge or topic understanding. • Lead a discussion that emphasizes how they can move from the lower levels to the expert level.
Human bar graph	Post signs on the wall to indicate levels of understanding. Students move in front of the sign that reflects their individual level, forming a straight line at each one. Compare the lines to the bars on a bar graph. Each student represents one section of a bar on the graph. Ask students to stand in place so the lines are straight both horizontally and vertically to create the bar graph.	• Each student in a line becomes a segment of the bar on the bar graph. • Compare and contrast the number of students in front of each sign. • Discuss their differences.
Show your number	The teacher asks, "Where do you stand on the line?" Students stand in front of a number chosen on a Likert scale of 1 to 5.	• Post the numbers 1 to 5 to form a Likert scale. Be sure the numbers are spaced. • Name the topic, skill, concept, or standard. Give students time to identify their knowledge levels. Students take their positions. • Groups discuss their reasons for choosing the positions.
Circle gab	Conversation circles are formed with students who have common beliefs, opinions, experiences, or backgrounds.	• Each student joins other learners on the same knowledge level. • They discuss and brainstorm to defend their view, opinion, thinking process, or background.
Energizing partner	Students choose partners and share the information learned. They meet in designated areas.	• Partners meet to discuss, share, review, brainstorm, read, or check an assignment. • The same partner teams meet periodically. • This gives them the opportunities to bond and develop mutual respect, trust, and friendship.

FORMAL FORMATIVE ASSESSMENT   ■

What Is Formal Formative Assessment?

Formal formative assessment is administered to gather specific, documented data for analysis. Patterns of strength, weakness, or needs are analyzed to identify the student's status in mastery of the standards. End-of-the-unit tests, rubrics, portfolios, and anecdotal records are examples of formal formative assessments.

What Are the Instructional Benefits of Formal Formative Assessment?

- The level of mastery is identified and recorded.
- The data gathered at the end of a learning segment are analyzed and used to develop instructional plans for students' identified strengths and needs.
- The analyzed data are used to make changes in the individual student's instructional program or placement in special classes.
- Students are instructed in the use of test-taking skills to use throughout their academic careers.
- Formal formative assessment results are used for reporting purposes because they are more objective and reliable than informal formative assessments.

Implementing Standards Using Formal Formative Assessment

- Collect formal assessment tools such as rubrics and checklists to use before, during, and after learning. Add new tools to your repertoire. Make a list of the assessments, and place a checkmark beside the tool each time you use it. This adds novelty and identifies assessments that require an introduction.
- Select the most effective and efficient assessment tool to yield the results you need for planning.
- Report formal assessment results to other teachers and to parents as needed.
- Use formal formative assessments to determine mastery of standards, facts, or skills for a segment of learning.
- Teach students the skills and strategies for checking their work for accuracy upon completion of assessments.

Demystifying Formal Formative Assessment

Use a lecturette similar to the following to introduce formal assessment:

> *A formal assessment is a test to find out what you know about a standard, topic or skill. It also reveals what you don't know or understand. Your responses inform the teacher with specific information to plan your lessons and activities. You may receive a grade, points, or a score on a formal assessment.*

★ ★ ★ ★ ★

**Five-Star
Tips for Formal Formative Assessment**

1. Use a formal assessment tool when an informal one will not provide enough information. Select the most appropriate formal tool to obtain the data needed to show the learner's needs, progress, and mastery. Use a variety of formal formative assessment tools such as the following:

Fill in the blank	Academic journals	Open-book tests
Open-ended responses	Products	Portfolios
Quizzes	Reports	Rubrics
Standardized tests	Teacher-made tests	True/false tests

2. Become familiar with the assessment's directions and guidelines before administering it.

3. Teach students how to use the selected formal formative assessment tool. Introduce the terminology. Model the specific guidelines or procedures while explaining your thinking process.

4. Use more than one formal assessment to make informed curriculum planning decisions to address the specific needs of each student.

5. Analyze data from formative and summative assessments to obtain the formal grade.

Examples of Formal Formative Assessments

Example A: Combining Formal Assessments

Students work in groups on an assignment and present the information learned as a team. The group members, peer observers, and teacher score the presentation using a rubric that addresses the cognitive and social aspects of the task's process and the presentation. After completion of the presentation and the unit, each student takes an independent test to show what was learned.

Example B: Develop and Administer a Pretest/Posttest

A teacher-designed pretest is administered to assess the identified standards 1 to 2 weeks before the unit of study begins. The data are gathered from the results to pinpoint the knowledge base of each learner. Instructional plans are designed to teach the standards according to the identified individual and group needs. At the end of the unit, the pretest is administered again as the posttest to measure growth and mastery.

Example C: Teacher-Assigned Portfolio

Each student designs a new paper or electronic folder. The teacher instructs the students to place assigned artifacts in their portfolios. A list of ongoing entries is the front page. During and upon completion of the gathering, students conference with a portfolio partner, the teacher, or their parents to discuss accomplishments, insights, growth, and needs. Individual entries can be graded and a portfolio grade assigned upon completion.

PRETEST/POSTTEST ■

What Is a Pretest/Posttest?

A pretest is given to identify what the learner knows before teaching the unit. The test can be administered 1 to 2 weeks before the unit is introduced. This provides time to analyze the data gathered from the pretest results and to tailor plans for each student. Use the same instrument as the posttest at the end of the study to analyze areas of growth and identify standards or skills that need further development.

What Are the Instructional Benefits of Pretests/Posttests?

- Teaching is more efficient when pretests and posttests are administered. The evidence shows what individuals, as well as the total class, need during and after instruction. A teacher can identify learning gaps or strengths and share the results.
- The data can be used to design flexible grouping strategies for the activities.
- Students know what is important in the study when they see the pretest information.
- Materials and resources can be gathered to match the students' strengths, learning styles, intelligences, and needs.
- Growth is evident to the teacher and student when the same pretest and posttest is administered.

Implementing Standards Using Pretest/Posttest

- Design the most efficient, effective test to show what the students know.
- Be sure the test covers the needed components in the study.

★ ★ ★ ★ ★

Five-Star
Tips for Pretests/Posttests

1. The best tests are designed by the teacher. Remember, you know the information and standards to assess!

2. Select questions from areas in the study. Check to see that the test covers the identified standards, skills, content, and objectives.

3. Disperse easy items among the difficult ones so students become detectives and search for items they know. Designing the test using simple-to-complex items gives a true picture of each learner's prior knowledge and potential. Using this design, no one should make a zero or score 100% on the pretest.

4. Tell students their answers help you plan each activity and strategy for individuals and small groups.

5. Compare the pretest and posttest results. Share needs and growth with students.

- Vary the questioning formats.
- Explain to students that the pretest will be used to identify their background and knowledge related to the standard. Tell them they will be taught the information they do not know during the study.
- Give the pretest as a posttest to analyze growth.

Examples of Pretests/Posttests

Example A: A Formal Pretest/Posttest Grid

Prepare a grid sheet with six subtopics, and tell the learners to write anything they know about each category. At the end of the study, students fill out another grid with the same categories and write what they know. It is exciting to see how much knowledge has been acquired. Lead a celebration cheer. YES! YES! YES!

Example B: Manipulative Pretest/Posttest

Prepare a checklist for a standard to be taught with each student's name on the grid. During the week, the teacher asks individuals to model different tasks and concepts using manipulatives. When each example is performed correctly, the student places a checkmark or star beside his or her name.

This revealing information is used to group students for an upcoming unit standard for small-group assignments. Place the manipulatives in a station during the study. By the end of the unit, the teacher observes that most of the students mastered the skills. This observation indicates that it is posttest time. An analysis of the data identifies standards mastered and needed interventions.

Example C: Using a Company Pretest/Posttest

Carefully read the company-made test. Identify questions to address during the unit of study. Questions not addressed in lessons are announced to the group by saying, "You do not need to answer the following questions or items: ___, ___, ___." All students will enjoy hearing that statement!

EFFECTIVE QUESTIONING   ■

What Is an Effective Question?

An effective question is a specifically designed, mental probe that guides a learner's thinking toward an appropriate response. Questions are designed for the learner to process information, predict, review, check memory, or apply higher-order thinking skills. For written responses, teach students to pretend they are talking to someone and to write every word. The responses reveal the learner's inner thoughts to provide data for immediate instruction and planning.

What Are the Instructional Benefits of Effective Questioning?

- Questioning is a valuable technique to check for understanding and to assess students' needs and strengths before, during, and after learning.
- Thought-provoking questions allow the teacher to guide a student's thinking, focus individual attention, generate curiosity, and challenge minds. While probing a student to process information, the teacher gains a clearer understanding of the learner's knowledge of the current standard.
- The student gains a feeling of achievement by independently finding answers. Each learner is encouraged to select his or her personal problem-solving approach for providing the response.
- Questions lead students to connect old and new learning.
- An effective question assesses understanding. Each response provides informational data to use in planning customized instruction.

Implementing Standards Using Effective Questioning

- Differentiate questions based on the learner's abilities, knowledge level, learning styles, preferences, and interests.
- Develop a variety of questioning techniques to use as assessments. This keeps students intrigued and challenged.
- Strategically ask questions as checkpoints for understanding before, during, and after learning segments. Adjust your instructional pace if necessary.
- Use Bloom's, William's, or an appropriate taxonomy as a guide to design questions that develop critical thinking and problem-solving skills.
- Ask effective questions to promote thinking that links new information to a student's personal world. For example, ask the learner how the information or skill is used in daily activities at home.

Demystifying Effective Questioning

Introduce effective questions by describing them as brain probes. Use dialogue similar to the following to discuss the purpose of questions:

Questions are asked to discover what you know and don't know. They give you opportunities to give your opinions and thoughts about information you are learning. They help you think in different ways. Often, questions lead you into more detail about what you know. All answers are accepted, honored, and valued in this classroom.

Five-Star Tips for Effective Questioning

1. Present questions in novel ways.

2. Occasionally give students unexpected techniques to respond to questions. Use each response strategy until they master or take ownership of it. The next time you use it, the learners will know how to respond without extensive directions.

   Examples:

   - Give partners time to whisper the answer to each other, agree on the best answer, and write it down.
   - Engage students in physical actions for responses, such as standing, sitting, or using hand signals.
   - Ask each student to write the response in or around a shape related to the study.
   - Use response cards in a multiple-choice format.
   - Have students record responses on individual sticky notes or small pieces of paper.

3. Use Bloom's or William's taxonomy:

   - Make a checklist of the key terms on each level of the taxonomy to monitor its use.
   - Introduce questions strategically throughout the lesson to develop better thinkers and problem solvers.
   - To differentiate, allow students to choose questions from a list designed for their knowledge base level.
   - Create questions from independent assignments or group work that requires written or oral responses.
   - Teach and post definitions of the verbs in questions. Provide time for students to brainstorm their interpretation of each term, and write it beside the word. Learners take ownership of the academic vocabulary when they use their own terminology.

   Examples:

   Sequence: Place in order.
   Contrast: Tell how they are different.

4. Vary the types of questions. Remember to ask both explicit and open-ended questions. Most students must be taught how to answer questions that require implicit responses.

   Literal: The answer is in the writing. You can identify the needed information by pointing to it. Remember, the answer to a literal question is usually "right there."

(Continued)

(Continued)

| *What* | *When* | *Where* | *Who* | *How* |

Inferential: The answer is not stated outright—it is inferred—so you have to read between the lines to discover it. It is like seeing darkness behind a door. You have to use clues to guess what is on the other side of the door. Read the sentence and use the clues in the text to produce an answer when you cannot point to it in the passage.

- How did the character feel?
- What was the weather during this scene?

Evaluative: The answer explains the importance or value of the information. It gives the benefits of the facts or ideas.

- Why is this information, character, or idea important?
- Will the characters become better citizens as a result of their experiences? If your answer is yes, how do you think they will improve?

Figure 3.8   Varying Questioning Techniques

Container Questions	Action Questions	Written Questions	Oral Questions
• Basket • Box • Bucket • Can • Compartment • Cup • Drawer • Envelope • Folder • Glass • Hat • Jar • Pan • Pouch • Sack • Sock • Suitcase • Tub • Tube	• Roll a cube with a question on each side. • Use a spinner. • Sing to favorite tunes. • Use game formats. • Select questions from a container. • Toss a to identify the question choice. • Race with a classmate to the question. The winner selects the question for the opponent to answer.	• In a survey • On the board/smartboard • In a PowerPoint presentation • In a journal • In a station • On a choice board • In a shaker or jar • In the book • On a test • Under desks or chairs • On ribbons • In a spotlight • In graffiti style • On the door • On a mobile	• Within the group • From partners • From individuals • From consensus • Read from written material • In a game format die • In a computer program • Recorded • In a rap

Examples of Effective Questioning

Example A: Pull My String

1. Sit in a circle with a small group of students.
2. Give each student one string tied to your ruler.
3. Ask a question. Give students time to think of the answer.
4. Pull a student's string for a response.

Example B: On the Ball

1. Create a list of numbered questions.
2. Write different numbers on small balls, and place them in a large container.
3. Call on a student to take a ball from the container, and read the question corresponding to the number on the ball.
4. Ask all students to prepare a mental response.
5. The student who selected the ball calls on someone to respond.

Example C: Mystery Question

1. The teacher or students prepare questions relevant to the targeted standard(s).
2. Hide the questions in a container, such as a jar, sack, or envelope.
3. Each student selects a mystery question to answer.

Differentiating Questions Across Content Areas

Intentionally select the best questions to uncover the information you need to probe the learners' thoughts and guide differentiated instruction. Figure 3.9 presents probing questions and statements to use across content areas. It is followed by Figure 3.10 that shows examples of classroom questioning techniques.

Figure 3.9   Right Question, Right Time

Purpose of the Question	Sample Questions and/or Statements
To focus attention, stimulate curiosity, and challenge minds	What do you think about when you see _____? What are the important facts? What will happen next?
To find out what they know in order to identify needs before, during, and after learning	What do you know about this? What do you remember? Brainstorm a list of related facts and important details.
To check mental preparation to work	Do I need to explain a part of the directions for you? Do you have any questions about the steps you need to take? What do you need before you begin this activity?
To check for understanding	What steps did you use to get your answer? What were you thinking as you created the _____? Explain this in your own words.

Purpose of the Question	Sample Questions and/or Statements
To discover opinions or views	What do you think about this? What is your point of view or opinion? Identify the problem or solution.
To pinpoint the most valuable Information	Can you tell me the most important part to remember? What was the main idea? What are the highlights?
To identify what the student wants to learn next	What would you like to learn next? What was the hardest part for you? How can I help you?
To connect old and new learning	How do you know about _____? Where have you used this information? Tell me about an experience you have had. How will your experiences help you learn this new information?
To organize ideas	What goes with this part? Brainstorm and categorize your thoughts. Name three highlights from the beginning, middle, and end of _____.
To address what the student needs to know	What would help you learn more about _____? What do you need to learn next? What was difficult for you?
To gather knowledge	How can you organize the facts you need to remember? Which memory tool can help you remember the important information? Design a graphic to record what you know about.
To give personal ownership	How can you use this information in another class? Compare our new learning to an experience in your life. What is the best way for you to learn _____?

Figure 3.10   Students' Responses to Questions

Questioning Technique	Directions for the Technique
Random call	Ask a question and pause to provide "think" time before calling on a student to respond. This keeps students in suspense as to who will be chosen to answer, so everyone prepares a mental response. Randomly call on someone for an answer.
Unison call	Ask a question and provide "think" time. Call for an oral group response.
Quick call pass	Ask a question. Call on a student to quickly call on a classmate for the response. If the student hesitates, call on someone for the answer.

(Continued)

(Continued)

Questioning Technique	Directions for the Technique
Cluster call	Distribute question(s) to groups. Each team selects a recorder and reporter. Students form a brainstorming cluster around the recorder. Each group comes to consensus on the best answer to the question. The reporter announces the team's best response to the class.
Partner call	Identify two students as A and B partners. The teacher asks a question, gives wait time, and calls on A or B partner to respond. The designated partner answers the question. The other partner verifies or corrects the response and adds information to it. This leads to a class discussion.

When the student is identified for an independent differentiated assignment, use questions similar to those in Figure 3.11 before, during, and after the tasks as conversation starters and feedback. These interactions place responsibility on the student to identify immediate needs and progress with the assignment. The responses provide ongoing feedback related to standards and skills the student is learning.

Figure 3.11 Conversation Starters

Before **The Designing Stage**	• What would you like to learn about this standard? • What tasks would you like to complete to learn more about it? • What resources or materials do you need? • How much time will it take to complete your tasks? • How will your final product be presented? • How would you like to be graded on your work?
During **The Assessing Progress Stage**	• What have you done so far? • What have you learned? • How can I help you? • Do you need more or different materials? • Have you made any new discoveries? • Is there anything that we need to revamp or change in your assignment? • Show me some examples of your work.
After **The Feedback Stage**	• What did you learn? • What were your favorite tasks? most challenging? most difficult? • The next time which segment would you want to keep? • What needs to be changed the next time? • Did you need more assistance? ___ yes ___ no When? • Did you understand each assignment, task, and procedure? ___ yes ___ no. If not, identify and explain the problem(s). • Were you given enough time? ___ yes ___ no. If no, explain. • Would you like to complete another assignment like this? ___ yes ___ no. Why or why not?

ANECDOTAL RECORDS   ■

What Is an Anecdotal Record?

An anecdotal record is a note written during the teacher's observations of a learner. The information is used to improve instruction for an individual or group. Consistent, organized notes and forms are the key to effective anecdotal record keeping.

What Are the Instructional Benefits of Anecdotal Records?

- Anecdotal records are the product of teacher observation. They can be used in all aspects of instruction.
- They reveal information about a learner's academic progress, behavior, attitudes, emotions, and physical strengths and needs. These records provide individual data in academic areas and in social interactions and may include developmental characteristics.
- The teacher can observe and record findings before, during, and after learning without disturbing the student's engagement in activities.
- Anecdotal notes supplement other forms of assessment data to ensure that individual needs are adequately addressed in lesson plans.
- Strengths and needs are observed over a period of time, revealing growth or evidence of backsliding in an area of learning.

Implementing Standards Using Anecdotal Records

- Establish a record-keeping system that works best for you.
- Use specific, observable comments, such as the following:
  o The student does not know how to use context clues.
  o The standard has been mastered by the learner.
  o The student needs more instruction on _____.
- Avoid adjectives or subjective phrases, such as the following:
  o Good procedures
  o Working successfully
  o Poor work
- Observe and gather data regarding every aspect of the learner, including the knowledge base, learning style, work habits, attitude, and interest level. Let students know that the notes are made to assist them with learning.
- Analyze the notes when developing plans to address significant patterns or target specific areas. Share your observations with students, parents, and colleagues during conferences.

Demystifying Anecdotal Records

Tell students you keep anecdotal records or notes as you observe one student or a group. Explain that the notes are made before, during, and after lessons so you can remember what to do to help students. Let them know they may see you make notes as they work. Discuss how you use the information to plan their assignments and activities.

**Five-Star
Tips for Anecdotal Records**

1. Establish a record-keeping system that works for you.
Example:

- Use a large 5 × 7-inch index card for each student.
- Create a title or cover card to place on top of the card set.
- Write the student's name in the upper right-hand corner of the card.
- Alphabetize the cards.
- Punch a hole in the upper left-hand corner of each card.
- Place a ring through the holes in the cards to form a class set.

2. When using observation as an assessment tool, make brief notes on the student's card.

- Record the date and time of day for each entry, and record your comments.
- Write specific observable statements.
- Beware of using adjectives and adverbs in your descriptions. Avoid subjective comments.
- Focus observations on work patterns, growth, needs, and task behaviors that hinder or enhance learning.

3. When a student's card is filled on the front and back, create another card for the learner and insert it on the ring. If you notice that a student has only one card containing a few brief comments while other students have multiple cards, this reminds you to observe this individual more carefully.

4. Inform students about the purpose of taking anecdotal notes. Show individuals their personal information when it is appropriate.

5. Refer to the accumulated data in team meetings, teacher discussions, and parent conferences as documented evidence to support your perception of a student's strengths and needs.

Examples of Anecdotal Notes

Example A: Observing Peer Tutoring

Circulate among students during work time with a ring of large index cards to record findings. An individual is working with a peer tutor on a skill that was not mastered. Write a note about the peer tutor's quality of instruction or easy-to-understand explanation of the skill. This shows that the tutor truly understands the concept. Write another note on the card of the student receiving instruction to outline the problems and accomplishments of the tutoring session. A note is made about gaps in learning or concepts grasped. This information helps you remember what this student needs to practice and learn.

Example B: Group Member Feedback

Students are working in groups on a cooperative learning activity. Write notes to each team and to individual team members, sharing specific observations about the level of cooperation and social interactions.

Specific observations help students become more aware of their actions within a group setting. The notes assist them in making positive changes to be more considerate and effective members of a learning team. Watch for work patterns. Use the information in student conferences.

Example C: Noting Subtle Actions and Reactions

Be alert to a student's body language, including facial expressions and gestures. While giving directions, observe and note signs of insecurity, misunderstanding, or concern. Make written or mental notes as reminders to praise students who listen, follow directions, work cooperatively, work independently, and engage eagerly in tasks.

■ SURVEYS

What Is a Survey?

A survey is a questionnaire designed to identify personal information about the student's feelings, likes, dislikes, knowledge base, and other information. Three types of surveys need to be administered throughout the school year: (1) personal preferences, (2) study habits, and (3) background experiences to identify knowledge bases related to the standard.

What Are the Instructional Benefits of Using Surveys?

- A survey identifies learner's personal preferences, attitudes, and feelings.
- This information is used to customize opportunities for the students.
- The collected data assists the teacher and students to connect new skills and information to their lives.
- By surveying students often, teachers can keep abreast of the learner's knowledge and changes in their lives.
- Students are more apt to reveal information when intriguing survey formats are used.

Implementing Standards Using Surveys

- Develop a questionnaire for the unit of study or learning experience.
- Survey throughout the year, because students are forever changing.
- Survey for different purposes at the appropriate time:
  - Strengths/weaknesses
  - Likes/dislikes
  - Habits/experiences
  - Attitudes/feelings/emotions
  - Content knowledge/background

- Tie the survey results to instruction. Remember, the brain learns by making links and connections between the known and the unknown—or new—information.
- Use the survey's data to build rapport, especially with struggling learners.
- Use the data to plan strategically.

Demystifying Surveys

Explain the meanings of the word *survey* using examples from the learners' lives. Here is an example:

Restaurants often use a form to ask patrons what they enjoyed or want to eat so that the restaurant can use the information to plan future menus.

In the same way, you may be asked to answer questions so specific lessons and activities can be planned to suit your needs and interests.

★ ★ ★ ★ ★

Five-Star
Tips for Using Surveys

1. Use three different types of surveys throughout the year to gain more knowledge about the learner.
   - Finding personal preferences
   - Examining study habits
   - Determining knowledge and experience about a standard

2. The most informative surveys are designed by the teacher.

3. Give parents surveys to reveal more detailed information about the students.

4. Design brief questionnaires. Divide the questions into small segments so students or parents can zero in on quality answers.

5. Analyze the learned information and use the results to plan learning opportunities that appeal to students while addressing their individual personal and academic needs.

Examples of Surveys

Example A: Personal Preference Survey

What is your favorite subject? Why?

List three ways you like to learn about new things or ideas.

Example B: Study Habits

Where is your favorite place to study?

Who helps you with your homework problems?

Example C: Standard Knowledge Base

What do you know about _____?

List experiences you have had related to _____.

■ JOURNALS

What Is a Journal?

A journal is a place where thoughts are recorded so they can be organized, saved, and read at a later time. A journal entry is a writing activity that may have details of an event, an experience, an observation, or a memory. The major purpose of a journal entry is to record the student's thoughts. Correct English usage and mechanics are not emphasized. The goals of journaling are for students to make their thoughts visable and to generate creative thinking.

What Are the Instructional Benefits of Using Journals for Assessment?

- A journal is an excellent learning tool for all subject areas and all grade levels. A journal assessment activity may be used for a daily lesson, weekly assignment, or unit with individuals, partners, or small groups.
- Journal assignments may ask the student to record important facts, steps, procedures, and other information during a study.
- The entries become resources for review and reference during independent study or test preparation.
- Writing new information leads the learner to focus and apply thinking processes.
- Journaling gives the teacher a clearer view of a learner's attitudes and beliefs in relation to a standard.

Implementing Standards Using Journals

- Identify the purpose for the journaling activity:
  - To gather information about the student's comprehension of the lesson
  - To explain step-by-step thinking
  - To record interests and attitudes about the topic
- Select a journaling strategy or genre. Use different forms, because some students write better in one format than another.
- Provide the necessary time, tools, and materials.
- Give lead-in statements to obtain specific information, and monitor journal entries to provide targeted feedback and appropriate interventions.
- Use specific guidelines, such as the following, with students to personalize journal experiences:
  - Follow the directions to decorate the cover of your journal.
  - Add drawings, stories, and thoughts to your journal when you have extra time.
  - Record the date, title, or purpose above each entry.
  - Keep your journal neat, organized, and in a special place so it is easy to find.
  - Use the journal as a study resource for reviews.

Demystifying Journals

Students may be confused the first time a journal activity is introduced outside of the English or language arts classroom. Adapt the following dialogue to explain that a journal is an effective learning and assessment tool for any subject:

> *A journal is a place to gather your thoughts. It is a special place to record important information, findings, facts, and ideas. Use journaling to note facts or things you are learning, concepts you don't understand, and what you would like to learn. A journal activity is an effective way for a teacher and student to communicate.*

**Five-Star
Tips for Using Journals for Assessment**

1. Give each student a sheet of colored paper for a journal cover. Tell students to personalize the cover by writing their name in large, colorful letters, using a graffiti style. Instruct them to add symbols, words, and phrases that reflect the journal's purpose. Use the following ideas for students to personalize their journals. See Figure 3.12 for related ideas.

   Personal journal: Add symbols, words, and phrases that represent your family, hobbies, and interests to decorate the cover.

   Content journal: Decorate the cover with symbols and themes related to the standard.

Figure 3.12　Journaling Ideas for Assessment

Graphics	Learn and Write
• Plot on an organizer	• Write about content information
• Draw the object and label it	• Answer a question
• Create a cartoon	• Brainstorm a list
• Illustrate a sequence	• Free write
• Create an advertisement	• Draw a timeline and plot the
• Cut, paste, and write	information
• Create a graph and explain	• Record a sequence
• Draw a map	• Write a sequence
• Diagram the parts	• Develop a fact sheet
• Design a caricature	• Add a log or diary entry
• Design a spreadsheet	• Write an editorial or news flash
• Create a PowerPoint presentation	• Write a letter
• Create a brochure	• Create a song, poem, rap, or cheer
• Design a puzzle	• Write reflections
• Create a game and its rules	• Develop a summary or critique
• Make a shape book	• Write a report
• Design a mobile	• Set goals
• Decorate a shirt	• Explain your thinking process
• Design a Webpage	• Create an ongoing progress report

(Continued)

(Continued)

2. Use a variety of strategies for independent journal assessments.

3. Use flexible grouping during and after the journal assignment.

   - Brainstorm with a partner and write _____.
   - Discuss _____ in your group and record the best ideas.
   - Write your opinion about _____ and share it with your group.
   - Use a double-entry journal. Draw a line to divide a sheet of paper into two columns. Write your thoughts in one column. Your partner responds to your comment(s) by writing in the other column.

4. Add novelty to the writing experiences.

   - Use a variety of writing implements, including the following:

Gel pens	Colored pencils	Magic markers
Crayons	Chalk	Glitter glue

   - Use a variety of writing materials:

Construction paper	Poster board	Chart paper
Wrapping paper	Word processor	Notepads

   - Use a variety of writing designs in assignments:

In a pyramid	Around the edges	On the outline of an object/picture
In a spiral	In a unique	Using calligraphy

5. Identify various ways for students to share journals during the year. Periodically present choices for individuals and small groups to present or share their journal work, similar to the following:

   - Display it on a table.
   - Share it with a partner, group, or another class.
   - Present it to family members on parent night.
   - Post a favorite page on the class website.

Examples of Journaling Activities

Students need time to write journal entries about their requests, comments, questions, and reflections.

Example A: Use "Aha" Boxes

Each student writes about an "aha" moment experienced while reading or working with a task, and draws a box around it.

Example B: Use a Likert Scale

Our Likert scales begin with the number 2 because we believe students deserve a score above 1 for being in school and for participating. See the examples in Figure 3.13.

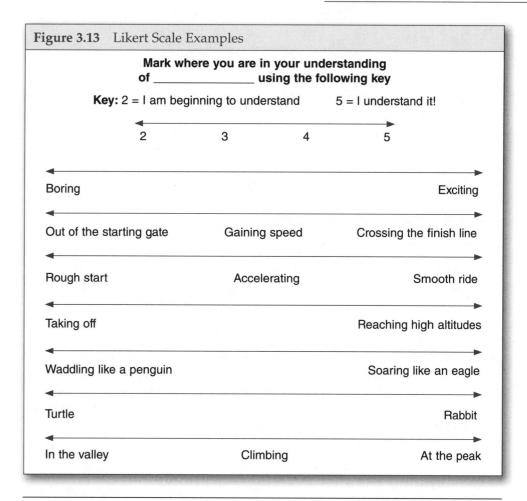

Figure 3.13   Likert Scale Examples

Example C: Draw It!

Draw a picture of an important place, character, or event in the lesson. Write a brief description of your drawing. Explain why it is important.

Example D: Color the Lesson Segment

Figure 3.14   Coloring Standards

Select a color that suits today's standards.	Tell why you chose this color.

Example E: Theme Song

Choose a song as a theme song for today's lesson. Explain why you selected this song.

■ PORTFOLIOS

What Is a Portfolio?

A portfolio is a place where student work samples are gathered for a specific purpose. The collection reflects progress and growth, needs and strengths. It is an evolving showcase of the student's best work.

Portfolios are designed by the teacher or the student using specific criteria and guidelines set by the teacher. Portfolios can be binders, notebooks, folders, boxes, tablets, zip drives, or other electronic devices.

What Are the Instructional Benefits of Using Portfolios?

- Portfolios can be adapted for all grade levels and subject areas.
- Each learner is given the responsibility to select his or her best work and determine which pieces need improvement or replacement. This gives students a sense of ownership and control over the learning experiences.
- Preparing a portfolio teaches self-assessment and reflection skills for improvement.
- A portfolio can be completed at the learner's individual pace.
- Progress points and a completion date teach the student how to set goals. Each successful portfolio experience generates a sense of pride and accomplishment.

Implementing Standards Using Portfolios

- Explain the purpose and goals for using the portfolio.
- Establish the criteria for item selection.
- Engage the student in various aspects of the procedure.
  o Planning the criteria
  o Selecting the samples
  o Assessing the work
  o Designing the presentation
  o Creating a display
  o Setting new goals
- Identify and explain the assessment tools used with the portfolio experiences.
- Establish a timeline with checkpoints and a completion date.
- The following ideas may be adapted and used as student guidelines for using portfolios:
  o Personalize your portfolio with your name. Decorate it following the directions provided.
  o Place the guidelines, assessment tools, and important dates in the portfolio.
  o Review the assessment tools and use them according to the timeline to assess your work and reflect on ways you can improve future assignments.
  o Add samples of your work to the portfolio throughout the study.
  o Select samples of your best work to showcase in the final portfolio conference.

Demystifying Portfolios

Share the meaning of *port,* meaning to carry, and *folio,* meaning "leaves" of paper. Display examples of portfolios, including a briefcase, a leather notebook, and a folder. Discuss portfolios that are required as part of many job applications. Show samples of portfolios the students will use.

Examples of Portfolio Assignments

Example A: Digital or Electronic Portfolio

Plan a portfolio assignment by identifying each of the following:

- The purpose and the audience
- The standards used as the organizing framework
- The electronic equipment and software available
- The technology level of skills possessed by the portfolio developer
- The electronic portfolio activities the student is to complete

The following are entry samples of an electronic portfolio selected over a 1- to 3-week period.

- ○ Introductory plan with purposes and timelines
- ○ Notes from active research
- ○ Reference bibliography
- ○ Term paper
- ○ PowerPoint presentation of findings

★ ★ ★ ★ ★

**Five-Star
Tips for Using Portfolios**

1. Identify the targeted standard(s), topic, and timeline for the portfolio gathering period.

2. Determine the purpose, guidelines, and process of creating and using the portfolio. Adapt the following steps for the portfolio experiences:

   a. Identify the type of portfolio:

   - Teacher selected: The teacher chooses the items for the portfolio.
   - Student selected: The teacher provides the criteria and number of samples for the portfolio. The student chooses the items.
   - Teacher and student selected: During a conference, the teacher and student come to consensus on the guidelines and criteria for the portfolio entries.

   b. Identify the form of the portfolio:

   - Electronic portfolio: tablet, personal computer, organizer, zip drive, or CD
   - Folder portfolio: pocket folder, large plastic bag, or homemade folder
   - Notebook or briefcase portfolio
   - Box portfolio: plastic, cardboard storage box; pizza box; or shoebox

(Continued)

(Continued)

3. Assign portfolio pals or teams. They conference at scheduled times during the process to discuss the portfolio selections, monitor progress, give and receive feedback, and determine areas of need. Teach students how to obtain quality results from a conference.

4. Use the following steps to prepare learners for the portfolio conference:
   - Place small tabs on four or five selections that represent the best examples of your work.
   - On each selection, identify and plan how to present or showcase evidence of the information you learned.
   - Highlight the important part to share.
   - Attach personal comments about the entry if you want to tell the teacher about it.
   - Use a self-assessment or peer-assessment form for the completed portfolio.

5. Celebrate completion of the portfolio!
   - Provide peer conference partners time to share specific accomplishments that are evident in the portfolio conference.
   - Plan a special portfolio showcase/conference for parents.
   - Invite students from another class to view the completed work.
   - Send electronic portfolios to family members or friends.

  o Digitized pictures of artifacts
  o Graphics organizers, including charts and graphs
  o Video streaming and recordings
  o Reflections
  o Summary of information learned related to the standard.

The student shares and discusses entry samples to show evidence of learning. The audience may be the teacher, or peers, or parents in a portfolio conference or class presentation.

Example B: Independent Portfolio
One Student Excels in the Upcoming Topic, Standard, or Skill

1. Hold a conference with the student to identify interest areas related to the standard.

2. Work with the student to identify appropriate portfolio activities from a list. Encourage the student to think of additional portfolio activities. Decide how many entries the student must complete. The student checks assigned activities in the first box. When the activity is completed, the second box is checked.

Examples:

☐ ☐ Essays   ☐ ☐ Graphic organizers

☐ ☐ Discovered facts   ☐ ☐ Illustrations

☐ ☐ Outlines   ☐ ☐ Self-assessments

☐ ☐ Poems   ☐ ☐ Study guides

☐ ☐ PowerPoint design   ☐ ☐ Summaries of video clip

☐ ☐ Procedure log   ☐ ☐ Web search findings

☐ ☐ Research findings   ☐ ☐ Writing samples

3. The student creates a contract proposal and submits the action plan.

4. The teacher approves the student's submission, accepts it with additions, or rejects the proposal. When the student and teacher come to consensus, each one signs the contract to indicate acceptance of the terms.

5. Create a timeline to monitor checkpoints, conference dates, and the completion deadline.

6. Identify the needed materials and resources.

7. Review the criteria and assessment tools with the student.

Example C: Cooperative Learning Project Portfolio

The following steps lead to a successful team portfolio:

1. Form groups of three or four to create cooperative working teams.

2. Provide a list of proposed topics for each group to select a topic by consensus.

3. Present a folder assignment with purposes, timeline, rubrics, and standards to address.

4. Establish roles and guidelines for each team member.

5. Complete the portfolio by collecting samples from each team member, as well as those created from the group. Some portfolio sample entries may include the assignments, individual contributions, notes from brainstorming, results of findings, graphics, artifacts, or group and individual reflections.

   NOTE: Grade each team member separately on his or her contribution during the cooperative learning experience. Individual tests may be administered on the information learned instead of giving a group portfolio grade.

■ GRADING IN THE DIFFERENTIATED CLASSROOM

What Is Differentiated Grading?

Differentiated grading refers to the combination of assessment data gathered from two aspects of a student's learning world. The school district and administrators must approve this grading procedure. Educators who value differentiated instruction see the impact of differentiated grading on each learner's success.

Grades are accumulated from a combination of knowledge-base work and grade-level assignments. This dual grading is necessary in the differentiated classroom. Some grades are gathered from the learner's work on knowledge-level assignments and activities. Students receive alternative assignments to zap gaps or to work at a higher degree of mastery. Some grades are gathered from these special assignments. When students work with activities and tasks tailored to their levels, they usually make high grades. If these scores are the only assessment results used in grading, a false picture of the learner is presented.

Other grades are recorded from data gathered on grade-level performances and assignments. Using only assessment results from grade-level work is not an option. These exclusive scores lessens the value of knowledge-level assignments.

In traditional classrooms, the number and/or letter grade is often the focus of all assessments. It reflects the learner's standing in relation to the class. In a differentiated classroom, the assessment reflects the student's knowledge level and progress. The final grade is a blending or combination of knowledge-based and grade-level assignments. This approach rewards progress and provides a fairer and truer picture of the learner.

What Are the Instructional Benefits of Differentiated Grading?

- Strategic grading from various sources provides data used as an integral part of planning customized instruction.
- Grades are gathered from different measures and types of activities.
- A more complete view of the learner's progress and growth is presented.
- Students are honored for effort and success.
- The gathered data reflect the learner's level of mastery and identify intervention needs for the targeted standard(s).

Implementing Differentiated Grading With Standards

- Understand the dual grading process thoroughly before using it in your differentiated classroom.
- Explain this process to parents, students, and other teachers. Do not gloss over the fact that a student is not performing at grade level. Be honest.
- Gather grades from all aspects of the learner's work, not just pencil-and-paper assignments. Use assessments from authentic tasks. Strategically select the grades that give the most complete report of

the student's overall performance and growth. Remember, it is not the quantity of grades included in the grade book list that is valuable but the quality of the grades.

- Analyze your belief system in relation to assessment.
- Share your differentiated grading philosophy in discussions with the grade-level or subject-area team and other faculty members so everyone is aware of your views on the differentiated grading system.

Demystifying Differentiated Grading

Explain to students that in a differentiated classroom, everyone is not graded or taught the same way. Grades are given on grade-level information and skills, but each person is also graded on knowledge level, effort, and progress. Everyone encourages and assists classmates. Remind students that someone who is struggling with a standard now may become an expert with more knowledge and experience.

Always remember that a grade is simply a checkpoint. Remind them that they can always improve.

Five-Star
Tips for Using Differentiated Grading

1. Be selective in choosing grades to record. They need to represent the student's progress, growth, understanding, weaknesses, and strengths. Do not grade every page or record each score. Choose a few quality grades that reflect the same results as a multitude of grades.

2. Use the appropriate assessment tools, such as rubrics and checklists, for authentic learning so students can show what they know. Ask yourself, "Which assessment tool will be the most effective in uncovering what the learner knows?"

3. Let students grade their papers so they receive instant feedback on correct answers and identify their own errors. Have students correct each mistake by drawing a line through the wrong answer and writing the correct response above it. The learner and the teacher use different-colored writing implements, so each one is able to target mistakes and focus on corrections.

4. Remember, students are motivated when a grade is accompanied with a note that explains how to improve.

5. Give two grades to present a more complete, blended picture of the student's abilities.

   - Base the first grade on the student's progress within his or her knowledge or ability level. Measure the student's progress with filling holes in learning or zapping gaps to complete understanding.
   - Use the second grade to reflect the student's ability in relation to grade-level expectations. This compares the learner to students in the same grade or subject.

Examples of Differentiated Grading

Example A: Dual Grading

- A student excels on the preassessment and is working on an individual academic contract assignment. Collect two individual grades, one from the contract assignment and one from the pretest.
- A group of four students demonstrate a lack of understanding of the skill on the preassessment. They receive two special assignments to reteach the skill. During independent work time, the remainder of the class works on grade-level practice assignments. A grade-level test is administered to all students. The grade is recorded. In this scenario, each student receives two grades—one from independent work and another from a class test.

Example B: Grading and Analyzing
Pretest/Posttest Results

A teacher-designed pretest is administered 1 to 2 weeks before the study begins. The results are analyzed to plan for individual needs. The preassessment results are not used as a grade but serve as a planning tool to address the diversity in the assessed group.

The pretest is given at the end of the study as a graded posttest. The results are analyzed to identify the learner's needs for future instructional planning. Students benefit when they compare the pretest and posttest results and realize how much they learned.

Example C: Gathering Grades From Various
Performance Evidence

Average and combine grades from various tasks such as written work, oral presentations, daily activities, lab experiences, portfolio samples, and the end-of-study test to create the final grade. In each daily assessment, including grading papers and collecting anecdotal records, be consciously aware of gathering the valuable information to plan strategically.

TEACHER-MADE TESTS   ■

What Is a Teacher-Made Test?

Teacher-made tests are formative assessments and evaluations created by the teacher to discover what the student knows before, during, and after instruction. The tests relate directly to the standards, skills, and concepts in a learning segment. They are designed using various formats, such as multiple choice, open-ended questioning, fill in the blank, matching, graphic organizers, and performance tasks. Each test is developed for learners to show what they know. The time involved in producing teacher-made tests is worthwhile because items are customized for the individual, group, or class.

What Are the Instructional Benefits of Using Teacher-Made Tests?

- Each item on the test relates to the current lesson, standard, or skill to emphasize the identified content information.
- Because items focus on previously taught information, teacher-designed tests clearly reveal parts of the lesson or unit the student learned or items that need to be revisited.
- A thorough pretest can be used as a posttest to identify individual growth and deficiencies.
- A teacher-made test compares students' knowledge to develop appropriate learning plans.
- If students incorrectly answer the same question(s), select a different instructional strategy to teach the standard or concept.

Implementing Standards Using Teacher-Made Tests

- Select the standard(s) to assess. Consider each piece of information to determine which test format in your assessment toolbox will be most effective.
- Choose the appropriate format to reveal information students know.
- Design and develop the test. Thoughtfully plot the order of the questions. Disperse easier and difficult questions throughout the test. This encourages learners to be detectives and work through the entire test.
- Give yourself an assessment rehearsal by taking the test as a learner. Check it to see that directions are clear. Eliminate irrelevant questions and replace them with items that focus on the addressed information. Create an answer key and revise it as needed.
- Select the most appropriate time to give the test. Explain the format, the grading scale, or weights that apply, and answer student questions. Share words and phrases to encourage and build confidence before learners take the test.

Demystifying Teacher-Made Tests

Inform the students when a test is teacher made. Use a lecturette similar to the following:

> *I made this test so we can see if you learned the most important information in our lessons. It will reveal the things you know. It will also show us the items you still need to learn or practice. I made the test and answered the questions to be sure it would be the best test for you. So . . . do your best on the test!*

★ ★ ★ ★ ★

Five-Star
Tips for Teacher-Made Tests

1. Remember, assessment drives curriculum when planning to teach the core standards. Preassess 1 to 2 weeks before the unit is introduced. Use an analysis of the data to develop lesson plans that work for the group. For example, when a student gets 100% on a test, this learner is exempt from the unit activities and assignments. The student engages in alternative tasks to extend thinking in areas related to the current standard.

2. Use a teacher-made test as a pretest and as a posttest to address the most important information in the content study. Be sure each question addresses the most important information. Give the posttest when a majority of the group knows the material.

3. Place two or three easy questions at the beginning of the test. Disperse easy questions throughout the test. Tell students to search for items they can answer.

4. Design the test so no one receives a zero, even on the pretest. This encourages the learner to search for questions to answer.

5. If there is not enough time to develop the test, adapt a commercial test. Tell students to mark and skip inappropriate questions. Learners should not be tested on information not taught in the unit. Add questions to address the standard..

Examples of Teacher-Made Tests

Example A: Using a Pretest/Posttest

The teacher designs a preassessment on an upcoming topic to administer. It also serves as the post-assessment tool. The assessment is divided into three parts on different levels of difficulty. The teacher may give each section of the test on a different day to avoid overwhelming students.

Example:

Part 1: Manipulatives
Show me so I can develop hands-on experiences for you.

Part 2: Open-Ended Questions
Tell me what you know so I can see how deep I need to go to develop ideas for you.

Part 3: Multiple Choice
Find and mark the right answer so I will know the information and facts I need to teach.

Example B: Using a Company-Made Pretest/Posttest

1. Examine the pretest/posttest provided by the textbook publisher. Use it only if it covers most of the material you plan to introduce with the upcoming standards.

2. Read each test item and decide if it is a keeper or loser.
   - Keep the item if it will show what will be learned during the study.
   - Mark the items that will not be addressed or that are poorly stated.
   - Be sure every student will be able to answer some items.

3. At the end of class, take 15 minutes to distribute and administer the pretest.
   - Explain how the pretest assists in planning their lessons and activities. Tell students to answer the items they know. Explain that they are not expected to know everything on the test.
   - Pass out the test. Identify the items students do not need to answer. No one will mind omitting questions.
   - Give the same test as a posttest. Add a blank page so they can write facts and details about anything not addressed on the test. Give one point for each correct statement.

Example C: Using a Box Organizer for Assessment During Learning

Tell each student to fold a piece of copy paper to create six sections or boxes.

Provide six subtopics and/or vocabulary words related to the current standard or study for students to place in each box. They fill in each box with information learned.

■ STANDARDIZED TEST PREPARATION

What Is Standardized Test Preparation?

Standardized test preparation begins the first day when students enter the classroom and continues throughout the year. Routine practice prepares students to work effectively and comfortably during formal testing. Each test follows mandated guidelines, directions, and time frames for each section. Use the established guidelines. Students must know how to follow oral and written directions, pace themselves, read statements, select the best response, and check their work.

What Are the Instructional Benefits of Standardized Test Preparation?

- Practicing test-taking skills using content information throughout the year builds confidence. This is more beneficial than extended preparation a few weeks prior to the test. Use the strategies for test success throughout the curriculum and in a variety of activities.
- Give students various ways to practice these skills without isolating them as preparation for the "big tests." They develop the skills without the anxiety some students feel before and during standardized tests. Play games highlighting vocabulary skills, and practice the skills with facts related to the standard. Periodically give unit assessments from time to time using standardized test formats.
- Test preparation is built into the class culture. Test takers realize their roles as important representatives in school success.
- When students know test-taking skills and apply them automatically, the weeks before the test become a celebration time.
- Students who experience test preparation throughout the year are able to do the following:
  - See tests as routine activities that reflect their knowledge.
  - Become familiar with words and phrases used in the directions.
  - Internalize test-taking strategies and apply them automatically.
  - Check their work.
  - Know the results are used to help them improve.

Implementing Standards Using Standardized Test Preparation

- Know your standards, your students, and the most effective ways to teach information so it is retained.
- Teach test-taking strategies, and use standardized test formats throughout the year using the content information.
- Motivate students, and build their confidence with testing skills.
- Teach students to become problem solvers and critical thinkers.
- Identify the test-taking needs of individual learners.

Materials:	Pencils	Erasers	Paper	Place marker
Personal:	Space	Lighting	Desk position	
Mental:	Familiar environment	Familiar administering voice		
Physical:	Water	Nutrition	Exercise	
Emotional:	Specific praise	Affirmations	Cheers	

Demystifying Standardized Test Preparation

Explain to students that each test provides opportunities for them to show what they know. The results reveal each learner's strengths and weaknesses. Discuss ways the information is used to plan the right kind of assignments and activities to prepare them for the state test. Use the following analogy to emphasize the importance of test preparation:

> *When a music teacher begins practice sessions with students, the focus is on basic skills. During each session, they improve and gain confidence. The performers begin to look forward to a successful recital to showcase their skills and talents.*

★ ★ ★ ★ ★

**Five-Star
Tips for Standardized Test Preparation**

1. Teach test-taking strategies throughout the year.
2. Use games or mystery adventures to help your students absorb information in their unique ways of learning.
3. Inform parents and students of the physical and psychological needs for top brain functioning.
   Examples:
   Rest   Eat nutritious snacks and meals   Be excited!   Be confident!
4. Maintain the look and feel of the daily learning environment during testing experiences. Use the same room, voice, and desk arrangement, if possible.
5. Design exciting activities the week before the test to celebrate what students know to raise their confidence levels and reduce pretest jitters. Then watch test scores soar!

Examples of Effective Standardized Test Preparation

Example A: Attacking a Passage

The students read a passage with new vocabulary words. They look for context clues such as antonyms, synonyms, or definitions. Discuss the value of using context clues on a test. After the lesson, place the passages in a learning station for extended practice in attacking a passage.

Example B: Eliminating Incorrect Answers on Multiple-Choice Questions

While reviewing for a chapter test, students play a game based on the popular television game *Who Wants to Be a Millionaire?* The questions are based on important facts from previous lessons. By playing the game, students learn multiple-choice strategies such as how to eliminate incorrect choices.

Example C: Experiencing the Testing Environment

Introduce various aspects of the standardized testing environment during chapter and unit tests throughout the year.

- Place and space desks in the standardized-test arrangement.
- Provide each student with two pencils and scrap paper.
- Place a "Do Not Disturb" or "Brain Drain in Progress" sign on the door.
- Time the test.
- Maintain a quiet environment.
- Use the available computer-generated test formats to practice.

■ CONCLUSION

Assessment is an ongoing process in the differentiated classroom. Remember that detective hat, and search for the most effective tools to assess the identified standard(s). Analysis of the gathered data is essential for planning a curriculum to address individual needs.

Effective differentiators know their students, standards, and resources. Then, using formative and summative assessment results to diagnose learners' specific needs, interests, and abilities, they create individual-appropriate activities. The learning segments are planned to continuously challenge but not overwhelm students. It takes time to learn about each aspect of the individuals, but the investigative work is rewarded as the "detective" discovers clues to students' learning and achievement.

- Preassess before planning curriculum for a given topic to engage students at their current knowledge levels. Avoid basing decisions for lesson plans on previous groups of students or preconceived notions. Use a preassessment to hit your mark.
- Assessing during the learning prevents boredom and saves valuable instruction time. Once information is mastered, no student is held back or forced to wait until a unit is completed before moving forward with more challenging activities.
- Evaluations show mastered learning and highlight the standard or concepts that require interventions for reteaching or reinforcing during the next lesson or study.

Remember, clues provide information for solving a case. In a similar way, assessment tools give you data to plan instruction for each student. Using the right formal or informal formative assessment, you identify needs and confidently plan for each individual, small group, or the entire class.

Figure 3.15   Personal Differentiated Reflections on Formative Assessment

1. How do you preassess students? How are the gathered data used to personalize instruction? Identify new preassessment tools you encountered in this chapter. When and how are you planning to use them?

2. Label 2 weeks of your lesson plans to identify the formative assessment tools used before, during, and after learning. Mark each type of assessment as (F) formal or (I) informal. After completing the task, tally your marks to see how many formal and informal tools were used. Ask yourself if you are using the appropriate type of assessment to gather data. Also, identify overuse of the tools that leads to assessment ruts!

3. Create survey entries to identify individuals' interests, study habits, and knowledge base related to upcoming units, standards, or topics. How can you incorporate the survey results to teach the standards?

4. How do you prepare students for standardized testing throughout the year?

5. Use Figure 3.3 as a checklist to assess your use of various assessment tools before, during, and after the learning. Identify a tool to add to your assessment toolbox.

Figure 3.16   Five Activities for a Professional Learning Community (PLC) Study

1. Brainstorming Formative Assessment Tools
   a. Form small study groups.
   b. Have each group identify a recorder, and tell other members to gather around the recorder.
   c. Direct the group to brainstorm formative assessment tools currently used for 3 minutes as the recorder writes each response.
   d. Ask the groups to label the tools using (F) formal and (I) informal.
   e. Compile a total group list of tools in columns of formal and informal tools. Provide a copy of the list for all PLC members.

2. Response Cards
   a. Tell individuals to create three response card samples related to their grade-level standards or skills using the directions in the Five-Star Tips on page 66. Form interest groups to share the response cards.
   b. Read and discuss the Five-Star Tips!
   c. Display the response cards on a rope or ribbon.
   d. Provide time for participants to copy and adapt the response card ideas as assessment tools for their grade-level standards.

3. Stand and Show
   a. Post or display the numbers 1 through 5 individually around the room.
   b. State a specific topic addressed in the chapter. Suggested topics:

   - Pretests/posttests   page 77
   - Effective questioning   page 79
   - Anecdotal records   page 85

(Continued)

(Continued)

○ Surveys	page 88
○ Journals	page 90
○ Portfolios	page 94
○ Grades	page 98
○ Teacher-made tests	page 101
○ Standardized test preparation	page 104

    c. Individuals identify their knowledge-base level in relation to the stated topic using a 1-to-5 scale (1 = low; 5 = high).

    d. Participants stand in front of the chosen number on the scale.

    e. The knowledge-level groups discuss and list what is known about the topic or content. Questions and related thoughts are added to address in future sessions.

4. Effective Questioning

    a. Read and discuss the Five-Star Tips for Effective Questioning, on page 80.

    b. Discuss the chart of novel ways to present questions, in Figure 3.8.

    c. Have participants check the ideas they currently use to present questions.

    d. Identify and discuss the least familiar ideas.

    e. Expand the list by brainstorming more unique ways to present questions.

5. Using Journals as Assessment Tools

    a. With a partner or in small groups, discuss when and how journals are used for assessment. Share advantages of journal experiences. After the partner activity, conduct a total class discussion.

    b. Refer to Figure 3.12 in the Five-Star Tips for Using Journal Assessments. Add journaling ideas, formats, and entries to your assessment toolbox.

    c. Form four member groups. Share ideas for using journals for assessment in various flexible grouping scenarios. Present highlights of the discussion with the total group.

    d. Read the various ways suggested on page 91 for hamming up writing experiences with a variety of writing implements, materials, and designs. Add more ideas to the lists.

    e. Discuss the benefits of using journals as differentiated assessment tools.

4

Differentiated Instructional Strategies

IN THIS CHAPTER, WE PRESENT PRACTICAL and effective strategies for differentiating instruction while addressing the content standards. We encourage all teachers to build an array of effective strategies. This is a challenging but rewarding task. Choosing the right hat for a specific occasion is valuable for making the perfect ensemble! Likewise, choosing the right strategy is necessary for making the activity a hit. Collect a variety of hats or instructional strategies and activities from which to make the best selection at the appropriate time and occasion.

> A goal of differentiated instruction is providing opportunity and support for the success of far more students than is possible in one-size-fits-all approaches to teaching and learning.
>
> —Tomlinson and McTighe (2006)

STRATEGY SELECTION ■

In the past, a teacher gave one assignment to the total group. This general approach did not work well because often some students were frustrated by the assignment's level of difficulty and some were bored. Thankfully, there has been a paradigm shift from "one assignment fits all" to designing activities that fit each student's needs. This increases the number of students who master the standards.

Like the magician, a teacher always needs a "bag of tricks." He or she can pull things out of the bag to stimulate, challenge, and intrigue minds. Each act is carefully planned with a beginning, middle, and end. Suspense builds throughout the performance. A magician turns attention into curiosity and anticipation. The audience hangs onto every piece wondering, "How did that happen?"

Each performance is tailored for the age and type of group in the audience. Each trick is strategically placed in the show plan. The format flow must meet the audience's needs. The trickster assesses throughout and after the performance for quality, adjusting and revamping. Like the magician, a teacher needs to constantly reassess the timing of activities, deciding which activities use time best to teach the standard.

Strategy selection is based on the assessment data gathered before, during, and after learning. Once the assessment results are analyzed and the students' strengths and weaknesses identified, determine the best strategy to present, practice, reinforce, or enhance the content standard for each learner.

Managing the differentiated classroom is easier when a repertoire of instructional strategies is maintained to use in planning customized lessons for individuals and groups. Have some favorite tricks to place in the strategy lineup, but constantly add new ones to ham up the act. Students are challenged by the wonderment.

Analyzing the Instructional Strategy

Strategy selection is a tactical process. When considering a new differentiated instructional strategy, ask questions similar to the following:

Is the instructional strategy . . .

- The most effective way to teach the standard to the student?
- Teaching the standard for the learner's understanding?
- Using accessible materials and resources?
- Appropriate for the learner's age and characteristics?
- Developing a successful, self-directed learner?

Remember, if the strategy is boring or frustrating for you, it will be more boring or frustrating for students! Be sure they understand the purpose of the strategy, have clear directions, and can complete the tasks independently.

Assessing the Instructional Strategy

Avoid using a strategy simply because it is in your collection. If you do not know a strategy's effectiveness, consider this well-known saying, "When in doubt, throw it out." In other words, if you do not recognize the benefits of a strategy, the student does not need to waste time using it.

After using a strategy, consider the following questions:

- Was the strategy effective for the learner?
- What part of the strategy was most effective? Why?
- How can I improve this strategy?
- What materials or resources do I need to make it more useful?
- Where and when can I use this again?

Evaluate the overall success of the strategy's use as a vital step in improving and planning curriculum.

Warning for Instructional Strategies

The most effective strategy becomes ineffective with an unconscious action. Use the following list to become consciously aware of these pitfalls.

Figure 4.1   Instructional Strategies: Warnings and Prescriptions

Warning	Pitfalls	Examples	Suggested Prescriptions for Prevention
Overkilling	Giving too many directions or too much information at one time.	All facts are presented in one teacher-directed lesson.	Present appropriate chunks of information for students to process before presenting the next fact.
Suspending in midair	Leaving learning fragments with no links. No bridging from one lesson to another.	There is no wrap-up for the lesson on Friday. A new skill or topic is started in the next class session.	Link the current lesson with the previous information.
Staying in a rut	Spending too much time on one aspect of the lesson.	This often occurs when the teacher or students are carried away with their interest in a topic.	Maintain the pace of the lesson by following the instructional plans.
Flip-flopping	Moving to a new standard or skill before the first one is mastered and flip-flopping between them.	The term *latitude* is introduced but not mastered. The term *longitude* is introduced. The discussion refers to latitude.	Complete a segment of learning and develop it before moving to the next one.
In a holding pattern	Pausing the lesson until one student understands a skill or procedure.	Everyone slows down or stops their work while one student receives special instruction or assistance from the teacher.	Maintain momentum by giving an alternative assignment.

Giving Effective Directions

Emphasize the importance of knowing and following directions. Observe students closely when it is time for them to concentrate and understand guidelines. Be aware of each student's focus or listening ability so you can give individual special directions or simple reminders such as a "heads-up" signal.

A student cannot complete an assignment independently without clear and concise directions that are easy to follow. Treat each direction as a commercial to build excitement for completing the task. Begin and end each set on a high note.

Use the following suggestions to design effective directions:

- Give an established signal so everyone knows it is time for a direction.
- Explain, demonstrate, or model each step separately using terms the student understands.
- Post directions in writing. Use color-coding, symbols, or pictures to emphasize each step.
- Make each direction clear, simple, and specific. Provide enough information to keep the students' attention. Too many details will overwhelm and confuse them.
- Provide time for students to repeat the directions before work begins. Partners may take turns going over the directions by restating them or role-playing the procedures.

Creating Buy-In to Instruction

The student has to buy in to new learning for the brain to receive and retain information. In other words, to benefit from instruction, the learner must first open the gate to the brain or processing center. The student's desire to learn opens and closes the gate. The individual must see a personal need for the information and want to learn it.

Use the following suggestions to generate buy-in:

- Build in discussion and reflection time that leads an individual to realize a need for the current or upcoming information. Give students opportunities to create meaningful connections from prior knowledge and experiences.
- Give students choices to demonstrate what they know and their thinking processes.
- Actively engage students in authentic tasks related to the learning. This creates vested, personal interest in working with the new information.
- Plan activities to target the learner's intelligences so the student works with the information in his or her zones of strength. Label the intelligences addressed in the activities to analyze the learning opportunities and methods used.
- Set high expectations. Show your passion and enthusiasm for the topic or skill. It's catching!
- Teach students to answer the following questions to create "buy-in."
  - Why do I need to learn this?
  - How will I benefit by investing my time in this activity?
  - What is the purpose of this information?
  - What is in this for me?
  - How can I link my experiences to this new information?

Don't forget to use the student's interests, sense of humor, and curiosity to create buy-in. Add mystery and suspense to build a sense of anticipation.

FOCUS ACTIVITIES ▪

What Is a Focus Activity?

A focus activity directs the learner's attention to the current standard or topic. Carefully design it to draw the student's mind to the instructional activity or experience. A focus activity introduces a standard, skill, or content. It brings a learner's attention to other learning segments, such as reviews, practices, and extension activities.

What Are the Instructional Benefits of Focus Activities?

A focus activity prepares the learner's mind for the upcoming standard. It leads the student to mentally engage with the task at hand. Use a focus activity to spark a discussion, bridge to new information, or create a brainstorming list.

Effective focus activities accomplish the following:

- Prepare students' minds for learning.
- Provide more time on task.
- Establish an expected daily routine.
- Serve as an engaging hook to the targeted information.
- Intrigue students so they are eager to explore the standard, topic, or skill.

Implementing Standards Using Focus Activities

- Plan a focus activity to mentally engage the learners ASAP!
- Post and introduce the standard and the focus activity in a creative way.
- Present a purpose and compelling reason for the learner to engage in the activity.
- Gather and organize materials and supplies learners need.
- Give students opportunities to do the following:
  o Identify their knowledge base, and link prior experiences with the standard
  o Remove the clutter from their minds and prepare to complete the task at hand
  o Ask questions and clarify the directions or guidelines
  o Do their best on the focus activity
  o Work independently, or with a partner or small group

Demystifying Focus Activities

Introduce focus activities by discussing the purpose of the focus mechanisms on cameras, binoculars, microscopes, and video recorders. Explain that they eliminate the people or objects outside of the larger view and make what is critical clearer and easier to see.

In the same way, the brain has the ability to focus. The brain can be trained to cut out thoughts, feelings, and visual images, and tune in to important information. Tell students to use focus control when their minds need to receive and work with vital information without interference.

Challenge students to list distractions they often experience during instruction or at home. (See Figure 4.2.)

Figure 4.2   Distraction in Action

Outside the Classroom	In the Classroom	Beyond the School Doors
• Classes changing • Custodians working • Bells • Hallway noise • Traffic • Talking • Weather • School events	• On the wrong page • Unrelated thoughts • Intercom messages • People coming in leaving • Movement of students • Talking • Social interests • Special guests	• Dispute with someone • New pet • New sibling • Family conflict • Illness • Upcoming event • Disaster • Performance • Holiday or birthday

---

Discuss how students can use their focus control to deal with distractions. Teach techniques to manage a focused mind.

Examples:

- **Practice active listening:** Focus all your attention on the person talking.
- **Probe with questions and restate response:** Ask for more details and clarification, if needed.
- **Be aware of the need to focus:** When the brain begins to wander off task, clear your mind and refocus.
- **Take notes:** Make eye, hand, and mind connections with the information through writing about it.
- **Take a break:** When confused or stressed, take a deep breath or mini mental break to reduce tension, and come back to the task. For example, remember your favorite joke or a funny movie bit.

★ ★ ★ ★ ★

Five-Star
Tips for Focus Activities

1. Establish general guidelines for focus activities. Choose a signal or identify a specific time for the focus activities to begin.

2. Select or design activities that challenge students to think about the upcoming lesson segment.

3. Determine the best way to give the directions to students. They may be written, oral, or displayed.

4. Engage the learner using higher-level thinking skills, including problem solving, questioning techniques, organizing thoughts, and gathering information.

5. Use a variety of grouping strategies to engage students in exciting and novel focus tasks. Include mystery activities, scavenger hunts, puzzles, or games.

Examples of the Effective Use of Focus Activities

Example A: Entering the Class

An artifact related to the topic or skill is displayed on a table in the center of the room. Give each student an index card with the following directions:

1. Record three words to describe the _____.

2. Predict three ways _____ is important in our study.

3. Share and compile your thoughts and predictions with a partner.

Example B: Moving From One Group to Another

The following directions are posted, distributed, and/or stated to students:

1. On your way to our group, think of a story you have read or heard that relates to yesterday's standard.

2. Jot your ideas on a sticky note.

3. When you join the group, take turns giving the highlights of your story, and tell how it relates to the information about the standard.

Example C: Ending Class

The lesson ends 10 minutes earlier than expected. Students use their books for a review scavenger hunt. The teacher names important facts, words, places, characters, or events for students to locate quickly in the text.

■   ## SPONGE ACTIVITIES

What Is a Sponge Activity?

A sponge activity fills gaps in instructional time caused by interruptions, early completions, or emergencies, and uses time wisely before, between, or after learning segments. It addresses student needs, such as reenergizing the brain. It does not address the standard. Sponge activities are designed to benefit learners. They can be challenging, exciting, or humorous, and may be presented as games, mind teasers, competitions, puzzles, or songs. Beware of overusing sponge activities. They can absorb valuable instructional time.

What Are the Instructional Benefits of Sponge Activities?

- A sponge activity is planned as a time filler to relax and recharge the brain. It gives the mind a break from the stress of learning a standard or curriculum information. This relaxes the body and mind and prepares the brain for learning.
- These activities use time wisely in the following situations:
  o An administrator, teacher, or parent needs to talk to you for a few minutes during a lesson.
  o The class is waiting to be called to an assembly or program.
  o The lesson ends before it is time for classes to change.
  o A scheduled speaker is late.
  o An emergency occurs that engages the teacher.
- Smooth transitions occur with activities such as games or songs.
- Specific skills are enhanced using fun and stimulating activities.
- Students can use the time to socialize and enjoy being with classmates.

Implementing Standards Using Sponge Activities

- Decide when to use a sponge activity instead of a brief assignment or focus activity.
- Build a repertoire of sponge activities to fill various lengths of time.
- Create activities based on students' interests, favorite songs, or current fads.
- Select novel sponge activities to suit specific purposes and student needs.
- Adapt the following guidelines for students to use during the sponge activities:
  o Listen to the directions and complete the activity following the rules or guidelines.
  o Assist classmates.
  o Suggest and demonstrate sponge activities the class can use.
  o Take advantage of the time to clear cobwebs from your mind.
  o Enjoy!

Demystifying Sponge Activities

Give students the following description of a sponge activity:

> *A sponge activity is used when there is extra time or a break is needed. It may give you an opportunity to take a walk, play a game, stretch, or engage in free-choice activities.*

Five-Star
Tips for Sponge Activities

1. Identify skills or activities students need that are unrelated to the lesson. Present sponge activities to enhance skills or citizenship, such as the following:

   Relaxation   Movement   Following directions
   Taking turns   Listening   Courtesy

2. Prepare a tool kit of sponge activities to use before and after lessons to include the following:

   Physical exercises Songs   Games   Competitions   Puzzles

3. Limit the time, and use sponges wisely. Keep activities handy to match the amount of time and tone needed for quiet and still or noisy and active times.

4. Allow students to lead their favorite sponge activities.

5. Socializing counts! Give students opportunities to interact. This is relaxing. It also gives students time to share and clear their thoughts before they need to concentrate on the next standard or skill.

Examples of Effective Use of Sponge Activities

Example A: Completion of a Difficult Assignment

Ask students to stand and participate in stretching exercises or a timed, 1-minute free stand and talk with peers.

Example B: An Emergency Occurs That Engages the Teacher

Appoint a student as the sponge activity leader for a familiar game or song.

Example C: Students Are Entering the Room

Let students engage in a quiet activity of their choice for a brief period of time. Set a timer.

■   ## ANCHOR ACTIVITIES

What Is an Anchor Activity?

An anchor activity is a privilege provided to engage the student in meaningful tasks when all teacher-directed assignments are complete. The task is linked to the current or upcoming standard or topic of study. For example, when a student completes the customized assignment, an anchor activity is available.

In a differentiated classroom, individuals and small groups finish tasks at different times. Carol Ann Tomlinson and Marcia Imbeau (2010) refer to this as "ragged time" (p. 127). Often, when students complete class assignments, the time is filled with busywork or downtime. An anchor activity keeps learners from wasting time and engages them in an intriguing task connected to the content standard.

What Are the Instructional Benefits of Anchor Activities?

An anchor activity is designed to reinforce, practice, or extend concepts and skills related to a previous, current, or upcoming study.

Anchor activities use the learners' time wisely because they

- are designed with meaningful activities.
- provide choices to develop self-directed, independent learners.
- offer opportunities in decision making for completing tasks thoroughly and correctly.
- are designed to enhance standards and skills.
- help learners know what to do when the assignment is complete.

Implementing Standards Using Anchor Activities

- Analyze the learning standards, skills, and concepts to design worthwhile, engaging anchor activities for students to use when they complete assigned tasks.
- Designate an area for the anchor activity that will not disturb other learners.
- Plan, explain, and post an appealing, enjoyable anchor activity so students will be eager to be engaged.
- Routinely remind students that an anchor activity is a privilege for learners who complete the assigned work to the best of their ability.
- Give simple directions for anchor activities that are easy for students to follow, such as the following:
  - Read the directions. Gather materials you need for the activity, and move to an appropriate place to work.
  - If choices are provided, read all options carefully to select the most interesting activity, and follow the directions.
  - Work quietly.

○ If you need assistance while the teacher is assisting other students, ask classmates who finished the assigned work for help.

○ Clean the workspace and organize materials before leaving the area.

Demystifying Anchor Activities

Discuss the common definitions of the term *anchor*, including "to hold in place and to keep a vessel from drifting." An anchor activity is tied to learning. It is available to individuals, partners, and small groups to review a standard, practice skills, or explore the major topic.

**Five-Star
Tips for Anchor Activities**

1. Design the anchor activity based on student needs. Make each experience appealing and rewarding.
2. Decide if the activity will be completed in one lesson, over multiple days, during the length of the unit, or in the grading period.
3. Avoid assessing anchor activities for a grade.
4. Teach students how to move to the anchor activity, when work is completed, without disturbing classmates. Give clear directions, answer questions, and have materials ready for smooth transitions from the assigned task to the anchor activity.
5. Identify a space for students to display finished products.

Examples of Anchor Activities

Example A: Using Content Art

A mural, collage, or poster related to the content study is designated as an anchor activity in a special area of the room. Students make creative additions to the ongoing project.

Example B: Using a Brainteaser Game

Students create or play games to reinforce information related to a standard.

Example C: Using a Scene Reenactment

Students design and write parts to role-play the important passages or scenes in a studied event.

■ CUBING ACTIVITIES

What Is a Cubing Activity?

Cubing is an intriguing organizational technique that uses an exciting game format to challenge the student's mind. Six options are provided that allow students to work with information from a current category, standard, skill, or topic. This strategy is designed to meet individual and small-group needs in all content areas and to address grade-level standards. Cubing activities enhance instruction across the curriculum, in student-centered and teacher-centered activities.

What Are the Instructional Benefits of Cubing Activities?

Cubing activities can be designed for individuals, partners, or small groups to do the following:

- Review, teach, reinforce, or extend lessons using content standards, concepts, skills, or steps in procedures
- Promote discussion, modeling, and information processing
- Assess before, during, and after learning
- Use in a focus activity, a learning zone task, an assessment, or a homework assignment
- Challenge students within their level of success so they will not be bored or frustrated

Implementing Standards Using Cubing Activities

Use the following directions for successful cubing activities:

1. Identify the purpose(s), and design the cubing activity to teach the standard.

2. Identify a noun or category from the current study, such as an artifact, date, event, character, term, or setting, as the focus for the activity.

3. Choose six activities or questions, and write each one on the sides of the cube.

4. Decide if students need to work alone, with a partner, or in a small group.

5. Select a method for students to identify their cubing number.

   Examples:
   o Roll the cube with an option written on each side.
   o Roll a die or numbered cube.
   o Use a spinner.
   o Write a secret number—1, 2, 3, 4, 5, or 6—before the six options are revealed.

6. Give materials and directions for playing the game.

7. Use the following explanation for students to complete during a cubing activity:
   o Determine the cubing number by following the teacher's directions.
   o Read the directions for the activity that matches the assigned or selected mystery number.
   o Complete the activity that matches your number.
   o Review the skills or facts learned during the activity.
   o Be prepared to share with your partner or small group.

Demystifying Cubing

Show students examples of cubes. Introduce or review the definition of a cube, emphasizing the six facets. Explain that there will be six ways to approach the selected topic:

When playing a board game that uses dice, the number rolled determines the number of spaces the player moves. In our activity, rolling the die, using a spinner, drawing a secret number, or counting off identifies your number on the cube.

★ ★ ★ ★ ★

**Five-Star
Tips for Cubing Activities**

1. Introduce cubing activities using a large numbered cube created from foam, poster board, or a box. Die cutters often include patterns for cubes.

2. Once students understand the cubing strategy, move to variations of the activity. Place the six options in a different form, such as a grid, a list, or a unique design.

3. Create the list of six activity options that match content noun(s). (See examples below.)

4. Use the cubing method to assign activities for centers, oral reports, projects, daily work, cooperative groups, or homework assignments.

5. Establish a second-chance rule. If the student does not want to keep the first activity number, a second roll or selection turn is an option. *The original number cannot be used if the student chooses to use the second-chance option.*

Examples of Cubing Activities

Example A: Cubing as a Research Activity

During or after a study, select six important subtopics, terms, events, or procedures that are a valuable use of time for the learner. Place the numbers 1 through 6 on small cards in a basket. Make numbered sets to match the number of individuals in the class. The students form research teams according to the drawn number. This may be used for independent research activities.

The following example can be used as a cubing activity for research of a city, state, province, or country:

Figure 4.3 Geography Cube		
1. Landmarks	2. Rivers	3. Major Cities
4. Famous People	5. Historical Sites	6. Products

Example B: Cubing With an Object or Artifact

At the close of a unit, place an object or artifact related to the standards. in the work area of each cooperative team. Give each group a spinner with the numbers 1 through 6. On the board, list directions using key words from different levels of Bloom's or William's taxonomy. Each individual spins, reads the corresponding activity, records the answer, and responds to the group.

Sample cubing list of activities:

1. Compare the object with another object.

2. Give a definition for it.

3. Ask someone a question about it.

4. Identify the object's attributes.

5. Predict what will happen to it.

6. Brainstorm uses of the object.

Example C: Communicate

Place the six choices on a poster in a center with a die.

1. Billboard   2. Editorial   3. Fictitious story

4. Newscast   5. Interview   6. Cartoon

Post the following instructions:

- Roll the die to identify the type of communication to use.
- Write about _____ using your selection.

Example D: Cubing With Homework

As students prepare to leave at the end of the day or class period, each one rolls a number cube to identify the homework assignment from the list of options.

Display a list of five to seven vocabulary words with six homework options:

1. Create a crossword puzzle using all the words. Use the meaning of each word as the key.

2. Design a graffiti board, writing the words and their definitions in various colors, fonts, shapes, and designs.

3. Write a mystery paragraph using at least three words and a synonym for each one.

4. Design an advertisement using at least four vocabulary words.

5. Create a silly story using all vocabulary words or their antonyms.

6. Draw a cartoon using at least three words in speech bubbles.

■ CHOICE BOARDS

What Is a Choice Board?

A choice board provides a selected list of activities that target the specific needs of students. Each activity is directly linked to the standards, skills, or unit and is student focused so it can be completed with little or no teacher assistance. The choices can be presented in a grid or on a list. They may be placed creatively on or around a subject-related object or drawing, such as a heart or rocket.

Choice boards or designs are flexible tools that may be used by the total class, individuals, partners, or small groups in all curriculum areas across grade levels. They may be placed in a learning zone or assigned as part of an agenda, project, contract, or other student-directed task.

What Are the Instructional Benefits of Using Choice Boards?

Students who are given choices become more responsible for transferring the information. When individuals choose activities in their areas of strength and interest, they are more comfortable with the learning process. They are more likely to show what they know when working in their favorite styles or modalities.

Choice boards

- are designed to meet the needs of individuals and small groups.
- teach, reinforce, practice, or enhance learning.
- give learners opportunities to select the ways they want to show what they know.
- enrich homework or class assignments, independent activities, or center work.
- give students ownership in their learning.

Implementing Standards Using a Choice Board

- Identify the purpose of the choice board in relation to the identified standard.
  Examples:
  ○ To teach, practice, or review a standard, skill, or topic
  ○ To debut a character, event, or artifact
  ○ To work with vocabulary words
- Determine the most suitable choice activity design to fit the learning situation and match the content information. For example, use an outline of a symbol from the unit or a seasonal design.
- Brainstorm a list of activities that will meet the learners' needs. Write each activity on a sticky note.
- Use the "Keeper and Loser" criteria checklist. The most valuable activities from the brainstormed list are the "keepers." Eliminate the "losers." Place the best activities, or "keepers," on the choice board or design.

- Help students understand the procedure for using a choice board using guidelines similar to the following:
  - Read or listen to the directions for the choice board or design.
  - Make a selection that's best for you. Don't allow others to influence your decision!
  - Follow directions to complete the selected activities.
  - If you need help with the activity, ask two classmates before going to the teacher.
  - Follow the directions to display, turn in, or store your work.

Figure 4.4   Choice Board Item Selection

Identifying Keepers and Losers

Ask yourself the following questions to see if the activity you are assessing "measures up" and should be a keeper.

☐ *Does the activity address the content standard and meet the student's needs?* The item must provide a learning experience in which the student practices, reinforces, enhances, or assesses the content focus. If it does not, eliminate it from the list of possibilities.

☐ *Is the activity a valuable learning experience?* If it is busywork and a time waster, omit it from the list of possibilities.

☐ *Will it take the "right amount of time" to complete the activity?* Analyze the time it will take most students to complete each activity. For example, if an item takes 5 minutes and other activities take 20 minutes, you probably need to eliminate the 5-minute activity. Be sure the activity can be completed in the allotted time frame.

☐ *Are materials and resources available for the activities?* If you must purchase materials or spend valuable time finding items for an activity, remove it from the list.

☐ *Can students work on the activities with little or no adult supervision?* Is each activity (a) student focused, (b) age appropriate, and (c) within the learner's range of success? If not, it is a loser.

☐ *Is it easy to assess?* If you have to design a separate assessment tool, eliminate the item.

Demystifying Choice Boards

Introduce the term *choice* by discussing the value of knowing how to make decisions. Ask students how and when they make choices in their daily activities outside of school, such as their selection of computer games, snacks, clothes, or television programs. Emphasize that it is a privilege to have a special assignment with choices. Talk to the class about the value of making wise activity selections.

Five-Star
Tips for Choice Boards

1. Create choice boards that use information related to the standard(s).

2. Provide activity choices that use a variety of intelligences or learning styles to ensure that the learner's individual needs are met.

3. When some students are on the readiness level and some are on the advanced/mastery level, try the following activity arrangement: Assign odd numbers to practice activities that are designed for students on the readiness level. Assign even numbers to activities that are designed for students on the advanced/mastery level.

4. Create choice boards to do the following:
   - Assess before, during, or after learning
   - Respond to a text
   - Solve a problem
   - Debut a character
   - Teach, review, or enrich

5. Present choice activities to work with the standards in novel, inviting ways so students are eager to work with them. Use intriguing graphics, colors, and fonts. Use designs or symbols from the content to present choices. Add interest-grabbing titles such as "Quick Pick."

Examples of Choice Board Activities

Example A: Choice Boards for Adjustable Assignments

Find your level. Select three activities in your level to complete.

Figure 4.5   Leveled Choice Assignments

Level 1	Level 2	Level 3
1.	1.	1.
2.	2.	2.
3.	3.	3.
4.	4.	4.
5.	5.	5.
Rewinding	**Grade Level**	**Fast-Forwarding**

Example B: Choice Boards for Presentations

Choose an activity from the list to present your research project.

Oral report   Mini-posters display   PowerPoint presentation

Simulation   Diorama demonstration   Booklet

Example C: Choice Activities as Test Bonus Points

Place five facts learned on a graphic organizer.

Make a list of _____.

Select a unit vocabulary word that was not on the test. Define it.

Draw pictures to illustrate _____.

Figure 4.6	Choice Board Themes			
August	**September**	**October**	**November**	**December**
Stars School items Summer items	Fall things Labor Day Trees	Leaves Pumpkin patch Apples	Thanksgiving Football Election items	Holiday items D-Day Traditions
January	**February**	**March**	**April**	**May**
Fireworks Snowman Martin Luther King, Jr.	Valentines Winter items President's Day	Kites Shamrocks Lamb/lion	Hats Butterflies Earth Day	Summer items Maypole Memorial Day

General Choice Activity Shapes/Designs

The following list of shapes may be used with content themes as choice designs:

Wheel   Book   Hand outline   Octopus   Pyramid   Star

Scroll   Grid   Bingo board   Flower   Tree   Steps

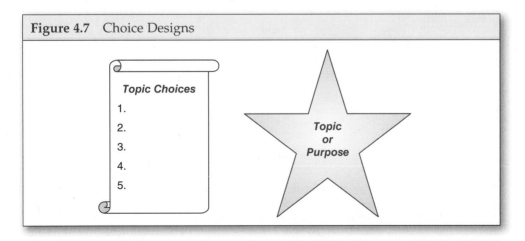

Figure 4.7	Choice Designs

Topic Choices

1.
2.
3.
4.
5.

Topic
or
Purpose

Figure 4.8   Book Report Choices

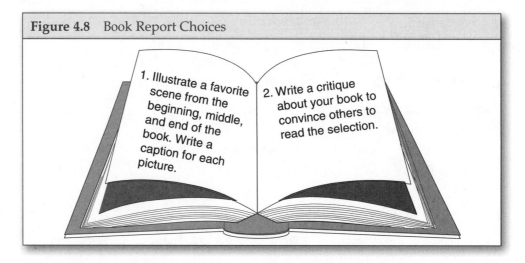

Figure 4.9   Wheel of Choices

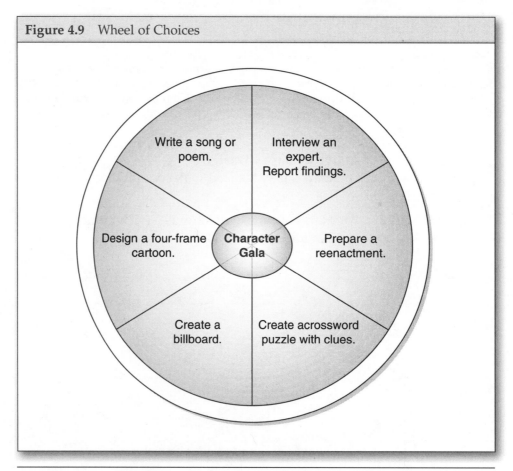

GRAPHIC ORGANIZERS ■

What Is a Graphic Organizer?

A graphic organizer is a design, drawing, or shape used to categorize or organize data related to a standard. It is a visual/spatial and logical/mathematical means of arranging thoughts and plotting key information.

A variety of graphics can be used as organizers, from basic grids and boxes connected by lines to more elaborate shapes for holidays and unit themes. The form chosen for the organizer depends on the intended use: to categorize facts and ideas, to retain information associated with a shape, or to plot data.

What Are the Instructional Benefits of Using Graphic Organizers?

A graphic organizer creates a picture for the mind to associate with the words placed on it. This mental image assists the brain as it stores and retrieves the associated information.

A graphic organizer provides a place to plot thoughts around an idea. Often, this is more exciting than writing sentences and paragraphs. Since organizers can be any shape or design, these graphics offer a variety of choices to fit the topic. Some learners discover that graphic organizers are easier to use for recording information than writing it in paragraph form.

A workable organizer that fits the subject matter is an invaluable tool for brainstorming ideas and plotting information. It can be used to sort, classify, and identify relationships between thoughts and ideas. It can stand alone as a writing activity or be used as an excellent prewriting activity.

Organizers present information in a design that gives learners the freedom to plot facts or data in their own creative way. These experiences teach students how to arrange information in a personal, logical format. Graphic organizers are beneficial note-taking tools for independent or group brainstorming. They can be used to present assignments for plotting key points of a partner or group discussion, a reading passage, a thinking process, a homework assignment, or a test question.

Implementing Standards Using Graphic Organizers

- Introduce and model each graphic organizer several times during direct instruction and while leading group discussions across the content areas.
- Have students work with a graphic organizer in partner, small-group, or independent assignments. Provide time for them to share their products and explain placement of the information.
- Allow students to choose their own graphic organizer from the designs previously modeled.

- Continually add to the list of organizers so learners expand their toolbox.
- Provide adequate time for a student to revisit an organizer to add new, learned information.

Five-Star
Tips for Using Graphic Organizers

1. Explain, model, and provide guided practice with each graphic organizer before using it as an independent assignment.

2. Watch for ruts! Familiarize yourself with a broad assortment of graphic organizers, and challenge yourself to use as many as possible during the year to present your students with many options.

3. Choose the organizer that suits the topic and standard.

4. Don't be afraid to create a new graphic organizer! Try it out before presenting it.

5. Remember, picture organizers appeal to the visual/spatial part of the brain, while matrix and sequence organizers appeal to the logical/mathematical part of the mind. To address the individual learning styles, it is important to allow students opportunities to select their graphic organizers from a choice board.

Demystifying Graphic Organizers

Explain to students that it is easier for the brain to remember information when it is placed on a graphic organizer because the design assists memory. Show students familiar graphic organizers such as family trees and television schedules. Discuss the gathered facts, where they are plotted, and why each piece of information is on the graphic organizer.

Examples of Graphic Organizers

Example A: T-Chart

Introduce the T-chart using two vocabulary words. Draw the letters in large, bold colors. Select two nouns from the content information to explore, and write them on each side of the T as category titles. From discussions or text reading, guide students to select information that gives more detail about each noun. At another time, assign a T-chart organizer and have partners list the facts related to the two standards.

Figure 4.10 T-Chart Plotting	
Noun A	Noun B

Example B: Picture Vocabulary—Word and Meaning

1. Each student folds a piece of paper into six equal sections.

2. The teacher assigns six new words with meanings that can be illustrated.

3. The students write one word in each box. After reading the meaning of the word in the text, each student draws a picture with the definition under the word in the box.

4. The completed pages are shared with a partner and used later as a study sheet for a test.

Example C: Weekly Journaling Hand

1. Have students draw a hand shape in their personal journals on Monday.

2. Instruct them to write the days of the week on each finger.

3. Above the finger tip for Monday, each student writes the most important fact learned that day.

4. Tell students to add a new entry each weekday. At the end of the week, they have five reflective facts for review.

■ CENTERS, STATIONS, AND LEARNING ZONES

What Are Centers, Stations, and Learning Zones?

Center, *station*, and *learning zone* are synonymous terms for designated areas where students find hands-on, learner-focused, problem-solving activities. Each experience is designed to provide students with opportunities to explore, practice, and work with a standard or content information. The activities reteach, extend, and enrich current learning areas or lead students to discover new subject matter. Refer to these activities with age-appropriate titles. For example, use *centers* for the younger students and *stations* or *learning zones* for older students. When the age-appropriate name is used, more students buy in to using the activities.

What Are the Instructional Benefits of Using Centers, Stations, and Learning Zones?

Centers, stations, and learning zones are designed to accomplish several objectives simultaneously to meet the diverse needs of individuals or groups. Structured and exploratory activities can be placed in centers. Each area is customized for students to work with standards, specific skills, and creative or critical thinking activities.

Other instructional benefits are listed below:

- A structured center is established for students to work with specific standards, skills, or procedures within their abilities and knowledge levels. The students must follow the activities' rules and guidelines.
- In an exploratory center, a limited number of rules are established and materials provided. Learners create or problem solve in their own way.
- The teacher is able to assess the learner's knowledge base and understanding as the student explains the thinking process.
- Choices are offered to address individual learning styles and intelligences to challenge minds.
- Students learn to take responsibility for staying on task, furthering their own learning, and using time wisely.

Implementing Standards Using Centers, Stations, and Learning Zones

- Plan, develop, and name each center or station. Label it with a title that coordinates with the subject area and/or grade level.
- While designing a center, use questions similar to the following to create a quality work area:

> o Is it student centered?
> o After receiving directions and rules, can the student be productive with little or no adult supervision?
> o Are multileveled activities included to fill learning gaps and present challenges for the students?
> o Does the work area provide practice and enrichment?
> o Does it promote critical and creative thinking?

- Decide and post the number of students who can work productively at each center.
- Introduce each center. Provide clear directions for the activities, and explain the rules. Topics to address include the following:
  - o Acceptable noise levels
  - o Proper use and care of materials
  - o Directions for moving in and out of centers
  - o Setup and cleanup procedures
  - o Directions for the activity, with expectations and adventures for exploration in each center
- Model! Model! Model! Illustrate the correct use of centers via role-playing and demonstrations.
- Adopt one of the following procedures for students to move to and from each work area:

Rotation: Each student works in a center for a set amount of time. Everyone moves to the next center at the sound of a signal.

Choice: The first group of students chooses a center. The next group selects an available center.

Assigned: The teacher assigns groups or individuals to centers with activities designed for specific learning needs.

Demystifying Centers, Stations, and Learning Zones

Explain to students that centers, stations, and learning zones are work areas set up to help them learn more about a topic or skill. Discuss the fact that they may be assigned to work there alone, with a partner, or with a small group. Emphasize that materials and supplies are shared with other classmates, so they need to be used with care and stored properly. Also, stress the importance of cleaning and organizing the area before leaving it. Point out that the learning zones are created for explorations, discoveries, and inventions. Use an explanation similar to the following:

When inventors or artists work, they explore and work in a specific area, where they use the materials and basic supplies. They rely on their knowledge and creative minds, often without assistance from experts in their field. They analyze the task to learn and improve their product, skills, or process. The tasks are completed in one or several sessions. The materials are stored properly so they are ready to use the next time.

Figure 4.11 Learning Zone Materials List

Brain Booster Center	Writing Center	Reading Center
Games Board games Card games Computer games Hand-held games Mind games **Puzzles** Board Floor Crossword Sudoku Logic Jigsaw Anagram **Television Formats** "Who Wants to Be a Millionaire" "Password" "Wheel of Fortune" "Jeopardy"	**Writing Implements** Pencils Pens Crayons Chalk Markers Colored pencils **Materials** Paper in varied colors, shapes, sizes Paper with and without lines Gel bags Salt trays Wipe-off boards **Reference Tools** Pictionaries Word walls Boxed word files Unit dictionaries and facts Thesauri Computers	**Reference Tools** Class-made books Dictionaries Thesauri Word lists Students' writing **Factual Materials** Trivia books Fact books Unit materials Newspapers Brochures Magazines Computer programs Web access Leveled materials Facts about interests **Fictional Materials** Student's writing Favorite books and stories Poetry Songs Comic books Personal
Skills Center	**Art Center**	**Listening Center**
Material Manipulatives Visuals Posters Games Puzzles Self-checking keys Electronic devices **Storage** Labeled folders Baggies Baskets Plastic containers Envelopes	**Variety of Art Media** Scissors Glue Paste Tape Easel and paints Markers Colored pencils Paper in various colors, shapes, sizes, and textures **Display Areas** Clothesline Table Doors Walls Bulletin board	**Equipment** Headphones/ear buds Listening stations CDs/CD player DVDs/DVD player Computer programs Recorded information **Sources** Class-written books Factual/fiction book Music

**Five-Star
Tips for Using Centers, Stations, and Learning Zones**

1. Begin slowly. Establish one or two centers to acclimate students to their use. Increase requirements and the number of centers as your students become comfortable with them.

2. Prepare more center and station selections than the number of students in the room. Make choice activities available when assigned activities are complete. This provides more options on free-choice center days.

3. Make resources and materials accessible. If there is no space to store materials in or near the center, designate a shelf, crate, or part of a supply cabinet as "student accessible." Tell students where to find their materials.

4. Provide places for students to proudly display completed projects and products.

5. Design "Open" and "Closed" signs.

   • When a center or station is not working because you observe a disturbance or a broken rule, post the "Closed" sign at the center. Do not give students second chances. As soon as a disruption is observed, "nip it in the bud." Reopen the center after you conduct a class meeting, discuss the problem, and review expectations. Make necessary improvements. Reopen the center with a celebration.

   • If students dread going to a center, close it. Negative feelings are evident by deep sighs and avoidance. Keep the center closed until you add pizzazz to it. Students often have ideas to improve the work area. Make necessary changes, and reopen the center with an enticing advertisement that reflects changes or additions.

Examples of Effective Centers, Stations, and Learning Zones at Work

Example A: Guiding Students From a Structured Activity to an Exploratory Option in One Work Area

Once a structured assignment is completed, add exploratory options to engage the student for a longer period of time in a productive center activity.

Structured Center Assignment

During a social studies lesson, students enter a center to invent something new in a designated category. They invent the new object using posted step-by-step procedures such as the following:

1. Invent a new _____ using the materials in the assigned box.

2. Draw a picture to scale of the new invention.

3. List the attributes.

4. Draw the background using the related information.

5. Display the product in the assigned space.

6. Return unused materials to the box.

Exploratory Option

Now it is the student's turn to use the available materials in the box to design and create anything. The learner moves from using a structured center to an exploratory option. This extends the learner's on-task time in the center.

Example B: Presenting Multiple Options

Create a choice board to support the center's objective. The students at the station complete the assigned reading selection. Each student selects an activity related to the reading from the "After Reading Choice Board" posted in the station. The student gathers required materials for the activity from the designated area before beginning the chosen assignment.

Example C: Transitioning From Center to Center

Give specific directions to follow when tasks are completed and the area is clean so the students know to automatically move to a specific center or area.

After completing an experience in the center, the group cleans the area and puts away any unused materials and equipment. Students move their desks together or go to a designated space to draw and/or write the steps used in the activity.

Remember, quality is more important than quantity.

AGENDAS ■

What Is an Agenda?

An agenda is a purposefully planned list of ongoing activities assigned to personalize independent or group work assignments that address the targeted standards. A list of activities is tailored for specific needs identified in the assessment results. It may be assigned to a student or group not ready for the class assignment, or it may be assigned to individuals who need more challenging tasks. It may be presented on paper, on a dry-erase board, in a folder, or on a chart. An agenda is usually given for a designated period of time. The teacher selects tasks. These activities are designed specifically for the student's needs: to fill in the learning gaps, to work with grade-level skills and materials, or to fast-forward the curriculum. In some schools and classrooms, the term *menu* is used for the list of agenda tasks.

What Are the Instructional Benefits of Agendas?

An agenda can be adapted to the needs of individual students at all grade levels in all curriculum areas. Design it for the student(s) to use during a class period, a day, a week, or a grading period.

- A list of activities is customized to meet the student's particular needs on his or her level of readiness.
- The order in which activities are completed is determined by the student.
- Students work independently, learning how to take responsibility for completing tasks with little adult supervision.
- Each learner is able to work at his or her appropriate pace.
- Individual students learn to manage personal time.

Implementing Standards Using Agendas

- Identify the students who need an agenda assignment using assessment data.
- Create a form with the list of teacher-selected activities and a timeline with expected completion dates based on the standard or unit of study.
- Customize the standards and skills for individual learners as an intervention tool, to work with grade-level tasks or challenge with extended learning.
- Vary assignments using the student's learning styles, intelligences, and modalities. An individual working with an agenda needs to work with appropriate activities and materials to promote thinking.

Examples of agenda items:

Complete your activity from the cube.

Choose two items from the choice board.

Write a journal entry related to _____.

Use the _____ to create a replica of _____.

Read the selection and take notes.

Complete a computer assignment.

Select three activities in the _____ station as tasks.

Plot the information on the graphic organizer.

Create a collage.

Record your step-by-step thinking as you complete _____.

Solve the following problem and explain how you solved it.

Create a song, rap, or poem using facts about _____.

- Talk to students about agenda work using the following suggestions:
  - Explain the agenda's guidelines for each activity on the list, the assessment tool, and the expectations.
  - Let students ask questions or state concerns about the agenda assignments.
  - Explain that agenda tasks may be completed in any sequence or order.
  - Teach students how to pace their time so they are able to complete each task within the time frame.
  - Assign a completion date and designate an area to place or display products.

Demystifying Agendas

Introduce the various uses of the word *agenda* in terms students understand, such as the following:

An agenda is a list of items. When you attend a function, there is often a program of planned events. When you plan your after-school activities for an afternoon, this becomes your list or agenda. Lists are taken to the grocery store so items can be checked off as they are placed in the basket. Recipes consist of a list of ingredients with steps to complete.

Explain to students that everyone has different learning experiences and enters each topic with varying background knowledge. Agendas provide everyone with tasks they are able to complete.

**Five-Star
Tips for Using Agendas**

1. Use preassessment data to identify the student(s) who needs an alternate, differentiated assignment.

2. Select student-focused activities that address the learner's assessed needs.

3. List activities the student can easily read and follow. Thoroughly explain each one so the learner can work independently to complete them.

4. Specify places, times, and materials for the agenda work.

5. Give students an opportunity to showcase products created during their agenda assignments. This builds self-esteem and encourages them to do their very best work.

Examples of Agendas

Example A: An Agenda for All Grades and Curriculum Areas

During this agenda assignment, students select activities from a teacher-made choice board or agenda list.

NAME _____ Due Date _____

My Tasks _____

Activity 1: _____

I learned _____.

Activity 2: _____

I learned _____.

Activity 3: _____

I learned _____.

Checkpoint Date #1 _____   Checkpoint Date #2 _____

Agenda Completion Date _____

Signatures:

Student _____

Parent _____

Peer _____

Teacher _____

Example B: Agenda for Integrating Subjects in a Self-Contained Classroom

Give the following assignment to integrate subjects across content areas for all class members to complete during the week. Note that the activities are differentiated within this total group assignment because students may be on different pages or working with standards or skills on varying levels.

Student's Name _____ Due Date _____

☐ Read pages _____ in the social studies book and take notes.

☐ Complete the math manipulative sheet and check it with the key provided. Make corrections with the green pen, and place it in the teacher basket.

☐ Choose two activities from the science choice board. Place the completed activities in your science folder.

☐ Make a journal entry listing five things you learned this week.

Student Signature _____

Reflective Comments _____

Example C: Agenda for One Subject Area

Student's Name _____ Due Date _____

☐ Complete the computer program _____ and the response sheet.

☐ Make a puzzle with all vocabulary words. When it is complete, place it on the bulletin board.

☐ Observe the _____ and predict what will happen next. Draw or write your prediction.

☐ Practice _____ with a partner using the _____.

☐ Write ____ journal entries during the week to describe facts you are learning about _____.

ACADEMIC CONTRACTS   ■

What Is an Academic Contract?

An academic contract is a form outlining an alternative assignment related to the current study. The student presents it to the teacher for approval. It is specifically tailored to an individual's needs. A contract is usually granted to a student who demonstrates mastery of upcoming skills or topics and needs more challenging work. It may be used by a student who has an idea for an alternate grade-level assignment. The teacher and the student must agree on the contents of the contract. Once the teacher gives final approval, the tasks for the assigned project or study are outlined on a form with a set time frame.

The grade is determined by the content, process, and/or product. Grades can be assigned for the individual tasks and/or the total contract.

What Are the Instructional Benefits of Academic Contracts?

The heart of an academic contract is the focus on the student's interest area that extends learning in topics or skills related to the current standards addressed during the study. Contracts can serve two major instructional purposes in the differentiated classroom. (1) A contract avoids wasting a student's time and prevents boredom, because the learner is not required to repeat previously learned information. Remember, the student is assigned the academic contract as an alternative assignment because the learner has a strong background related to the information planned for class instruction. (2) Another way an academic contract can be used is to replace the regular assignments of a student, on any performance level. The student outlines and submits to the teacher the proposal for an alternative assignment. When a contract is approved, the learner is exempted from assignments given to the class.

Each academic contract is designed to intrigue and challenge the student. This differentiated contract gives learners opportunities to move on with their learning within a unit to expand their knowledge and specific interests.

Implementing Standards Using Academic Contracts

Before the Assignment Begins: The Designing Stage

- Preassess the class to gather data on the learners' knowledge base, attitudes, and interests related to the planned standard and topic. Use the results to identify students who need an academic contract.
- Conduct a preconference with each student.
   o Explain the purpose and value of the special assignment.
   o Present the guidelines and procedures for an academic contract assignment.

Examples:

You'll need to work in _____ or _____ areas.

Do your work when _____.

You have permission to go to _____ or _____ to obtain more information.

○ Discuss the learner's interest areas related to the current topic that are worthwhile for in-depth study. Once you agree on a subtopic, ask the student the following:

What tasks would you like to complete to learn more about _____?

What resources or materials do you need?

How much time will it take to complete your tasks?

How will you present your final product?

How would you like to be graded on your work?

○ Tell the student to develop a proposal for approval using directions similar to the following:

1. *Identify the standards, skills, and concepts you plan to include and address.*

2. *Develop challenging but doable tasks to address the standard or content information.*

3. *List the necessary materials and resources.*

4. *Set a timeline for conferences, checkpoints, and due dates.*

- Allow the student time to gather ideas and outline the tasks.
- Conference with the student about the contract proposal, and give your consent if appropriate. Approve the contract if the plan is student focused, uses time wisely, and teaches the student more about the standard(s) or current study.
- Create or select appropriate forms to use as monitoring and assessment tools.
- Come to consensus on the topic of the assignment, assessment tools, grading system, and timeline. You and the student sign the agreement.
- Assign a personal place for concentration, with adequate workspace. Be sure this space is not distracting or disruptive to the work of other students. Consider a remote area with a desk, table, computer station, lab, reference area, media center, or just the floor for personal space.
- Designate a space for artifacts that is out of the way of normal classroom traffic. Place printed computer findings and products in a personalized folder. Keep completed paper assignments in a separate portfolio folder designated for the project, with the signed contract

agreement, the timeline, and any activity logs. Include self- and teacher-assessment pieces as integral parts of the portfolio.

During the Academic Contract Work: The Work Stage

- Follow progress checkpoints as designated on the timeline. Hold a midpoint conference to discuss solutions to any problems or concerns. Adjust the assignment or timeline, if necessary.
- Be sure needed materials and resources are available during work time.
- Support, encourage, and provide appropriate feedback.
- Provide uninterrupted time for the student to work on the assignment. Independent contract work usually occurs when a majority of the class is engaged in other activities. If extra work sessions are needed, consider using time before or after class, study periods, or homework assignments.
- Periodically ask questions or use prompts from the following list:

  What have you completed?

  Tell me important information you are learning.

  How can I help you?

  Do you need more or different materials?

  What new discoveries have you made?

  Do we need to revamp or change anything in your assignment?

  Show me examples of your work.

After the Completion of the Academic Contract: The Feedback Stage

- Schedule a conference for the student to present the completed academic contract.
  - Obtain the student's evaluation of the contract as soon as tasks are complete.
  - Use the list of questions during the conference that are not addressed in the evaluation.

    What did you learn?

    Name your favorite task. Tell me about it.

    What did you find most challenging?

    If assigned another contract, which segment would you want to keep?

    What needs to be changed the next time?

    Did you understand each assignment, task, and procedure? If not, identify and explain the problem(s).

    Did you need more assistance? If yes, when?

    Were you given enough time? If you answered no, please explain.

    Would you like to complete another assignment like this? Why or why not?

- Assess the final product and give specific feedback to the student.
  - Identify new information standards or skills the student learned.
  - Does it meet the specified goals and objectives?
  - Identify the effective tasks and segments.
  - What aspects of the contract need improvement? Why and how?
  - Was it worth the time? Why or why not?
  - What will you change before you make a similar assignment?

- Provide time for the student to respond to your feedback, and revise or revamp as needed.
- Decide if it is beneficial for the student to present the contract activities to the class or special guests. If so, provide time for the learner to prepare the presentation.

Demystifying Academic Contracts

Introduce the term *contract* by discussing formal agreements such as those used in hiring employees or signing professional athletes or actors. Emphasize the agreement's importance and the significance of the signatures.

Explain that a contract is used as an option for some class assignments. It may be selected by the student or teacher.

★ ★ ★ ★ ★

Five-Star Tips for Academic Contracts

1. Analyze the student's contract proposal to see that it addresses the learner's needs, enhances content information, and is a valuable use of the student's time. Make additions and deletions as needed.
2. After approval, organize tasks cooperatively and strategically with the learner.
3. Select the monitoring and assessment tools.
4. Schedule conferences to monitor and discuss progress, new discoveries, and needs during the work according to the timeline. Praise accomplishments.
5. Keep notes during each stage of the contract. Record the things that work and areas needing improvement for future contract assignments.

Examples of Academic Contracts

Example A: An Expert on the Unit of Study

A preassessment reveals that a student is an expert on the information planned for instruction. It is obvious that this individual will be bored with the lessons.

With the teacher's invitation, the student submits a written proposal with alternative assignments to complete as an independent study. The teacher approves the proposal or works with the student to create more acceptable tasks or topic-specific activities.

Example B: An Expert With a Skill or Concept

A new student joins the class. You are planning an upcoming unit to teach specific math skills and concepts. A preassessment indicates that this student has mastered the standards, skills, and concepts. The student designs a contract to illustrate how the information is applied in everyday situations. The findings are presented to the class in a creative way to enhance understanding of the standard or skill.

Example C: Expert Beyond the Grade Level

- A student enters the class knowing how to read the grade-level material. This student is provided with challenging reading assignments during independent work time. The contract may include an assignment on a computer program, illustrating a favorite story, or preparing a read-aloud session for a special time or class.
- A class in the upper grades is learning to design webpages in a computer class. The teacher discovers that one student is designing webpages for local businesses. The teacher asks this student to submit an academic contract proposal to further his webpage knowledge in an independent study while other students learn basic information.

Example D: An Academic Contract

Name _____   Date _____

Student Explanation of Proposal

My Plan

Resources and Materials Needed

I need _____ amount of time.

My due date will be _____.

Conference Date _____

Teacher Approval _____ **Teacher Denial** _____

Teacher Suggestions, Comments, and Additions

Signatures:

Student _____   Date _____

Teacher _____   Date _____

■ MANAGING PRODUCTS

What Is a Product?

A product is an object or *artifact* created by the student. It is visible evidence of student work and learning. Often products are in the form of an exhibit, diorama, PowerPoint presentation, computer printout, booklet, or report.

What Are the Instructional Benefits of Products?

The most valuable components of a product activity are the learner's thinking processes that take place during the tasks. The tasks engage the learners' creative as well as organizational skills. Products are designed to be teacher directed, student centered, or a combination of these approaches. Each product assignment is customized to meet the unique needs of learners. Products serve as effective instructional tools when they are shared with other students.

Creating a product accomplishes the following:

- Actively engages the student's mind.
- Takes the learner through thinking processes.
- Provides a purpose and goal for tasks.
- Teaches the student to follow directions, steps, and timelines.
- Allows the student to showcase his or her learning accomplishments.

Implementing Standards Using Products

- Determine which product assignment provides the most effective way for the student to learn the standard or content information.
- Utilize the student's strengths to make product assignment choices.
- Designate specific checkpoints and assessment tools.
- Provide materials, and establish the time allotted for the student to complete the product.
- Instruct the students to
  - review the directions provided,
  - give their best effort to create a quality product,
  - check the guidelines to be sure the directions are followed correctly,
  - make necessary revisions or adjustments,
  - review the procedure and identify information learned from the process, and
  - showcase, present, or store the product.

Demystifying Products

A product is anything created or completed by the student. It is evidence of a learning experience. Emphasize that everyone has different strengths, talents, and interests, so each product will be unique. Use the following artist analogy to introduce products to the class:

Some sculptors are experts in working with marble, while others work best with bronze or clay. Each artist has skills in specific areas and approaches the work in a different way.

Explain that product assignments may be given to individuals, a small group, or the total group.

Five-Star
Tips for Products

1. Emphasize the thinking processes used in creating the product. Provide time for students to develop their plans. Assign a processing partner so they can discuss their procedures, progress, and needs.

2. Establish checkpoints for teacher–learner conferences so students can explain their thinking process. This keeps the students' progress on the right track. At the completion of the product, give feedback on the thinking used as well as the product created.

3. Vary the ways products are displayed. Use the products to teach, reinforce, review, and enhance learning.

   Ways to display the product:

   Hang It

Ribbon	Rope	Yarn	Clothesline
Wire ring	Coat hanger	Hook	String

   Glue, Tack, or Staple It

Poster board	Butcher paper	Wallpaper	Cardboard box
Construction paper	Bags	Boxes	Bulletin board

   Tape It

Doors	Shelves	Windows	Shades	Blinds	Easel	Floor
Posts	Desks	Chairs	Ladder	Wall	Ceiling	Chart stand

   Exhibit It

Table	Shelf	Desk	Floor	Windowsill
Box	Rug	Bulletin board	Computer	

   Create special audiences for product presentations!

Parents	Community leaders	Guest classes
Grandparents	Review team	Administrators

4. Let students know their efforts and work are valued. All learners need encouragement and praise for their best work.

5. Because the value of a product is not completely objective, use a variety of assessment tools and strategies to determine a student's grade. Avoid using only A+ work for displays.

   Examples:

Peer evaluations	Self-assessment rubrics	Likert scales
Journals	Tickets out the door	Presentation

Examples of Products

Example A: Math Visual

Each group creates a visual to show the steps in a math problem. Students solve it. They discuss the thinking used in the process and create a visual to display the step-by-step procedure.

Give each group a math problem that requires multiple steps to solve. Provide the following directions:

1. Place each step on a separate, large strip of paper.

2. Color-code the steps. For example, Step 1 is purple, Step 2 is green, and so on.

3. Challenge students to display the steps in a unique way. For example, use a shoebox and write the steps on each side.

Example B: Showcase Display

Use an ongoing or growing product display to showcase important details in a study and reflect information learned. Students can add their products to a covered refrigerator box, timeline, wall, chair, or table.

Example C: Create Sack Products for Presentation Displays

Students decorate the outside of sacks to reflect information learned in a unit, using symbols, drawings, facts, captions, graphic organizers, and pictures. They place artifacts and/or props in the bag.

Figure 4.12   Product Assignments

Visual	Auditory	Tactile	Written	Mathematical
Draw a graph, symbol, or design to "represent" . . .	Listen to a partner's direction to create an example	Use the yarn to outline or "make" _____	Write a song using 10 terms that you learned	Place the fractions in sequential order from the lowest to the highest number
Color-code	Discuss information in a group	Record information on individual white boards	Write the important information in the genre of your choice	Develop a matrix
Make an editorial cartoon	Create a forum and debate . . .	Select a folder game	Research and write a report	Plot the information on a Venn diagram
Design a graphic organizer	Tell a partner the highlights	Write in . . . Salt JELL-O Sand Pudding Shaving cream	Respond to the questions: Who? What? When? Where? How? Why?	Create a graph and explain it

Visual	Auditory	Tactile	Written	Mathematical
Illustrate it	Create and interpret sounds for the setting	Show and explain using a manipulative	Create a word game or puzzle	Design a timeline that depicts . . .
Make a collage	Create a rap and share it with your group	Demonstrate a simulation	Write and perform a reenactment	Choose a formula and prove it
Create a diorama	Interpret a passage or song	Mix the ingredients	Design and write a mini-book	Write the sequential steps
Design a shoebox float	Create the background music for the topic	Feel it and name attributes	Brainstorm in a group and plot ideas on a graphic organizer	Design a number game
Create a mini poster display	Write lyrics	Collect artifacts	Come to consensus and write an editorial or point of view	Interpret appropriate data
Create a mural	Listen to instructions to create a product	Use a prop	Write step-by-step process thinking	Conduct a web search
Make a book	Create a riddle	Develop a display	Interpret a graph	Categorize and sort
Decorate the sides of a paper bag	Write a poem	Work in a learning zone	Identify and label an example	Solve a problem and draw the procedure

Adapt the following independent product assignments for agendas, choice boards, academic contracts, or anchor activities (see Figure 4.12).

■ CONCLUSION

Choosing the Correct Instructional Strategy

Remember, like the magician who chooses the tricks in an act with the audience in mind, it is important to purposefully select instructional strategies. Keep your students hooked by pulling out many different hats from your strategy repertoire and using a variety of activities and techniques. Constantly explore novel ways to intrigue and engage students. Try new approaches to reach learners in a differentiated, standard-based classroom.

Refer to each strategy with its title or special name, and be sure students understand related terms and phrases. Use each strategy until learners "own it" so well they use it in other subjects.

Develop a broad repertoire of tricks or instructional strategies to teach the standards and meet the unique needs of learners. Every time you pull out your "magician's hat," you are reminded to take all student needs into account. In a differentiated classroom, each strategy must be accessible and ready to use as soon as a need is recognized. While planning, keep a strategy list (see Figure 4.13) in sight for quality selection. Continuously add to the list as you implement new strategies and delete those that are not effective. This avoids overuse and nonproductive instructional time.

Use the students' interests and areas of strength whenever and wherever possible. Instruction must be meaningful and meet the needs of the students in each learning episode. Like a magician's trick, the perfect strategy will make a lesson, assignment, or activity a successful learning performance!

Figure 4.13   Differentiated Assignments Promoting Active Learning

The following list of follow-up activities may be used as differentiated assignments after students learn information by reading a passage or listening to a lecturette. Use these ideas to develop agendas, choice boards, homework, anchor activities, centers, or projects. Use differentiated assignments to intensify the learners' knowledge of a standard, skill, concept, or unit.

Record findings	Discuss with a partner
Hold a small group text talk	Develop questions
Write a song	Create a rap
Develop a chant	Write a limerick
Write a poem	Create a commercial
Develop a collage	Role-play
Create background music	Create a reenactment
Make a caricature	Draw a picture
Develop an editorial cartoon	Make a diorama
Write a cartoon strip with speech bubbles	Color-code
Illustrate the ____	List the attributes
Create a timeline	Write phrases to describe _____
Develop a mural	Design a new game to review _____
Play a game	Design a poster
Design a puppet	Draw the setting
Find the missing piece(s)	Draw a map
Write an editorial	Design a brochure
Scavenge for information	Write the main idea and supporting details
Plot facts on a graphic organizer	Prepare a point of view
Develop a key	Create a vocabulary game
Act out the vocabulary words	

Make a mobile	Write a summary
Write the directions	Develop a critique
Write your opinion	Write the fact(s)
Label the parts	Name examples
Develop the sequence	Debate the issue
Invent a new way to _____	Identify the sounds
Conduct an interview	Teach someone how to _____
Design a puppet	Draw the setting
Find the missing piece(s)	Use a manipulative
Write an editorial with your point of view	Create and interpret a pie chart
Make a bar graph and interpret the data	Develop a key
Prepare a point of view	Act out the vocabulary words
Name the causes	Create a vocabulary game
List the reasons	List the synonyms or antonyms
Teach someone how to _____	Write a summary
Write the directions	Develop a critique
Draw a conclusion	Write your opinion
Write the fact(s)	Describe how it works
Name examples	Develop the sequence
Debate the issue	Invent a new way to _____
Identify the sounds	Conduct an interview

Figure 4.14   Personal Reflections on Using Instructional Strategies

1. Select an instructional strategy addressed in the chapter that you want to implement or improve. First, study the information related to the strategy, and then place it with your instructional plans. After using the strategy, analyze its effectiveness and identify ways to improve it. Celebrate your professional growth!

2. Select 3 weeks of lesson plans for one class in the same subject area to assess your use of varying your instructional strategies. List and tally the types of activities used. Place a star beside the most effective tasks. Be aware of activity overkill and ruts.

3. Refer to the Differentiating Assignments chart on page 150 for new ideas to promote active learning. Identify activities or strategies to use with the standards in upcoming lesson plans.

4. Develop a cubing activity or choice board to teach a targeted standard. Follow the directions provided with each strategy.

5. Develop independent agenda assignments for students with varying knowledge base levels in relation to a standard.

Figure 4.15   Five Activities for Professional Learning Community (PLC) Study

1. Meeting the Instructional Strategies
   a. Make a list of the instructional strategies in the chapter.
   b. Form partner teams. Have each team sign up for one strategy to present.
   c. Tell partners to study, and highlight their findings.
   d. Call on each partner team to present the strategy with the total group.
   e. Celebrate.

2. Designing a Choice Board
   a. Divide the class into small working groups.
   b. Have each group identify a targeted standard.
   c. Tell groups to design choice boards, following the steps on pages 124–128.
   d. Label the targeted intelligences in each activity. Analyze the results to see if all intelligences are addressed.
   e. Share the completed choice board activities. Discuss the value of designing choice boards for interventions and for students on high and low knowledge levels related to their identified standard.

3. Creating a Cubing Activity
   a. Call on participants to name cube-shaped objects they can use as examples when explaining the cubing activity.
   b. Read and discuss highlights from the cubing section in the chapter.
   c. Form subject-related groups. Have each team identify one focus standard.
   d. Create six tasks to learn about the identified standard for the cubing activity following the suggested procedure. Share completed activities with the total class.
   e. Discuss other techniques for presenting six activity options to students, including the following:

   | Lists | Sticky notes | Drawing from a container | Spinners |

4. Graphic Organizer Sharing Gala
   a. Divide participants into team groups.
   b. Each group selects a graphic organizer from a web search or list.
   c. Have groups plot data from a standard or study on the organizer, using unique fonts and various colors.
   d. Call on each group to share the organizer with the total class. Explain highlights and other uses of the organizer.
   e. Provide time for the audience to add ideas for using graphic organizers to teach the standards.

5. Adaptable Agendas
   a. Discuss the rationale for using agendas.
   b. Form partner teams to create three 5-step agendas.
   c. Select a standard to target in each agenda.
   d. Design the first agenda with tasks or activities for one lesson. The next agenda includes activities for a 3-day period. The last agenda lists activities that extend through 1 week. See the agenda examples on pages 137–140.
   e. Include agenda experiences from the following:

   | Cubing activities | Centers | Graphic organizers |
   | Electronic devices | Computer programs | Free choice activities |

5

Flexible Grouping Strategies

JUST AS A BASEBALL COACH GIVES INFORMATION TO AN ENTIRE team, a teacher gives information to a classroom of learners. The team is brought together to receive general directions, to discuss the techniques and to review statistics of the opposing players. They also receive performance feedback and pep talks.

Wear a baseball hat to assume the coaching role. Bring students together to receive directions, learn new skills, or practice before a test.

Just as players work alone to practice their batting skills, students may work independently to gain more confidence with a specific skill. Players and students may also work in small groups or with a partner, based on their current needs.

One crucial and complex management task in the differentiated classroom involves making grouping decisions. Since instruction is student centered, the savvy differentiator continuously strategically identifies the most beneficial grouping scenarios.

Many questions must be answered during the planning process for grouping students to learn the standard(s):

- Which preassessment tool will be the most effective in guiding grouping decisions? Will it be administered to the total group, individuals, partners, or small groups?
- What is the most beneficial instructional approach to reach the student with the needed information?

- For each activity, what is the best way to arrange the room for group instruction, material distribution, and transitions?
- Who will be in each group?
- How much time must be allotted for group work?

Students benefit from having time to actively process information. Divide the class into small groups according to the results of the assessment data. Using this highly effective strategy, the groups receive content material and skills related to the identified standard on their knowledge levels. They receive specific directions with appropriate monitoring to engage productively.

As students engage in various types of group and independent work, the teacher becomes a coach, facilitator, or guide on the side. The students must understand the assignment's purpose and have clear directions with the necessary materials. When learners know how to carry out activities with little or no adult supervision, the teacher is free to assess and monitor other students or provide direct instruction or an intervention.

Teachers taking their first steps into differentiated instruction are advised to become familiar with the playbook of various grouping scenarios and the occasions when each is most effective in enhancing instruction. This will ensure that the most appropriate approach to grouping is selected and adapted for students during specific periods of study.

FLEXIBLE GROUPING   ■

What Is Flexible Grouping?

Flexible grouping gives students opportunities to learn information in a total class, alone, with a partner, or with a small group. The teacher selects the grouping strategy or scenario to provide the best learning experience for each participant in an activity based on the assessment data.

After determining the need for a partner or small-group activity, the teacher decides if students are grouped according to knowledge base, ability, or interest. Other alternatives include random groupings, peer-to-peer tutoring, multiage teams, or cooperative learning situations.

Grouping scenarios are fluid because students move in and out of the groups as needed based on continuous assessment. For example, if several observations reveal that a student is excelling on the beginning level of a skill, the learner moves to a group to work on more challenging tasks.

What Are the Instructional Benefits of Flexible Grouping?

- Flexible grouping decisions are made with ongoing assessments to meet the identified academic, social, and emotional needs of each learner.
- The teacher can zero in on the specific standards or skills for each group to maximize learning for every student.
- Groups may be created with common interests and abilities. This allows students to feed off of one another's experiences and excitement. They are more likely to contribute when they do not feel overshadowed by classmates.
- When individuals engage in a variety of grouping designs, they learn to work independently and cooperatively with a variety of personalities.
- Groups are formed to reinforce strengths and/or diminish weaknesses.

Implementing Standards Using Flexible Grouping

- Familiarize yourself with each grouping option and its benefits to make the most efficient and advantageous planning decisions.
- Plan instruction to engage learners through a blending of activities in a total group, alone, with a partner, or in a small group. Be alert to the student's growth in knowledge and skills! Move individuals into groups tailored for their needs.
- Avoid ruts by varying the grouping designs with teacher-assigned and student-choice arrangements.
- Share the following suggestions for guiding learners in flexible group work:
  - Follow the directions for teamwork and assignments.
  - Be an active, productive participant to gain information and increase knowledge of the standard from each experience.

o Be respectful! Communicate! Listen to ideas, and contribute to group discussions.
o Ask questions for clarification.
o Move in and out of groups promptly without disturbing classmates.

Demystifying Flexible Grouping

All students need to know what to expect in their classroom. If learners are not familiar with flexible grouping, they need to understand the rationale for using it. Use an analogy such as the following to introduce flexible grouping:

The baseball coach is using a practice session to improve individual and group skills. Two girls are working on pitching and hitting the ball, while other players practice passing the ball. One player is perfecting his catching skills. The remaining players are running and sliding into bases. In the next special practice session, all players engage in a scrimmage game.

In the same way, in our classroom, we work on skills individually and in small groups. Our scrimmage will take place when we have a practice session for a major test.

★ ★ ★ ★ ★

**Five-Star
Tips for Flexible Grouping**

1. Identify the most effective grouping design for the learners. Decide how many students to place in each group from an analysis of the assessment data during the planning phase.

   Examples:

   Base group: A group of students who sit at the same table or near one another move their seats together to form a cluster or place their desks together to work.

   Gender: Some groups work better when they are composed of all girls or all boys.

   Previous relationships: After working together on several activities, members usually bond as a team. They get along socially and respect one another. They learn to use one another's individual strengths and talents to reach the group's goal.

   Student selection: Students choose classmates they can work with to get the job done. *Example:* Choosing an energizing partner.

   Teacher selection: The teacher places students together based on their needs. *Example:* Creating a cooperative learning group or a project team.

2. Observe group dynamics. If the members of a group cooperate socially, they are more likely to be successful in completing the assignment.

3. If group members do not want to work with a student, try this prescription: Hold a private conference with the learner to identify and discuss the reasons for the personal rejections. Develop a plan for improvement.

4. Move a learner to a more beneficial group when assessments, including observations, indicate that his or her needs have changed. For example, if one student is struggling with the skill practiced in a group, this individual moves to a new scenario for intervention to learn the skill.

5. Select reflection activities for groups and individuals to obtain feedback and to create learning summaries.

Examples of Flexible Grouping

Example A: Fast-Forwarding

Assessment data reveal that a small group of students mastered the information in the upcoming lesson. During independent work time, these students receive an alternative assignment to research related to the standard.

Example B: Ready for Grade Level

A student has been meeting and doing the assignments with the readiness group. He understands the concept and now is given the assignments with the grade-level groups.

Example C: Rewinding

From a checkpoint during the learning, it is evident that a group of students still do not understand the information. Give specific assignments during independent work time to address the gap. Also, bring this group together for in-depth explanation during a time when the other students are working on an independent assignment. This is an example of the teacher responding to a need with an intervention.

■ TOTAL GROUPS

What Is a Total Group?

A total group activity involves the entire class. Though this tactic might seem counterintuitive in a book about differentiation, it is an excellent means of reaching and engaging every learner in the classroom when used appropriately. The teacher analyzes each whole-group activity to be sure every student benefits from hearing or using the same information. This is the time to assess, introduce, and teach the fundamentals and basic information related to the standards, with the appropriate content and resources.

What Are the Instructional Benefits of Using Total Groups?

In the differentiated classroom, total groups are strategically planned. The sessions benefit learners when they are designed for the following purposes:

- Sharing the same information all students need. This includes introductions, background information, or procedures needed in a standard, skill, or concept.
- Providing explicit guidelines, directions, schedules, and announcements.
- Engaging students in brainstorming opportunities that produce ideas to explore. The class can hear the views, ideas, and processing alternatives to learn information during discussions.
- Celebrating and enjoying learning experiences. Examples include playing team games, using drill and practice activities, listening to visiting speakers, presenting reports and demonstrations, and beginning and ending activities for the lesson.
- Administering grade-level assessments and evaluations.

Implementing Standards Using Total Groups

- Plan each total group session strategically. Use this instructional arrangement when it is the most effective and efficient way to reach each learner.
- Divide lectures into manageable chunks or lecturettes for optimal comprehension of the standard information.
- Actively engage all students during total group sessions. Intersperse opportunities, similar to the following, for students to work alone, with a partner, or in a small group during a total group session:
  - Work independently to practice a newly introduced procedure.
  - Turn to a partner to model, restate, and discuss a difficult concept or skill.
  - Brainstorm possibilities with a small group.
- Let students see and experience your enthusiasm. Use novelty and your passion for a subject to capture and maintain students' interest and attention.
- Use the following suggestions to guide students while working in total groups:

○ Use the learner's terminology to present and teach the standard.
○ Provide expectations for on-task behaviors during total group sessions.
○ Encourage an open forum for appropriate questions at appropriate times.
○ Link new information to their personal experiences, and use memory hooks for easy recall.
○ Teach note-taking strategies, such as using symbols, shapes, colors, tabs, and graphic organizers.

Demystifying Total Groups

Explain the purpose of total group sessions to your students using an analogy similar to the following:

When the coach introduces a new play or strategy for the team, all players come together to listen to the explanation so they can carry it out in the next session.

During total group sessions, everyone needs to be engaged, giving complete, undivided attention to the instruction.

Five-Star
Tips for Total Groups

1. Replace lengthy lectures with lecturettes or mini-lectures. Be sure you convey information everyone needs to hear or see such as the following:

   • An introduction to vital background or facts related to the grade-level standards, content, and materials
   • Motivational hooks or focus activities for the lesson
   • A "how-to" demonstration or simulation
   • Directions for upcoming activities
   • Reviews, assessments, evaluations, and feedback sessions

2. Vary instructional strategies and activities according to the students' learning styles, modalities, and intelligences.

3. Actively engage learners in total group discussions. Establish rules for listening and responding similar to the following:

   • One person speaks at a time.
   • Respond when called on to contribute.
   • Speak so everyone can hear your response.
   • Listen to each person's statements, questions, and responses.
   • Be respectful and open to the views of others.

4. Employ questioning techniques that make each individual accountable for a mental, written, or oral response. Remind students to put on their thinking caps before questions are presented. Provide thinking time before calling on

(Continued)

(Continued)

someone for a response. Establish note-taking procedures. The best question-ers do the following:

- Vary types of questions
- Give students novel ways to respond individually
- Allow partners time to compose brief written or oral responses in the form of lists, phrases, or sentences
- Engage all students by requiring that each one give a visible response using dry-erase boards, signals, or response cards
- Ask students to whisper answers to a neighbor, agree on the best answer, and prepare to give their response in unison with the class at the sound of a signal

5. Vary ways to call for individual responses in total groups:

Random selection	Volunteers	Secret number
Alphabetical order	Birth dates	Seating arrangement
Drawing names	Signals	

Examples of Effective Total Grouping

Example A: Beginning a Lesson

The teacher provides an intriguing introduction to the upcoming topic of study, with emphasis on the appropriate standards for the whole class. This may include a debut of important facts, new vocabulary words, a discussion of characters, or highlights to stimulate or excite minds for new learning.

Example B: During Learning

After students work independently and in small groups for a period of time, the teacher brings the whole class together to review, celebrate, and summarize the learned information. Then the teacher may introduce the next activity by setting the purpose, explaining directions, and establishing the grouping scenarios.

Example C: After a Learning Segment

Students are brought together to review and prepare for a posttest on the standards in the current unit. The teacher provides study tips and reviews important facts and concepts. The total class plays a game to review information.

STUDENTS WORKING ALONE   ■

What Is Working Alone?

Working alone refers to a student who independently completes an activity or task. The student works in an assigned seat, a designated area, or a comfortable, self-selected place.

The teacher periodically monitors and assists the learner. If the teacher is engaged in direct instruction with a group, another adult or study buddy may serve as the teacher. If no assistant is available, the student is told how and when to interact with the teacher or other classmates.

A student who is working independently needs to be within the teacher's vision. Avoid placing a student in a secluded, unsupervised place.

What Are the Instructional Benefits of Students Working Alone?

- Intrapersonal learners need quiet work periods. It takes time for them to think. They yearn for alone time to conceptualize and problem solve.
- Some students prefer to work with others but occasionally need assignments to complete independently. Working and learning alone is a life skill everyone needs for success.
- When students work alone, they are able to show what they know, how they process information, and what they can accomplish on their own.
- When a student is successful during independent assignments, the time on task increases.
- The learner is able to work at his or her own pace.

Implementing Standards Using Working Alone

- Give an individual assignment when a specific, unique need is identified to teach the standard.
- Provide assignments and tasks students can complete with little or no assistance.
- Make materials and resources accessible to complete the task.
- Explicitly state how the student is to be held accountable for completing the assignment. This may be accomplished by stating something similar to the following:
  - "Make a journal entry of your learning."
  - "Show me your work in our mini-conference."
  - "Complete the rubric form."
  - "Place completed work in the 'IN' basket for grading when you finish."
  - "Place your peer review in your portfolio."
  - "Check your work using the answer key. Correct it, and place it in your folder."
- Be sure the student understands the purpose of the assignment and each direction. Establish clear rules, rituals, and routines. See Figure 5.1.

Figure 5.1   Work Alone: Trouble Shooting

What if . . .	Options for the student	Suggestions for the teacher
I have a question.	• Raise your hand. • Place the question on a sticky note and place it in an assigned area. • Ask a study buddy.	• Establish rules and procedures for the student to ask questions during independent activities. • Realize that when a student asks too many questions, the individual did not receive clear, appropriate directions; seeks attention; or experienced difficulty.
I need some supplies.	• If the supplies are located in an area that is open to students, quietly go and obtain the needed supplies. • If not, ask the teacher for permission.	• Have needed supplies accessible and available for students. • Designate some closet, basket, or shelf areas with supplies available to learners.
My pencil point breaks.	• Obtain a pencil from a container of sharpened, extra pencils. • Borrow one from a neighbor or the teacher.	• Collect pencils from parents and neighbors. • Place containers of sharpened pencils around the room so a pencil is easily available.
I need to go to the bathroom.	• Use a hall pass. • Obtain the bathroom tag or necklace prepared for a pass.	• Establish bathroom rules and procedures. Be consistent and persistent with everyone.
I do not know how to work a piece of equipment.	• Ask appropriate questions or request a demonstration. • Ask for help from a peer, then the teacher. • Move to another assignment or spot to complete another task until the teacher is available.	• Make sure that students are taught and practice with adult supervision before given an independent assignment on a new piece of equipment. • Assign a knowledgeable student to be in charge to assist others.
I know a classmate needs help.	• Help by asking probing questions to pinpoint the problem. • Show and tell your step-by-step thinking.	• Establish guidelines for giving assistance. • Explain and model how to assist others.

What if . . .	Options for the student	Suggestions for the teacher
		• Students who have an "aha" moment often are the best tutors because they know the steps.
I finished my assignment.	• Check over your work. • Move on to the next task. • Return materials to their designated area. • Complete a self-assessment activity. • Find something to do on your own that will not distract others.	• Have alternative activities for students who finish their work early. • Teach students to review their answers. • Provide ways for students to check and correct their own papers immediately after completion.

Demystifying Working Alone

Use a lecturette similar to the following to explain the purpose of working alone:

> *There are going to be times in your life when you have to work by yourself. When you work independently, you learn to stay on task, to have patience, and to complete assignments with little or no assistance. Consider the time an athlete spends working alone to perfect skills.*

★ ★ ★ ★ ★

**Five-Star
Tips for Working Alone**

1. Use an individual assignment to address an identified need. The task(s) should be designed to reinforce, practice, extend, or assess the standard.

2. Be sure the student understands the purpose of the assignment and directions to complete the tasks with little or no assistance.

3. Establish parameters that include the following:

   • Options for places to work, such as a rug, floor, table, or desk
   • Movement to other work areas

(Continued)

(Continued)

- Obtaining the materials and resources necessary to complete the task
- Talking to a study buddy
- How and when to seek answers to questions

4. Teach the student how to check and correct work.

5. Place the student engaging in independent tasks in a visable area where you are working. Proximity gives you opportunities to use a signal such as a "thumbs up" to encourage and support the learner.

Examples of Working Alone

Example A: Agenda Assignment

A student receives an independent agenda assignment with three tasks to complete. The learner works at his or her own pace, selecting the order of the activities and moving freely to stations or areas to complete the tasks. The student selects two completed work samples to place in a portfolio or folder. One selection is checked and corrected. It is placed in an assigned tray for teacher viewing.

Example B: Project Assignment

A learner has an ongoing, independent project assignment. The student completes a web search on the computer to gather research for the selected topic. During the next two independent work sessions, the student works at a desk reading, taking notes, and compiling valuable facts for the project.

Example C: Personalized Assignment

Analysis of a student's pretest data on a standard in the current study reveals a specific need. The learner works with materials to fill a gap or enhance learning. The student returns materials to the storage space. The student makes oral or written reflection statements and creates a journal entry about the learning experience.

PARTNER GROUPS ■

What Is a Partner Group?

A partner group consists of two students working cooperatively to complete a task or reach a goal. They are placed together as a team to share ideas, cooperate, and assist each other. The students must be socially compatible to be successful partners.

What Are the Instructional Benefits of Using Partner Groups?

- Partner work actively engages more students in learning. For example, when the total group is divided into partner teams for a task, half the class talks while the other half listens. Then the partner roles are reversed.
- All students have opportunities to share ideas, revise, and work with someone.
- Learners experience the value of "two brains working as one."
- Every student receives immediate feedback, assistance, and encouragement.
- Some students work better with a partner than alone or in a larger group.

Implementing Standards Using Partner Groups

- Identify the appropriate assignment for partner teams.
- Vary the way partners are identified.
    - Assign partner teams according to academic need and social interaction.
    - Allow students to work with a friend. Establish the understanding that only friends who stay on task and follow the rules have the privilege of working together.
    - Use random grouping techniques such as drawing names or counting off. Students will enjoy forming partner teams using a match game with one of the following categories: book titles with main characters, states with capitals, landmarks with cities, inventors with their inventions, or songs with the lyrics.
- Provide rules and regulations for productive, interactive learning. Model, practice, and role-play these guidelines.
- Teach students how to question each other to stimulate thinking while working together. Provide opportunities for partners to interact and get to know each other so they form a respectful, productive working team as friends.
- Devise a personal reflection activity for partners to use in summarizing information they learned together.

Demystifying Partner Groups

Teach your students that two heads are often better than one:

Every person has unique life experiences and different strengths and weaknesses. When working and learning with someone else, you have a bigger knowledge bank with two brains communicating.

Working together, Orville and Wilbur Wright invented the first powered airplane capable of carrying a man. Brilliant scientists and inventors working on their own for centuries had been unable to accomplish this feat. The Wright brothers made history because they worked well as a team. They respected each other and valued each other's ideas. Remember, you have a right to your own opinion or way of doing something, but so does your partner.

Five-Star
Tips for Partner Groups

1. Use partner teams wisely and purposefully. Prepare partner teams or small groups for specific assignments. Here are some suggested guidelines:
   - Select assignments and activities that enhance the current standard or topic of study.
   - Be sure the partners receive thorough directions for the assignment so they can complete it independently as a student-focused activity.
   - Give learners opportunities to ask questions related to the assignment.
   - Teach partners options for solving their own problems.
   - Make materials and resources accessible to minimize partner movement.

2. Establish energizing partners to work together throughout the day, class period, unit of study, or grading period. Permit students to choose someone they can work with effectively, or assign the partner teams.

3. Keep the same partners together long enough to cultivate mutual respect, trust, and team spirit.

4. Assign tasks that allow partners to choose a favorite place to work. If possible, let the team decide if they want to sit or stand to complete the tasks.

5. Ask students to write on their own papers even if they are discussing or checking answers with a partner. In this way, they learn to identify their personal mistakes and take responsibility for making the corrections.

Examples of Effective Partner Grouping

Example A: Drill

Two students who need to learn facts use flash cards or an electronic game for drill and practice.

Example B: Reading Reflection

Students work together to complete a writing activity to summarize their reading assignment. They brainstorm the information learned and compile the highlights.

Example C: Read, Share, Design, Report

Partners select or are assigned a topic related to the standard or current area of study to explore in depth. They read, share, and compile the ideas gathered. The partners design an innovative display to report their findings to the class.

SMALL GROUPS ■

What Is a Small Group?

The meaning of the term *small group* probably seems obvious, but the word *small* is a relative term. A teacher who has a large class may consider 15 students a small group, so clarification is needed here.

In a differentiated classroom, the most effective student-directed groups are composed of three or four members. The number of students in a group receiving teacher instruction is determined by the number of students who need to work with the information.

What Are the Instructional Benefits of Using Small Groups?

- Because small groups are formed for cooperative activities or for learners to work on common tasks, students can engage in separate, simultaneously occurring activities specifically designed for their needs.
- The teacher can introduce, review, or guide the practice of skills for more than one learner.
- Students who need support, interventions, immediate feedback, and encouragement are monitored.
- When engaged in group work, learners are actively processing information for understanding and retention. Pathways to memory are created as they share, hear, and mentally manipulate information during interactive activities.
- Each learner is given the opportunity to work, communicate, brainstorm, and be creative as a team member. Students are making decisions with others and learning how and when to compromise for consensus. These skills are necessary to be successful in nearly all aspects of life. Note: Make a banner or poster to remind students to respect, assist, and encourage team members.

Implementing Standards Using Small Groups

- Use the assessment data to decide when the students need to be in a group to learn the standards and content in the most effective way. Strategically plan assignments that build a knowledge base and create curiosity by presenting a focus activity, providing an anticipatory set, or introducing an engaging activity.

  Examples:

  o Find the facts related to the standard or topic.
  o Use the experiment to explore the information.
  o Discover the mysteries surrounding the standard.
  o Find out why you need to know this information.

- Establish appropriate, beneficial roles that accommodate group needs and showcase individual talents. Introduce one way to select a group leader, recorder, reporter, and other necessary roles. Explain the purpose and responsibility of each role assignment. Introduce a new technique when students are comfortable with their roles. When students understand two or three ways of selecting team members to fulfill the different roles, let each group choose the technique for assigning responsibilities or roles. Here are a few suggestions:

Use a spinner	Draw names	Ask for a volunteer
Use alphabetical order	Use birth dates	Take turns

- Provide groups with a clear purpose, expectations, and directions for the activity.

Example:

1. Name your group, and establish individual roles.
2. Review the assignment to be sure everyone understands the goal. Discuss the best way to carry out the assignment.
3. Obtain needed materials and resources.
4. Complete the assignment.
5. Share, reflect, and celebrate!

- Teach students how to transition in and out of groups efficiently and effectively, or Quickly and Quietly (Q & Q).
- Allow enough time for each step of the process, presentation of the learning, and reflection. During the reflection period, individual members share cognitive and social aspects of the learning that occurred during the group work. Emphasize the steps in the process more than the product produced.

Demystifying Small Groups

The following analogies assist in explaining the benefits of two major forms of group collaboration:

In some groups, each member is assigned a different task to complete a large job. In a committee planning a large party on short notice, for example, one member may be responsible for choosing and purchasing decorations, another may be responsible for hiring a band or DJ, and a third may be responsible for designing and printing flyers to advertise the party.

Small groups may brainstorm to solve a problem. Members of the president's cabinet, for instance, gather together periodically to discuss the pros and cons of laws the president is considering. Each member has a different specialty and unique viewpoint to offer. This helps the president consider all sides of an issue and determine the best course of action before making a decision.

Emphasize that each member has a different practical, analytical, or creative viewpoint to share with the group. Discuss quality decision making and problem solving, which relies on respecting and thoughtfully considering each individual's contributions.

Teacher-Directed Small Groups

- Bring together a group of students who need a common learning time based on an assessment of their knowledge in relation to a standard or skill. For example, a group may be formed for a response to intervention or enrichment.
- Avoid directing more than three groups in a class period, because it is difficult to plan and manage activities for more than three learning experiences. When too many groups are created, busy work assignments are often added to keep them occupied. Meet with different groups on different days.

Five-Star
Tips for Teacher-Directed Small Groups

1. Gather the small group in a designated work area. Name the purposes of the day's standard. Hook students into wanting to learn! Present directions and explanations in language they understand.
2. Teach standards and content in varied ways to keep each mind engaged.
3. Assess continuously to know what learners need next.
4. Provide immediate feedback.
5. Before leaving the group area, do the following:
   - Give an independent practice assignment as a follow-up activity.
   - Celebrate successes!
   - Lead a discussion to review the day's learning.
   - Ask students to state what they want to learn next.
   - Introduce highlights of the next small-group meeting.

Five-Star
Tips for Student-Focused Small Groups

1. Remember, group members must get along socially to complete an assignment successfully. Teach, model, and discuss the skills a productive team member must possess.
2. Vary group formations to meet student needs and to add novelty to learning. Avoid creating a group with more than four students. If the group will make a decision, use an odd number of members so it will be easier to come to consensus.

(Continued)

(Continued)

3. Establish clear, specific directions for the assignment, with roles and duties for the group members so each student has a specific task. Design assignments so they require little teacher oversight. Customize the activities for each group to suit specific member needs, such as the following:

- Review and practice essential information related to the standard, skill, or topic.
- Provide personalized, meaningful experiences.
- Build speed and accuracy.
- Move to mastery and automaticity.
- Apply information in a new way.

4. To be a better facilitator and monitor during small-group activities, try the following:

- Be visible and stay in close proximity with students.
- Keep moving among groups and avoid forming a walking pattern.
- Use nonverbal body language to emphasize messages.
- Position yourself on the opposite side of the group or behind it when a student is speaking to other members.
  Be careful about making promises to students that may be difficult to keep, such as, "I'll be there in a minute." In a differentiated classroom, you never know when a greater need will appear.

5. Avoid giving group grades. Assess learning during independent tasks. Group activities are best used for brainstorming sessions, producing products, making presentations, reviewing, discussing facts, reading, or practicing skills.

Design an effective combination of the various types of grouping to target the standard(s) and meet the student's cognitive and social needs. The activities in Figure 5.2 are suggestions for varying grouping scenarios for differentiation.

KNOWLEDGE-BASE GROUPS　■

What Are Knowledge-Base Groups?

In differentiated classrooms, knowledge-base groups are formed according to the student's assessed level of understanding on the topic, skill, or standard. Like a coach practicing specific skills at different levels, a teacher must take into consideration where students are in their current levels of understanding. This knowledge is acquired over a lifetime through personal and academic experiences. Create knowledge-level groups by analyzing the formal or informal preassessment data.

> **Curriculum rewinding:** Students on this level need an introduction to the basic information. They have little or no knowledge of the new standard, topic, or skill.
>
> **Grade level:** These learners are ready for the new grade-level information related to the standard. They possess the proper background, experiences, and understanding.
>
> **Curriculum fast-forwarding:** Students on this level know and understand the basic information. They are ready to extend their knowledge and explore related areas.

The adjustable assignment model is designed as a planning tool to use in selecting and customizing instructional strategies and activities for knowledge-base groups. See more about this planning tool in Chapter 6.

What Are the Instructional Benefits of Using Knowledge-Base Groups?

- Each student relates prior experiences to the new standard, skill, or topic because instruction begins with the learner's current knowledge.
- Lessons are customized for individuals and groups. Students receive instruction and challenges on their success levels.
- Students are more eager to learn because they are not bored or frustrated.
- The groups are fluid. Responding to analyzed assessment data and observations, the teacher moves a student to a more appropriate group working on a higher or lower knowledge level.
- A student may work on the fast-forwarding level on one standard and the rewinding level on another standard. This establishes an accepting tone and addresses the learner's cognitive knowledge base, including strengths and needs.

Implementing Standards Using Knowledge-Base Groups

- Select the best formal or informal preassessment tool to identify each learner's background and prior experiences. Analyze the data to form and plan knowledge-base groups using instructional activities to address the needs of each individual.
- Identify ongoing assessment tools for the unit, topic, skill, or standard to monitor each learner's ever-changing needs and appropriate group placement.

Figure 5.2   Grouping Scenarios

Group	Total Group	Alone	Partner	Small Group
When	☐ Topic introductions ☐ Modeling ☐ Skill demonstrations ☐ Focus activities ☐ Presentation of background information ☐ Drill and practice ☐ Directions and procedures ☐ Wrap-up sessions ☐ Lecturettes ☐ Guided practice ☐ Media clips ☐ Electronic presentations ☐ Performances ☐ Reports ☐ Celebrations of learning ☐ Reflections	☐ Contracts ☐ Agendas ☐ Menus ☐ Choice boards ☐ Journals ☐ Diaries ☐ Logs ☐ Practice/drill ☐ Information processing ☐ Questions/ responses ☐ Manipulative use ☐ Note taking ☐ Reviews ☐ Reflections ☐ Computer work ☐ Research ☐ Performances ☐ Assessments	☐ Manipulatives ☐ Reviews ☐ Practice/drill ☐ Cooperative learning ☐ Performances ☐ Listening and speaking activities ☐ Sharing information ☐ Questioning/ responding ☐ Checking work ☐ Games ☐ Puzzles ☐ Computer activities ☐ Problem solving ☐ Research ☐ Study buddies ☐ Revising/editing ☐ Double-entry journaling ☐ Reflections ☐ Conversations ☐ Summarizing	☐ Text talk ☐ Conversation circles ☐ Literary circles ☐ Cooperative learning ☐ Consensus building ☐ Applying information ☐ Practice/drill ☐ Brainstorming ☐ Performing ☐ Discussing/explaining ☐ Reflections ☐ Reviewing ☐ Problem solving ☐ Researching ☐ Presenting ☐ Previewing materials ☐ Publishing ☐ Using manipulatives
Where	☐ Desks ☐ Rugs ☐ Labs ☐ Media center ☐ Gymnasium	☐ Learning zones ☐ Center ☐ Station ☐ Lab	☐ Learning zones ☐ Centers ☐ Stations ☐ Labs	☐ Learning zones ☐ Centers ☐ Stations ☐ Labs
	☐ Tables ☐ Outside ☐ Standing cluster ☐ Commons areas ☐ Bleachers ☐ Hallway	☐ Desk ☐ Floor ☐ Rug ☐ Chair ☐ Glider ☐ Rocking chair ☐ Study carrel ☐ Loft ☐ Cubicle ☐ Large ball	☐ Chosen space ☐ Floor ☐ Desks/chairs ☐ Table ☐ Standing or sitting back to back to work. Facing each other to share and discuss.	☐ Grouped tables and/or chairs ☐ Clustered desks ☐ Floor ☐ Standing cluster ☐ Outside

- Schedule time to meet with each level. Give feedback with specific instructions, support, and encouragement.
- Realize that the individual student's prior knowledge and experience are unique for each learning segment. Use your best judgment to select the most opportune time and place to use knowledge-base groups.

- Use the following suggestions to help students effectively work in knowledge-base groups.
  - Give learners an opportunity to recall their experiences and what they know about the upcoming topic. Guide them to link what they know to the new information.
  - Teach them to accept the assigned knowledge-level tasks and realize they can grow and excel in this area.
  - Emphasize the importance of seeking standard mastery.
  - Adapt the following dialogue for your learners to understand knowledge-base grouping:

    Know what you know and what you don't know. If you discover that you have learning gaps, fill them in so you can move quickly to grade-level material. If you know the grade-level information, see how much more you can learn about it. Share what you know with others.

Note: For more implementation ideas refer to the Adjustable Assignment Model on pages 194–200.

Demystifying Knowledge-Base Groups

Understand that learners may be on different knowledge levels with each topic and skill. Lead a discussion comparing game and knowledge-base levels. Introduce students to knowledge-base groups using an explanation similar to the following:

When you turn on an electronic game, you select the level of speed or accuracy. You consider previous scores to choose the best level for you. In the same way, our preassessments and your daily work determine your level for each assignment or activity.

★ ★ ★ ★ ★

**Five-Star
Tips for Knowledge-Base Groups**

1. Use an appropriate formal or informal preassessment tool. If an informal assessment will identify the information needed to form the groups, use it instead of the formal assessment. Gather the information before planning the unit so you can tailor instruction and select the appropriate activities and materials for the success of knowledge-base groups.

2. Implement knowledge-base groups when the preassessment indicates that the class has a broad range of knowledge on a standard, skill, or topic. In other words, the results reveal that some students have a high level of understanding, many learners are on grade level, and others are on the beginning level.

3. Select tasks that generate buy-in from the learners and meet their specific needs.

4. Adjust groups continuously for effective instruction. For example, when a learner demonstrates that instruction is needed on basic key elements, that student should receive the basic information and quickly move to a higher level once the learning gap is filled.

5. Remember, knowledge-base groups are fluid, changing with the learner's needs.

Examples of Knowledge-Base Grouping

The following examples illustrate four ways a teacher can use adjustable assignments to divide a class into three groups according to the student's knowledge base related to a standard, skill, or topic.

The number of lessons needed for the learner to reach the objectives determines the number of sessions and the time allotted.

Example A: Grade-Level Instruction for the Majority of the Class

The teacher preassesses learners on new information. During the first 2 days of the unit study, the total class works together. Figure 5.3 illustrates a possible scenario for the third day of the study.

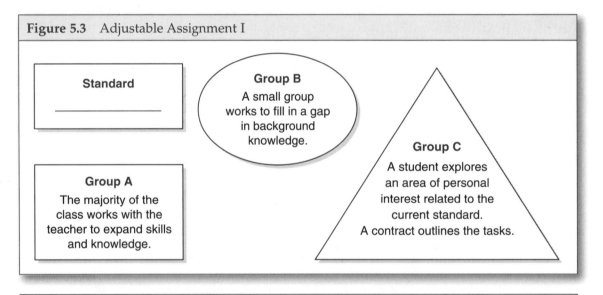

Figure 5.3   Adjustable Assignment I

Standard
_____

Group B
A small group works to fill in a gap in background knowledge.

Group A
The majority of the class works with the teacher to expand skills and knowledge.

Group C
A student explores an area of personal interest related to the current standard. A contract outlines the tasks.

Example B: Rewinding Instruction for a Small Group

A posttest reveals that most students have mastered the new skill. Three students had very low scores. Two students had perfect scores.

Both groups work on their individual assignments simultaneously within the same time frame.

Group A contains students who need the intervention.

1. The teacher reteaches the common need to members of Group A for part of the designated time frame.

2. The students work with an assignment to practice the retaught information. This gives students a chance to show their level of understanding.

3. The teacher leaves them to work alone and monitors the rest of the class by walking around.

Group B contains the students who are ready to work with the grade-level material. This group completes an independent assignment while Group A works with the teacher.

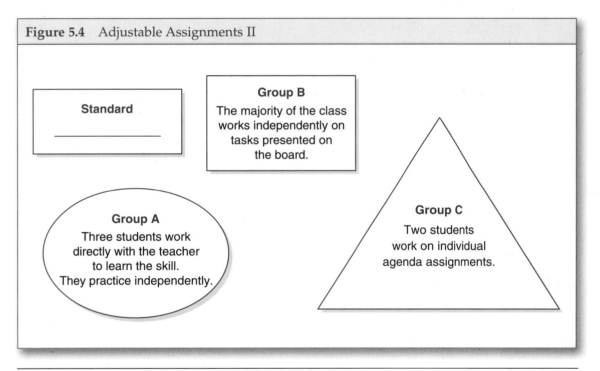

Figure 5.4   Adjustable Assignments II

Standard
_____

Group B
The majority of the class works independently on tasks presented on the board.

Group A
Three students work directly with the teacher to learn the skill. They practice independently.

Group C
Two students work on individual agenda assignments.

Example C: Curriculum Rewinding and Fast-Forwarding

The teacher designs two different group assignments to target the students' needs revealed by the assessment data. The groups complete the assignments in the same time frame.

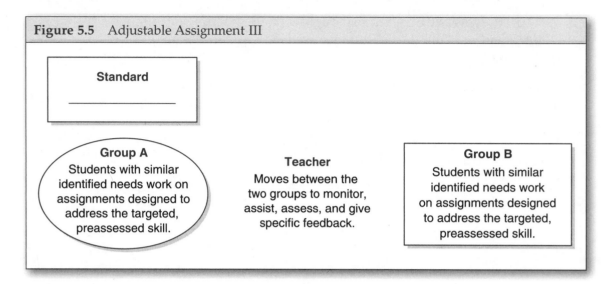

Figure 5.5   Adjustable Assignment III

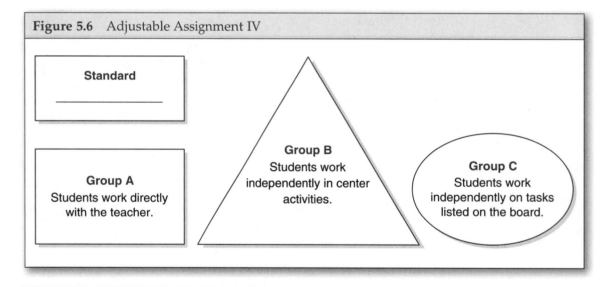

Figure 5.6   Adjustable Assignment IV

Example D: Three Rotating Groups

Students are engaged in three different group configurations occurring simultaneously. All groups rotate through a work session with the teacher, independent work, and center activities.

INTEREST GROUPS ■

What Is an Interest Group?

Interest groups are formed with learners who are eager to learn more about the standard, topic, or skill. These study teams are appropriate for all grade levels and curriculum areas.

What Are the Instructional Benefits of Using Interest Groups?

- Students gain an opportunity to investigate and explore an exciting topic in depth.
- Interest is a strong motivational tool that increases the student's desire to learn more.
- Learners are given the opportunity to delve into favorite related topics using their most comfortable learning styles and strongest intelligences.
- Students develop a sense of ownership in their education and are guided to become self-directed, independent learners.
- Students learn information and assume more responsibilities when engaging in assignments of interest.

Implementing Standards Using Interest Groups

- Assist the individual or group in selecting an interest area that focuses on information or skills related to the grade-level standards. Probe for ideas through discussion and brainstorming sessions, or use surveys and inventories.
- Analyze the chosen interest area to plan activities to challenge and enrich learning. These student-focused groups work with engaging activities that can be accomplished with little adult supervision.
- Select a method to form interest groups, such as the following:
  - Sign up for an area of choice.
  - Write a contract with interest-related activities, and obtain teacher approval.
  - Use a survey, and compile the data to identify interest areas.
  - Allow teams to select an interest topic related to the current study.
- Provide adequate time for the group to share what they know and to delve into new information on the topic. Celebrate learning!
- Set expectations to include the goals, guidelines, timelines, and assessment tools to use before, during, and after learning.

Demystifying Interest Groups

Explain interest grouping to your students as a great opportunity to explore a topic of interest.

Your favorite pastime, hobby, or activity is something you enjoy. It appeals to you and keeps your attention. You will have opportunities to choose a specific area of interest within our current topic and work with others who share your interest.

★ ★ ★ ★ ★

Five-Star
Tips for Interest Groups

1. Survey students to identify their areas of interest related to the current study. Use this information to provide appropriate choices and enhance learning.

2. Strategically provide choices to broaden each individual's knowledge. Match standards with interest assignments.

3. Learn as much as you can about your students. The more you know about individuals, the easier it is to plan effective, meaningful learning opportunities in an interest area.

4. Allow students who are working together on a subtopic to showcase their extended learning experiences.

5. Remember, when students have an affinity for a topic and have rewarding experiences in their study, they are more likely to retain the information.

Discuss a few categories, such as movies, songs, sports, and books. Ask students to name their specific areas of interest in each one. Wrap up the session by presenting a few upcoming unit topics or standards.

Examples of Interest Grouping

Example A: Research Dig!

The class is beginning a study of the ocean. Five students select an area of interest to explore for more information. Their study takes them through the following procedure:

- Individuals select a role or task to accomplish during the investigation and research.
- The members compile the information.
- The group highlights important facts learned in the investigation.
- All members participate in a presentation of the new information.
- Each student completes a rubric as a self-assessment tool.

Example B: Jigsaw

Individual learners select an area of interest from a choice board and joins the designated team. Each group has a different topic to explore. The team works, discusses, and studies the information. The group shares its results and findings with the class.

Example C: Contract

Students select a skill or topic of interest related to the current study. They design a contract or agreement to extend learning in this area. The contract identifies the tasks, time frame, product, and assessment tool. The teacher makes appropriate additions or changes in the contract. The teacher and students sign the agreement.

ABILITY GROUPS ∎

What Is an Ability Group?

Everyone has personal talents and weaknesses. An ability group is formed with students who have similar capabilities for working with a standard, skill, or procedure. Each individual's achievement scores, academic performance, and/or daily work are used as indicators of the learner's capability. These experiences provide opportunities for a homogeneous group to work with materials and activities within its members' ability range.

When students work to the best of their ability, with no cap on their potential, they become proud, hard workers. Ability groups often are composed of learners who are at risk, on grade level, or in the gifted and talented group. Some districts use these levels for homogeneous grouping within classrooms or schools.

What Are the Instructional Benefits of Using Ability Groups?

- The teacher can plan the appropriate pace with challenging strategies and activities on the same instructional level that focus on a skill needed by the group.
- Students usually receive direct instruction in an ability group. It is often easier to plan for those who have a common weakness or need.
- The learners develop a bond as they work on the same standard, skill, or procedure.
- Learners who work at a slower pace are not threatened with frustration and failure. High achievers are not bored during lessons.
- The activities match the students' ability level, so they are more likely to grow in learning and experience success.

Implementing Standards Using Ability Groups

- Analyze and compile assessment data to identify specific, common needs to establish groups. Plan activities to target individual needs, incorporating the learner's strengths.
- Strategically plan activities for the standard(s) on the group's ability level.
- Provide opportunities for students using a variety of learning strategies.
- Use flexible grouping and move students to the group that meets their needs.
- Adapt the following guidelines for students to use in ability groups:
  - Work to learn as much information as possible.
  - Show what you know.
  - Ask appropriate questions.
  - Show respect for each team member.
  - Complete your independent assignments and tasks.

Demystifying Ability Groups

Explain to students that ability groups are used so they can work on their level with a specific standard, skill, or topic. Compare ability groups to the levels in swimming classes: beginning, intermediate, and advanced.

When people take swimming lessons, some are placed in beginning classes because they need to become accustomed to being in the water. They must learn the basics, such as breathing techniques and specific strokes. Swimmers are placed in the intermediate level when they can use the fundamental skills. Individuals may remain in the beginner's class for a long period of time to learn the basic skills. Swimmers are placed in the advanced level because they have the physical and mental ability to use highly developed skills.

Individuals who do not advance in swimming may excel in other sports or hobbies. Engage students in a discussion of their experiences with varying levels of difficulty.

Five-Star
Tips for Ability Groups

1. Assess! Assess! Use formal and informal assessment data to identify ability levels.
2. Address individual needs, and apply flexible grouping strategies.
3. Teach groups in varied ways so individuals have numerous opportunities to learn the information.
4. Provide groups time for practice, discussion, and processing.
5. Use ability groups when you want to "zap gaps" for students and challenge high-end learners.

Examples of Ability Grouping

Example A: Skill Groups

Skill groups for an academic area are created according to the results of a preassessment. Students may need an introduction to the basic information, the grade-level lesson, or an extension of the skill. The specific needs of each group are addressed through direct instruction and specific assignments to advance learning on each level.

Example B: Reading Groups

The teacher and students compile reading materials to reinforce a unit on the Revolutionary War. The teacher divides the reading materials into four stacks (red, blue, yellow, and green) according to the level of difficulty. Before the lesson begins, students are assigned to groups based on their reading ability level. The Red Group chooses books from the red stack, the Blue Group chooses books from the blue stack, and so on. All students learn because they are capable of reading the assigned material.

Example C: Academically Gifted Groups

A special class session is designed for students according to their ability level. For example, students identified as academically gifted and talented meet twice a week for problem solving, educational field trips, projects using technology, and other challenging activities.

MULTIAGE INSTRUCTION   ■

What Is Multiage Instruction?

Multiage instruction is designed for students of varying ages who are placed together for learning experiences. They are grouped by knowledge levels, interests, or skills. The productive learning atmosphere that develops is similar to that of a one-room schoolhouse or a team of football players. For example, a dynamic freshman quarterback can lead a team of older players to victory and success. Mutual respect is formed, and age is not important. They are proud to be players who wear the helmet and represent the team.

Multiage programs are most often found in self-contained classrooms. Teachers let go of their traditional thinking about learners' ages and grade levels. Begin multiage groupings by taking small steps. For example, use the approach on Fridays during one class period or on 2 weekdays. Gradually make adjustments and add ideas to the effective strategies and activities.

What Are the Instructional Benefits of Multiage Instruction?

- Planning focuses on the standard and the learner's needs.
- Learners progress through content or skills at their individual pace.
- Students improve social skills as they interact.
- Students of different ages learn the value of working cooperatively to reach goals.
- Individual and group needs become the focus of all learning experiences.

Implementing Standards Using Multiage Instruction

- Select the instructional focus for the multiage groups: knowledge base, topic, skill, or standard.
- Use the most efficient assessment tool to identify group needs.
- Use intriguing instructional strategies to build a community of learners.
- Continually assess the multiage sessions to make placement and academic changes. Include students in the assessment process using the following probes:
  - List the facts you learned.
  - What do you need to do next?
  - How did your group work together?
  - Identify problems you experienced. What solutions do you suggest?
  - How can we make improvements before our next lesson?
- Use the following suggestions to guide students in multiage group work:
  - You can learn with and from classmates of different ages.
  - Give and show respect to other team members.
  - Be a valuable contributor to learning experiences.
  - Model what you learned with the group.
  - Ask the right questions that lead to better understanding.

Demystifying Multiage Instruction

If students have never worked with others outside of their age range, they may be initially uncomfortable with the idea. Dispel any fears by explaining the following:

> *Just as adults of different ages work together in a job, in our class, you will work with older or younger students. One group may have several members of different ages. Multiage groups are formed so you learn from one another.*

Discuss multiage groups familiar to the students, such as scouts and sports teams. Students often participate in events with others of different ages.

**Five-Star
Tips for Multiage Instruction**

1. Create teams with teachers who believe in the benefits of multiage grouping. Elect a team coordinator who will treat each adult as a valuable, instructional member and involve everyone in the decision-making process. Use time wisely by sharing responsibilities. For example, if one individual creates a manipulative activity, make duplicates for the other teachers.
2. Constantly check the standards of each grade level represented in the group to be sure the appropriate information is addressed.
3. Group students according to their academic and social needs, not age or grade.
4. Select flexible grouping strategies that fill in learning gaps and keep students moving smoothly in their learning journeys.
5. Explain multiage grouping to parents and other members of the learning community.

Examples of Multiage Instruction

Example A: Area of Difficulty

Students from several classes and grade levels are having difficulty with a targeted skill or standard. The students meet with a designated teacher to receive more hands-on opportunities to learn the information. Each session provides the group with active, engaging experiences. Each introduction, discussion, and assessment emphasizes the learning process.

Example B: Theme Project

Multiage groups are formed for a schoolwide theme project. Everyone in the school becomes a member of a team. Each participating teacher is assigned a group and a place to work with the group during the scheduled time. After completion of the project, the student body participates in a schoolwide learning celebration.

Example C: Self-Contained Classroom

Students are placed in a self-contained, multiage classroom with one teacher for an academic school year. Academic growth, rather than grade or age, is emphasized.

COOPERATIVE LEARNING GROUPS ■

What Is a Cooperative Learning Group?

A cooperative learning group is heterogeneous, with two to four students working together as a team. Each member has a vital role. On a football team, each player has an assignment and fulfills a role for the team's success. When one member lets the team down, the play may not gain yardage or score. In the same way, each member of the cooperative group completes his or her tasks and participates fully. The teacher strategically assigns students to groups so they are balanced in ability levels, learning styles, and/or intelligences.

What Are the Instructional Benefits of Cooperative Learning Groups?

- As a student engages in discussions during interpersonal activities and cognitive tasks, the brain creates memory pathways to enhance long-term memory.
- Participants' social skills are enhanced as they contribute, compromise, and respect the ideas of other individuals in a group setting.
- Students learn to share ideas, problem solve, make decisions, and come to consensus.
- Members learn the value of using individual strengths to reach the group's goal.
- Individuals learn to give and take, creating win–win situations for the team.

Implementing Standards Using Cooperative Learning Groups

- Identify the purpose(s) of using the cooperative learning strategy.
- Assign students to their cooperative teams based on diverse abilities, backgrounds, intelligences, and/or learning styles.
- Present the task with the guidelines, expectations, and assessment tools.
- Identify specific roles and responsibilities.

   Examples:

Captain	*Leader*	*Director*
Recorder	*Secretary*	*Scribe*
Messenger	*Supply person*	*Gopher*
Time keeper	*Pacer*	*Checker*
Illustrator	*Designer*	*Design director*
Reporter	*Newscaster*	*Narrator*

- Explain the assessment tools for the team and individual members. Engage the group in discussing what they learned and in identifying the productive social skills used by the team.

Demystifying Cooperative Learning Groups

Introduce cooperative learning groups by discussing productive teams that are familiar to students, such as sports teams and dance troupes.

Lead a brainstorming session for responses to the following:

- What makes a team successful?
- How is the team affected when a member fails to complete his or her assigned responsibilities?
- Why are roles identified for cooperative work?

**Five-Star
Tips for Cooperative Learning Groups**

1. Create groups with two to four students who are socially compatible so they will be cognitively productive. Smaller groups make students more accountable for completing tasks.
2. Establish roles and responsibilities for tasks. Be sure students understand their individual roles and are accountable for carrying out specific assignments.
3. Give clear, specific directions with individual and group expectations.
4. Make materials and supplies accessible.
5. Select an assessment tool that places more emphasis on individual learning than on group evaluation.

Examples of Cooperative Learning Groups

Example A: Jigsaw

A class is ready for a new chapter in the text. A section or important passage is selected for each group. The team members select or are assigned specific roles to carry out the tasks. They read the assignment, brainstorm the findings, and compile important information. Each group prepares a presentation for the class to showcase the most valuable details in the assignment. During each presentation, class members take notes.

Example B: Think, Pair, Share

Students individually list facts learned in a lesson. They meet with an energizing partner and decide who will be Partner A and Partner B in their cooperative team. They take turns sharing and compiling facts and then brainstorm together to add facts to their list. The combined list is posted to share with the class.

Example C: Unit Review

Students form cooperative learning groups to review content information received during a unit of study. Each individual shares important facts from the lessons and activities. The students assume individual tasks such as recording the information, writing a summary, or designing a graphic organizer, exhibit, poster, or game. The information is shared or displayed to contribute to the review.

RANDOM GROUPS   ■

What Is a Random Group?

A random group is a team formed arbitrarily using luck of the draw or chance. When the task can be accomplished without consideration for the learners' commonalities, use this approach.

Students have opportunities to work in heterogeneous teams and complete tasks with classmates who are not usually in their group. The emphasis is on the novel or unique way the group is formed. Random grouping promotes sharing ideas, pulling on individual strengths, and cooperating.

What Are the Instructional Benefits of Using Random Groups?

- Students practice skills and learn how to work cooperatively with standards.
- Success in working with a variety of groups builds self-confidence, respect, and pride.
- Communication skills improve as students interact in various learning situations.
- The mystery and novelty of the unknown grouping arrangement generate curiosity and anticipation for the upcoming lesson.
- The teacher is able to assess learners as they participate in challenging assignments in unique grouping scenarios.

Implementing Standards Using Random Groups

- Select the most effective random grouping scenario for students to work with the identified topic, standard, or skill. Explicitly state and model the purposes, guidelines, roles, and expectations for the activity.
- Use a variety of strategies and techniques to form random groups. Use the same approach until students become accustomed to it. Introduce a new random grouping technique and add it to the mastered list. Here are some common random grouping strategies:

  Counting off: Students number themselves by counting off to form the number of groups needed. Example: If six groups are needed, ask participants to number by counting off from 1 to 6. Ask the 1s to form a group, the 2s to form a group, and so on.

  Alphabetical: Use the class roll to call names sequentially. Ask students to line up alphabetically by first or last name. The first three students form the first group. The next three students form the second group, and so on.

  Birth date: Line up according to each student's birth month or day. The first four students form one group. The next four students form the second group. Continue until all students are in a group.

Drawing names: Write each student's name on a strip of paper, Popsicle stick, shape from the unit, or blank card. Place the names in a hat, basket, can, envelope, box, bag, mug, or holiday container. The teacher or designated student draws names for each group.

Matching categories: Students form groups by finding matching pairs. Distribute a matched set from categories similar to the following:

Animal/habitat	Historical figure/quote	Picture/caption
Problem/solution	Question/answer	Word/definition
Question/answer	River/country	Word/antonym

- Ask students to quickly and quietly (Q & Q) form their groups and complete the assignment.
- Identify a reflection tool for the groups to summarize their learning from the activity.
- Be actively involved as a facilitator. Monitor and assist while students work.

Demystifying Random Groups

Gain your students' interest in random grouping by telling them the following:

In our classroom, we will form groups in many different ways to study and learn. When we form random groups, no one will be able to identify group members before the random selection. Everyone will know who is in a group by "luck of the draw."

★ ★ ★ ★ ★

Five-Star
Tips for Random Groups

1. Prior to the assignment, prepare group directions, procedural steps, group formation, movement, and materials.

2. Vary the ways random groups are formed. Use the same scenario until students are familiar with the strategy's rules and guidelines.

3. Select a strategy that involves little movement if students have had few experiences with transitions three.

> Examples:
> *Form a group with three students who sit near you.*
> *Create a group with two students at your table.*
>
> 4. Use random groups often to allow students the opportunity to work with different classmates. If a group is not productive, disperse the team and assign individual tasks.
> 5. Reflect on the cognitive and social lessons learned by each group member, as well as by the team as a whole. Provide opportunities for teams to present information in novel ways, and give cheers to celebrate.

Examples of Random Grouping

Example A: Vocabulary Sort

As students enter the classroom, give each individual a word from the unit of study. When it is time for group work, each student finds three other students who have words in the same category.

Example B: Sound Off With Numbers

Seven groups are needed to work on different sections of content information or to work with activities related to a standard. Students count off from one to seven. Individuals with the same number form a group and select the best place to work.

Example C: Team Challenge

The class is divided into two equal teams for a review challenge using a game, such as Hangman or Jeopardy.

■ PEER TUTORING

What Is Peer Tutoring?

Often, a coach assigns a player to teach, demonstrate, or give pointers to another team member on a particular skill or play. A peer can often help more than a coach, especially if the two players share mutual respect. Peer tutoring works in the same way, engaging one student in teaching one or more classmates. Assign students as tutors when they have the "aha" experience. This is when you hear statements that indicate understanding, such as, "Yes! Now I know how to do it." As this occurs, students are excited about learning and sharing their understandings.

Peer tutoring needs to be a valuable experience for all students who participate. The strategy should not be used to keep students busy.

What Are the Instructional Benefits of Peer Tutoring?

- A peer-tutoring session provides extra practice for the tutor and for the student who needs the extra help.
- Immediate, special assistance is given to a student when the teacher is engaging in other tasks.
- Participants develop a sense of responsibility for learning.
- Tutors gain a feeling of accomplishment and confidence.
- The tutor is presented with an opportunity to take the information or skill to a deeper processing level.

Implementing Standards Using Peer Tutoring

- Carefully select the tutor using criteria similar to the following:
  - o The student will benefit by processing the information while sharing with a peer.
  - o The student needs to build confidence through the teaching experience.
  - o The student is able to share the information in a beneficial way.
- Explain directions and guidelines.
- Designate a place and time frame for the tutoring experience.
- Provide the tutor with appropriate teaching materials, including visuals and manipulatives.
- Check with the tutored student to find out what was learned in the experience. Express appreciation to the teaching peer for sharing.

Figure 5.7 Peer Tutoring Roles

Student Tutor Role	Student Tutored Role
Review the information or skill you will teach. Identify important terms, steps, or phrases, and choose the best way to teach them. Prepare the supplies and the work area. Teach the skill or information in small steps or chunks using your own explanations and examples. Assist, encourage, and praise the student you are tutoring.	Learn all you can from the tutor. Take advantage of the opportunity to learn more about an area of weakness or trouble spot. Show respect for your peer. Realize that this is a way to get the assistance you need. Stay focused on the explanation! Ask questions to get clarification. Model your learning to show understanding.

Demystifying Peer Tutoring

Define and discuss the term *peer* as meaning "an equal." Emphasize the value of learners helping learners.

> *When an individual is working on a computer, assistance is given by someone who has a better understanding of a program or techniques. Help is provided by a classmate to learn information, practice skills, troubleshoot, solve a problem, or review. Always thank each other when the peer tutoring experience ends.*

Five-Star Tips for Peer Tutoring

1. Choose a tutor who can explain the information in a way the student will understand. Give the tutor teaching guidelines and tips.

2. Provide the teaching supplies.

3. Use a student who has had a "light bulb" cognitive moment as the tutor. Avoid overuse of high-end learners as peer tutors. They need opportunities to expand their knowledge base, too.

(Continued)

(Continued)

4. Give the tutor specific directions, such as the following:

- Work with the information on pages _____.
- Collect the materials and supplies for the task, then find a comfortable place to work.
- Sit side by side when you work together, check work, or read from the same page or article.
- Work quietly for _____ minutes.
- Explain the information so the learner understands it.
- Move to the computer and use the _____ game for practice.
- Follow the steps from the poster, paper, or book.

5. Require a product, an explanation, or another form of accountability. Examples:

- Meet with me during _____ to report on your session.
- Place your work in the "IN" basket.
- Complete the rubric, and place it in your portfolio.
- Display completed work in your exhibit space.

Examples of Peer Tutoring

Example A: Catch-Up

A student was absent when a new skill was introduced in a center. A peer guides the learner through each step in the activity.

Example B: Sharing an "Aha" Moment

A student reveals a "light bulb" moment in a math class, saying, "Oh! I know how to work these problems now. I answered five correctly." This student is placed with a learner who is struggling with the problems.

Example C: Using an Expert

Two students need to complete an assignment using a word-processing program on their computers. A student who completed the assignment successfully is assigned as a tutor for the two learners.

CONCLUSION ■

The effective blending of total group, alone, partner, and small-group activities is a great way to meet the needs of interpersonal learners and independent thinkers for each standard. Put on your baseball caps to "coach" each student with the rules and guidelines for moving in and out of the grouping scenarios quickly and quietly to maximize learning time. Model the rules and guidelines. Use a variety of grouping designs, such as knowledge base, ability, random, or interest. This gives students opportunities to work with information in different ways to meet their diverse intellectual, social, and emotional needs—and it gives you a cohesive, winning team.

Figure 5.8   Personal Reflections on Using Flexible Grouping

1. What new grouping strategies and ideas did you learn from reading this chapter?

2. How do you currently use an effective blend of grouping scenarios for instruction: total group, alone, partner, and small group? Identify a grouping strategy that needs improvement using Figure 5.2. Collaborate with colleagues to develop new ideas. Set a goal(s) to increase your implementation of the grouping strategy.

3. Which grouping techniques will you incorporate in your plans for students who have mastered the standard(s)?

4. Identify new techniques for forming groups to Identify add variety to your interventions and to differentiate approaches with customized instruction.

5. How do you explain the purpose and value of flexible grouping to students and parents?

Figure 5.9   Five Activities for a Professional Learning Community (PLC) Study

1. Meeting the Grouping Strategies

   a. Form six teams.
   b. Participants move chairs to create conversation circles. Individuals bring the book, notes, a pen, and a highlighter with them.
   c. Each team selects or is given one of the following grouping strategies:

Knowledge base	*Interest*	*Ability*
Multiage	*Random*	*Peer tutoring*

   d. The teams read, discuss, and compile important information for planning flexible groups using their chosen or assigned strategy.
   e. Each team shares highlights from its study, with application suggestions for the strategy. Other participants take notes and add ideas to the discussion.

(Continued)

(Continued)

2. TAPS

   a. Introduce the flexible grouping acronym TAPS using the information on page 211.

   b. Divide the class into groups of four.

Total Group	Alone
Partner	Small Groups

   c. Tell group members to "letter off" using T-A-P-S so each individual receives one letter in the TAPS acronym.

   d. Have each group fold a sheet of chart paper to create four sections and label it as seen in the following example:

   e. Collectively, as a team, identify a targeted standard. Add activities to use in teaching the selected standard in the appropriate sections of the chart. Post the chart so other participants can collect new ideas for their grouping strategies.

3. Managing Multiple Groups

   a. Discuss techniques for students to use when working in multiple groups.

   b. Have the teachers list ideas they can use to help students stay on task to complete assignments while they work with other learners.

   c. List rules, expectations, and routines to assist students as they transition from task to task.

   d. How will you plan activities and strategies to actively engage students when they complete assignments?

   e. Assign energizing partners to create five mini-posters with highlighting tips for managing multiple groups.

4. Using Knowledge-Base Groups

   a. Read p. 172.

   b. Join a colleague in the same subject area or grade level.

   c. Create a graphic organizer similar to the examples on pages 174–176 to represent the grouping scenarios currently implemented with your learners.

   d. Establish the amount of time needed for groups to complete the assigned tasks. Note: Assignments are completed simultaneously.

   e. Write an assignment for each knowledge-base group.

5. Grouping Analysis and Growth

   a. Brainstorm a list of grouping strategies used throughout the school.

   b. Discuss strengths, concerns, and needs for improvement.

   c. Develop feasible prescriptions as solutions and growth for each concern or need.

6

Planning With Differentiated Models

WHAT IS A MODEL? ■

A formal hat is worn for a special occasion. This type of hat is chosen to fit the occasion and add a personal flare to the outfit. A model, a blueprint for organizing instruction, is selected for the specific learning event. It offers the finishing touch and a little "oomph" in planning a lesson for teaching a standard(s). It provides a pattern with steps to follow.

The differentiated models presented in this chapter were selected and designed to assist teachers in planning for specific learner needs. Each one can be adapted to the unique needs of a class, small group, or individual. A theory or belief serves as the foundation for each model.

The models are frameworks for managing instruction in a differentiated classroom. Each model can be used to organize strategies and activities. Become familiar with the models so it is easier to select and use it in your customized plans.

The adjustable assignment model is presented first because it is recommended as a master plan or map for differentiated instruction. When used effectively, everyone benefits from the outlined details because this information identifies each student's knowledge level in relation to the new learning. The remaining models are guides for carrying out instruction for standards.

It takes time to assess the learner in relation to the standard. Also, much time must be given to selecting the appropriate model for the specific group of learners. Matching the planning model with the student's assessed knowledge base is similar to selecting the right hat for the outfit. The same hat does not fit all occasions, and the same model does not fit all planning needs!

■ ADJUSTABLE ASSIGNMENT MODEL

What Is the Adjustable Assignment Model?

The adjustable assignment model is a planning tool designed by Gayle Gregory and Carolyn Chapman (2012). It uses a grid with special features to plan assignments according to the diverse needs of students. It was adapted from Carol Ann Tomlinson's tiered model (Tomlinson & McTighe, 2006).

A formal or informal preassessment identifies each student's background knowledge and experiences in relation to the upcoming standard, information, concept, or skill. The time used to administer a preassessment is well spent because the data guide and customize planning.

The first step in completing the grid is to analyze the preassessment data to discover the students' background knowledge or experiences in relation to the upcoming information. This gathered data is recorded in the area of the grid that matches the student's knowledge level: beginning, approaching mastery, or high degree of mastery. In the second step, the teacher lists what the learners on each level need to know next. This list determines the entry points for instruction.

In the third step, the teacher identifies the most effective instructional strategies and/or activities for each level, and lists them for each group so all students learn the targeted standard(s). The adjustable assignment model is a keystone of differentiated instruction because the learners' needs guide strategic planning. For examples of adjustable assignments using knowledge base groups, see Figures 5.3, 5.4, 5.5, and 5.6.

What Are the Instructional Benefits of Using Adjustable Assignments?

- Lessons are designed and customized for learners based on their knowledge levels.
- Students are not bored with previously learned information or frustrated with lessons that are too difficult.
- Students who need to "zap gaps" in their knowledge of a topic or skill receive the instruction they need.
- Students who demonstrate readiness for a grade-level standard receive instruction on the approaching mastery level.
- Students who know the information have opportunities to extend their knowledge in the current study.

Implementing Standards Using Adjustable Assignments

- Introduce adjustable assignments and discuss their value, purposes, and organizational procedures for using this model.
- Discuss the varied experiences and knowledge levels students will bring to each new standard.
- Emphasize the value of learning basic information, knowing the grade-level standards, and expanding knowledge.

- Use ongoing assessment to identify students who need to move to a more productive level during a unit of study.
- Adapt the following dialog to introduce students to adjustable assignments:
  - Each time a new topic or skill is introduced, think about the past experiences you have had related to it. Ask yourself about the knowledge you have that will help you in this new study and what else you need to know about it.
  - Realize that assessment results are based on your experiences and what you know, not how smart you are.
  - Be honest and do your best on each preassessment, because the results are used to design lessons to help you.
  - You may need to zap a gap, ask a question, or move to a higher challenge level.
  - Respect and honor classmates who work at a different pace or level.

Demystifying Adjustable Assignments

Introduce adjustable assignments to students by discussing the term *knowledge base*. Explain that each student's knowledge of a standard, topic, or skill varies because it is based on background, interests, and attitudes formed during past experiences. Ask students to identify their level of expertise in several sports and hobbies, such as soccer, swimming, cooking, and carpentry.

Remind learners that all experts begin on the lowest level of knowledge and experience. Discuss the journeys their favorite movie stars and sports heroes took to success. Emphasize that it takes desire and practice to move to a higher level.

Compare the levels for adjustable assignments with levels on computer and video games. Students of all ages understand levels of difficulty because they play games that move them from the beginning and average levels to the highest degree of expertise and speed. Give examples of adjustable assignments they may encounter.

★ ★ ★ ★ ★

**Five-Star
Tips for Adjustable Assignments**

Remember, the adjustable assignment model is a planning tool designed to address the needs of students on multiple knowledge levels. It is best used when deemed the most effective way to identify learners' needs. It takes more time to develop plans for more than one level, but the extra effort benefits each student.

1. Use a large sheet of chart paper to create the planning grid.
2. Work with a team whenever possible to generate more valuable ideas.
3. Use the adjustable assignment model to plan for two or three groups. It is difficult to plan, organize, and manage effectively for more than three groups.

(Continued)

(Continued)

4. Use a different color for Levels 1, 2, and 3. Students in each level may receive an independent, partner, or small-group assignment.

5. Use a word or phrase to build confidence with each color-coded level. In the following samples, notice how each color represents a stage of growth in knowledge. Give students opportunities to select the color and a phrase for their level.

Level 1 (Beginning Level) GREEN— I Am Growing: Zap the Gaps

Students in the beginning level have little or no prior knowledge and experiences related to the new standard(s). They need to master the basics or procedures to prepare them for the grade-level information. Develop intriguing activities to zap the gaps in learning early in the introduction of the standard.

Five-Star
Tips for Level 1 Adjustable Assignments

1. Target the important knowledge or skills the student must have to understand the grade-level standard.

2. Present Level 1 assignments as activities for "zapping the gaps."

3. Develop choice assignments by placing specifically planned activities on a design or in a grid. This provides students with options to work on their areas of need and be successful. They do not feel isolated when they work with choices.

4. Design an agenda with a list of specific assignments and activities to fill holes in learning. This gives the student an opportunity to back up and learn a skill or knowledge that was missed. Place the agenda in the student's green folder.

5. Build time in your teaching plan to provide basic, personalized instruction for individuals in this group while other students engage in Level 2 and 3 assignments. Remember, each leveled group works simultaneously within the same time frame to complete their assigned task(s).

Use Curriculum Rewinding to Zap the Gap

Curriculum rewinding takes instruction back to the basic information, skills, or standard a student lacks. Use it when a preassessment uncovers a gap or hole in the fundamental information the student failed to learn. Analyze the student's needs. Rewind the curriculum to the point where the learning gap occurred, and plan instruction to zap the gap.

All grade-level and subject-area teachers are responsible for student progress. They must rewind the curriculum as needed. Too often, teachers feel responsible for their subject and fail to realize their responsibility to assist students in mastering the missing pieces. This often occurs when the learning gap is unrelated to the subject or the teacher's expertise. For instance, if a science experiment requires measurement and a student cannot use or read the appropriate instrument, the teacher must rewind to teach the learner how to use the measurement tool.

Rewinding often requires specific instruction through an intervention in skills below grade level. The educator is professionally obligated to find ways to assess each student's needs and improve the specific skills or ability to learn. If several learning gaps are evident, select the most critical information for understanding grade-level material.

Teach students to be aware of their own learning gaps. Guide them in understanding the value of going back or rewinding to master standards they failed to learn.

Consider the following scenario that demonstrates the need to rewind the curriculum:

The teacher plans to teach two-digit addition. A pretest reveals that several students are not ready for this skill because they do not know the addition facts.

Questions to consider include the following:

- What skills do these students need?
- How am I going to assess these learners?
- How can I plan instruction to help them learn how to add single digits?
- Do I have programs or lessons to meet their needs?
- Do these students need to go to a new assignment, an intervention session, or another classroom to learn and practice addition facts?

At some point in planning the unit, time is built in for these students to learn addition facts. These sessions and tasks replace assignments given to the rest of the class.

Reasons for Learning Gaps

Learning gaps can occur for any of the following reasons:

- The student was never exposed to the needed information.
- A former teacher exposed the student to the standard, skill, concept, or information, but it was not understood or processed.
- The information was learned for the moment or for a test. The student did not have opportunities to take the skill to the level of mastery or automaticity.
- Memory cues or hooks were not used to store and retrieve the information.
- The student did not have opportunities to make meaningful, personal connections.

It is frustrating and disappointing when teachers realize that students are not prepared for the new information or skill. It is easy to dwell on the various reasons for the learning gaps. Students benefit when this valuable time and energy is used to design plans and activities to fill the gaps.

**Five-Star
Tips for Level 1 Adjustable Assignments**

1. Use a preassessment to discover the student's skill level or knowledge base in the topic.
2. Identify a gap in learning as soon as it occurs.
3. Hit the "Rewind Button" and plan a time and place for a response to intervention.
4. Zap the gap by strategically choosing instructional strategies and activities for the learner. Use an instructional approach that is different from the approach that led the student to failure.
5. Present students with ways to identify and zap their own gaps. This includes reference materials, computer programs, peer assistance, and instructional tools such as informative tables, charts, or posters.

Level 2 (Approaching Mastery) YELLOW— I Am a Ray of Sunshine: Grade-Level Ready

Students in the approaching mastery level are ready for grade-level information and need to work with the new standard, concept, or skill. This group demonstrated on a preassessment that they possess the background information to be successful.

If all students came to class on this level, there would be no need to differentiate. But we know this does not occur in the real world. Do not lose these individuals in the shuffle. Teach and nurture them.

Give Level 2 learners instruction to build on their current, bright rays of knowledge. Select activities to excite and stimulate their minds.

**Five-Star
Tips for Level 2 Adjustable Assignments**

1. Design activities in the Level 2 or yellow folder(s) to reinforce skills and provide practice with grade-level standards, competencies, and concepts.
2. Display the assignment in a visible area because Level 2 learners usually make up the majority of the class.
3. Continue to move this group forward in learning. Avoid holding these students back to tutor their peers.
4. Occasionally give these students choices to generate interests as they learn and practice.
5. Remember, boring or busy work does not produce a payoff for anyone!

Level 3 (High Degree of Mastery) RED— I Am Fired Up! Ready for the Challenge

Level 3 students know the grade-level information and can become bored or unmotivated during instruction. They may need quick reviews but do not need explanations and practice lessons. Plan productive activities and assignments for these learners to expand their knowledge and skills in an area related to the current topic. Design these opportunities to engage their minds in creative, challenging tasks and higher-level thinking skills.

★ ★ ★ ★ ★

Five-Star
Tips for Level 3 Adjustable Assignments

1. Preassessment is crucial. It identifies the student who knows the upcoming standard. Use fast-forwarding when it is obvious that the learner would be bored with the planned assignments and activities.

2. If a student proves the standard has been mastered, valuable learning time is wasted when the learner is asked to complete the class assignment. Give the learner opportunities to use this time on alternative assignments.

3. Ask the learner, "What do you want to learn next related to our topic of study?" Involve the student in selecting and planning activities.

4. Do not expect students working with Level 3 tasks to complete Level 2 assignments. Use the time productively to expand their knowledge and improve thinking skills.

5. Be cautious about assigning Level 3 students as peer tutors. Often, the information and skills have become automatic for these learners. It is difficult for them to explain the fundamentals, because they have moved beyond the basics. When students on this level are asked to explain an operation or skill, they often say, "I can't explain it. I just do it."

Fast-Forwarding the Curriculum

Curriculum fast-forwarding provides the student with opportunities to learn new information and skills related to the current standard. The teacher analyzes the student's strengths and needs and fast-forwards the curriculum to new areas for research and exploration. This requires planning instruction to teach skills and facts beyond the required grade-level expectations.

Place the curriculum on fast-forward when the preassessment results reveal that the students know the information. For example, if students can give you correct change from a $5 bill for a $2.79 purchase, they do not need to study coin value.

When the preassessment indicates that a student knows and understands the grade-level information, challenge the learner to select one of the following fast-forwarding strategies.

1. *Run quickly through each bit of the scenes.* Move through the new information quickly to review. Observe to check for understanding of each segment. Students who give correct answers may go through the introduction and explanations with a small or total group to review. They move to a new segment or challenging activity while classmates work in practice sessions.
   Example:
   > The learners are asked to identify the subjects and predicates in five sentences. Individuals who respond with correct answers and explain one example move to the next learning level.

2. *Turn off the picture and fast-forward quickly to a specific point.* Move to a new level after a preassessment when there is no need for the learner to review. The student skips a level and moves immediately to new learning.
   Examples:
   - A coach is teaching the skill for dribbling a basketball. Students who know this skill practice passing the ball.
   - A math instructor is teaching the process of multiplying with one-digit numbers, and the students participate in the initial explanations. The independent assignment is made for a small group to work with two-digit multiplication while another group practices with one-digit multiplication.

3. *Fast-forward through familiar scenes of a recorded show or movie.* Skip the first level of the standard when the student knows the introductory information. The learner moves to a higher level within the current study.
   Examples:
   - At the end of second grade, a child is socially, emotionally, and academically ready to move to fourth grade.
   - A student knows basic Spanish and moves to Spanish II.

THE CURRICULUM COMPACTING MODEL ■

What Is Curriculum Compacting?

Many educators place gifted and talented students in special classes or pull-out programs to work with challenging activities using higher-order thinking skills such as problem solving and critical thinking. The students do not become bored because they are involved with intriguing activities.

Curriculum compacting has evolved over the past few years. This presents more challenges because teachers are required to meet individual student needs within the classroom walls.

In differentiated instruction, curriculum compacting is implemented with students who are beyond the high-degree-of-mastery level. They are exempt from grade-level instruction. Their needs can be addressed through projects, agendas, academic contracts, personal discoveries, and investigations that intrigue the mind. Each assignment is designed to provide a productive, challenging learning experience.

Curriculum compacting may involve a major change in placement and assignments, such as skipping a grade or a subject exemption. A new placement is rarely implemented, but it can be the most beneficial experience of a student's academic life.

What Are the Instructional Benefits of Curriculum Compacting?

- A student who knows the upcoming standards and skills has an opportunity to be exempt from the mastered unit or subject. The learner uses time wisely with an alternative assignment or placement.
- It provides productive learning time for the student who knows the information and skills.
- The student engages in high-interest activities that challenge his or her mind.
- When learners engage in selecting the activities and are responsible for completing assignments with little or no adult instruction, they have opportunities to become self-directed learners.
- The cap on a learner's potential is removed.

Implementing Standards Using Curriculum Compacting

- Identify students who need to be exempt from the upcoming standard or skill.
- Brainstorm ways to provide alternative, productive assignments for the learners. Select the most effective strategy.
- Identify the purpose, timeline, activities, and assessment technique. Assign roles and responsibilities for each individual.

- Explain, discuss, and obtain approval from other teachers, administrators, parents, and students involved in the alternative assignment or placement.
- Create buy-in. This is critical for everyone involved.

Demystifying Curriculum Compacting

Introduce curriculum compacting by leading a discussion similar to the following:

If you prove you know and can use the information and skills in an upcoming study, you will have opportunities to participate in more challenging adventures that come with new learning.

**Five-Star
Tips for Curriculum Compacting**

1. Use curriculum compacting as an option for a student who knows the upcoming information and skills. Be sure the learner will benefit from an alternative assignment or placement rather than a Level 3 extension or enrichment activity.
2. Analyze all gathered data, including observations and input from other teachers, to make major placement or assignment changes.
3. Design a special, new assignment that is the most valuable use of the learner's time. Select high interest activities that are beneficial for the student.
4. The teacher who designs instruction in the learner's new placement or assignment is responsible for the grade.
5. Do not require the student who engages in alternate assignments to complete work missed in the regular program.

Examples of Curriculum Compacting

Example A: Subject Placement

A first-grade student working on a higher level in a certain subject is placed in a second-grade class for daily instruction in that area.

Example B: Alternative Assignment

A group of fluent, comprehending readers receive alternative assignments, while other students receive direct instruction. The high-performing readers form a learning community for a novel study group. This may take place within a class or with students from other classrooms.

Example C: Exemption

A high school student is exempt from the senior English program. He attends a university English class and receives college credit.

THE PROBLEM-BASED MODEL ■

What Is the Problem-Based Model?

The problem-based model provides students with an opportunity to select and solve an identified problem. It may focus on the classroom, school, community, state, national, or international concerns. The teacher guides students in choosing a problem they can investigate and solve with little or no adult assistance. The responsibilities, roles, and assignments are identified and assigned to individuals and/or small groups. For example, during a study of an endangered species, partner teams engage in a data-gathering session to investigate the causes for the problem. Each team creates a list of causes and presents it to generate a class list.

What Are the Instructional Benefits of the Problem-Based Model?

- Engages students in authentic activities that may evolve into a service project for the school or community. Problem-based tasks are designed to teach standards, skills, and concepts.
- Develops critical, creative thinkers. During participation, students usually realize there are several steps to finding solutions.
- Students learn problem solving processes that extend over a period of time.
- This instructional approach easily adapts for use with the total class, small groups, or individuals in all curriculum areas.
- Each step in the process presents valuable learning opportunities when students have a sense of pride in their accomplishments and they see the results of their efforts. See Figure 6.1.

Figure 6.1 Problem-Based Ideas

Classroom	School	Community
• Obtain donations for a game station, research nook, or reading corner. • Learn to recycle. • Establish rules for a classroom citizen. • Select a Yuk Spot to beautify. • Organize a "Say No to Drugs" campaign.	• Design an outdoor trail. • Develop a new study area such as a station or lab. • Establish a schoolwide recycling program. • Improve the cafeteria's menus. • Raise funds for a new piece of equipment.	• Beautify or clean a park or corner lot. • Go to local commissioners to state a case for change. • Adopt a grandparent. • Conduct a food drive. • Stop pollution in a local creek or lake.

(Continued)

(Continued)

State	National	International
• Develop a campaign to change a state law. • Identify a law that needs to be changed. • Examine ways to improve factory pollution. • Adopt an animal or plant in a state park. • Communicate with legislators related to a concern for improvement. • Compare your school with another one in the state. Analyze the results.	• Investigate ways to assist endangered species. • Study the reasons gas prices rise and fall. • Examine shortage of a product and the consumers' role. • Investigate ways to help a community or school that is dealing with a major disaster. • Identify solutions to assist homeless individuals.	• Identify steps for world peace. • Explore solutions to global warming. • Investigate a possible disaster and set up a preparedness plan. • Identify items needed by soldiers on battlefields. Collect the items and send them with personal notes. • Participate in a fundraising project for a specific cause.

Implementing Standards Using Problem-Based Learning

- Introduce and carry through the steps in the problem-based model with guidelines and a time frame. See Figure 6.2 on page 205.
- Assume the role of facilitator and guide. Ask questions during each stage of the process to stimulate thinking and discussion.
- Set aside time for students to carry out assignments, report progress or findings, and share their stumbling blocks and successes.
- Give students opportunities to present their findings, recommendations, suggested solutions, and results to administrators, legislators, parents, or other appropriate groups.
- Guide reflective discussions about the process, and celebrate success throughout the procedure.

Demystifying Problem Solving

Explain to students that every day, problems are solved by working teams in the business world and in daily situations. Discuss the importance of learning how to address and solve minor and major problems throughout their lives in any situation. Emphasize the importance of following problem-solving steps to guide their thinking and address problems in their world.

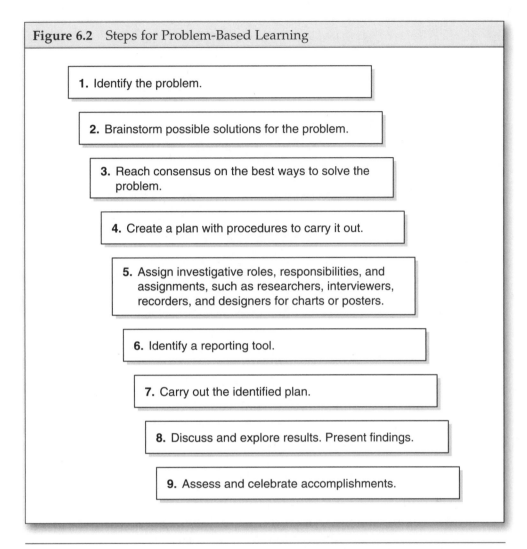

Figure 6.2   Steps for Problem-Based Learning

1. Identify the problem.

2. Brainstorm possible solutions for the problem.

3. Reach consensus on the best ways to solve the problem.

4. Create a plan with procedures to carry it out.

5. Assign investigative roles, responsibilities, and assignments, such as researchers, interviewers, recorders, and designers for charts or posters.

6. Identify a reporting tool.

7. Carry out the identified plan.

8. Discuss and explore results. Present findings.

9. Assess and celebrate accomplishments.

Examples:

- In the middle of a party, the host announces that pizza is ready on the patio. Everyone runs to the area, pushing and shoving as they grab slices of the treat. The pizza is gone before some guests enter the patio. What steps could be taken to solve this problem during the next party?
- A grocery store establishes a recycling program with designated containers for customers to drop off plastic or glass products. Discuss why the store provides this service and the problem this solves. If a local store does not have a recycling program, this can be an ideal place to begin a community-based, problem-solving project.

★ ★ ★ ★ ★

**Five-Star
Tips for Using the Problem-Based Model**

1. Analyze the current study to identify standards and skills to teach in a problem-solving activity.
2. Introduce the model using a high-interest problem in the classroom, school, or community that will lead to visible results.
3. Introduce the problem-based learning approach by discussing the importance of knowing how to solve problems in daily activities and various careers.
4. Model and guide students through the planning steps so they understand the process.
5. Remember, students carry out the plan, but the teacher approves each step.

Examples of the Problem-Based Model

Example A: Problem Solving in the Classroom

Students identify a reading corner to make comfortable and inviting. They find people to donate a rocking chair, beanbag, rug, lamp, and large pillows. Books and book characters are displayed in the area.

Example B: Problem Solving in the School

Students identify a dirt-covered section of the school grounds to improve. They want to eliminate the mud and dust that interferes with their outside activities, so they select this problem to tackle. The teacher approves this problem-solving project.

The group brainstorms and comes to consensus on ways to develop the area. They decide that grass and plants will solve the problem. The students outline a plan with assigned roles and data-gathering techniques. The students conduct a parent and community survey to find volunteers to donate grass seed, fertilizer, and shrubs. The school's parent organization agrees to prepare the area.

Example C: Problem Solving in the Community

The teacher leads a brainstorming session for students to create a list of local problems that affect them. The group selects one problem to solve from the brainstormed list: A busy intersection near the community recreation center needs a traffic light. The teacher invites the city traffic engineer to share the steps needed for approval of the light's installation.

The teacher and volunteer parents take students on a bus to an area a safe distance from the thoroughfare. They observe the vehicles as they pass through the intersection during the specific time period. The students gather data and create graphs to report the information. Selected graphics and a data summary are placed in letters to the local newspaper and community leaders. Within 2 months, the new traffic light is approved and installed.

THE PROJECT-BASED MODEL ■

What Is the Project-Based Model?

A project is an assignment designed to take a student into an in-depth study to learn a standard. A project may be assigned to a total class, small groups, partners, or an individual student. It is tailored to the learner's age and interest, so the assignment requires little adult supervision. Projects are a wise use of class time when individuals or small groups engage in tasks directly related to the current topic and content standards or skills.

What Are the Instructional Benefits of Using the Project-Based Model?

- Projects provide exciting opportunities to actively engage more students in learning.
- As a project develops over a period of time, students learn to carry out a plan using a timeline, accept responsibility, develop independence, pace their work, and make decisions.
- Students select interest areas that engage their strengths and intrigue their individual minds.
- Options allow students to apply their favorite modalities, genres, styles, or intelligences.
- Presentation choices provide decision-making experiences in selecting ways to share the products or project information.

Implementing Standards Using Project-Based Learning

- Identify the grade-level standards, content topic information, and skills to address.
- Select the grouping strategy:

  Total group   Alone   Partners   Small groups

- Prepare the requirements, including guidelines, purposes, expectations, assessment tool(s), and timeline.
- Provide choices for the research format, presentation, and display.
- Give each group an opportunity to share the project information and thinking process in displays or presentations.

Demystifying Projects

Explain the term *project* as an activity or product created by following a plan. The verb form of the word *project* means "to predict results." Discuss how specific steps or procedures are outlined and followed in a project to obtain desired results. Challenge students to discuss familiar projects such as organizing a closet, painting a room, or cleaning a yard.

Lead students through a class, independent, or small-group simulation of tasks in a project. Walk them through the planning process, procedures, and timeline for designing a product. Remember to identify and model your inside thinking for each step.

**Five-Star
Tips for Using the Project-Based Model**

1. Compile the project topic list around the current standards and content topics. Give students an opportunity to choose their projects.

2. Assist students by providing a Project Packet similar to the following to guide their plans. Model and guide students through each step so they understand the process.

   Project Packet:

   - Purpose and guidelines
   - Timeline, checkpoints, and due dates
   - Assessment tools to use throughout the project
   - Procedure checklist for project partners
   - Presentation and display options

3. Schedule accountability checkpoints or conferences for project partners or groups to share findings. During these sessions, students go through the process, review the information, describe the procedures, and analyze their learning.

4. Emphasize the thinking and learning processes involved throughout the project.

5. Schedule information celebrations for students to demonstrate or present the final product as evidence of their learning. Ask them to emphasize the steps and procedures used in the thinking and learning process during their presentations.

Examples of the Project-Based Model

Example A: In-Class Project

The teacher divides the class into cooperative groups during a social studies unit. Each group chooses a project from a teacher-made list.

1. Introduce the project purposes, directions, and timeline of the assignment.

2. Assign each learner a person, event, place, or artifact from the study.

3. Periodically, give an assignment that fits each student's project, similar to the following:
   - What significant role does _____ play in history?
   - List five characteristics or attributes about _____.

○ Research _____ from five sources, including the textbook.

○ Teach students the research card format to use while gathering notes from their reading material.

4. Establish a log or journal for personal comments. Identify specific times for journal entries.

5. Create a display about your project.

6. Present the key points learned to the class using a choice board activity. See Figure 6.3.

Figure 6.3 Project Choice Board			
Prepare a Webpage news report.	Design a poster.	Role-play.	Design a PowerPoint presentation.
Interview.	Be a stand-up comic.	Create a song.	Create a brochure.

7. Conference with students about their experiences. Discuss the thinking process used in the project.

Example B: Home/School Projects

After guiding students through the project process, assign some activities for completion at home and others to complete during class time. The same procedures are followed as for the in-class project.

Example C: Home Projects

Project partners are assigned to work together to complete individual projects at home. Again, the in-class procedures may be followed. The partners meet periodically to discuss the stage of their progress. On the due date, each student brings the project to class. They share accomplishments and information they learned during the project work.

■ THE MULTIPLE INTELLIGENCES PLANNING MODEL

What Is the Multiple Intelligences Planning Model?

The multiple intelligences are verbal/linguistic, musical/rhythmic, logical/mathematical, bodily/kinesthetic, visual/spatial, naturalist, intrapersonal, and interpersonal, according to Dr. Howard Gardner (2006) at Harvard University. Intelligence is the ability to solve a problem, create a problem to solve, and contribute to one's culture. Use Figure 6.4 to incorporate the students' intelligences in strategies and activities.

Figure 6.4   Multiple Intelligence Planning Model

Steps for Implementation	Directions
1. Name the topic or unit.	List the content standards, information, skills, and/or concepts to be learned.
2. Assess students to find out what they know.	Use the most effective formal or informal tool to identify the learner's prior knowledge, background, attitude, and interests.
3. Brainstorm a list of strategies and activities related to the topic.	List all the activities and strategies that teach the content standards, information, skills, and concepts. Record each thought in writing to create a quantity of ideas.
4. Write the lesson plan.	Analyze the preassessment data and select the "best" activities from the brainstormed list to teach the information needed by this individual or group of students. Write each activity in the order you plan to teach it. Create a smooth flow or transition between instructional segments.
5. Label the targeted intelligence and the supporting intelligences for each activity.	Identify one "intelligence" as the target of the activity. A task usually engages more than one intelligence, so identify one or two supporting intelligences. Use the abbreviations: V/L – Verbal/Linguistic L/M – Logical/Mathematical M/R – Musical/Rhythmic B/K – Bodily/Kinesthetic V/S – Visual/Spatial N – Naturalist Intra – Intrapersonal Inter – Interpersonal
6. Tally the targeted and supporting intelligences. Check overkills and omissions.	Design a form or checklist similar to the following to monitor how often the learner engages in a targeted intelligence and one or more supporting intelligences.

V/L	L/M	M/R	B/K	V/S	N
卌I	IIII	卌	IIII	卌	III

7. Identify the grouping arrangements.	Label the flexible grouping strategy using the TAPS acronym. **T** = Total group **A** = Alone **P** = Partner **S** = Small group Examples: When the activity begins with a total group and then learners work alone, label it TA. When the activity begins with students working in cooperative groups and then each student writes an individual summary of what was learned, label it SA.
8. Tally the use of the grouping scenarios.	Check for an effective blending of different grouping scenarios. If overkills and omissions are evident, refer to the brainstormed strategy and activity list.

Total Group	Alone	Partner	Small Group
⁷ℍⅬ ΙΙ	⁷ℍⅬ ΙΙΙ	ΙΙΙ	ΙΙΙΙ

|
| 9. Teach the unit. Use ongoing assessment to monitor and guide the plan. | Constantly monitor and assess students and the plan. Revamp and readjust the plan according to the student's needs. Remember to refer to the brainstorming list for activity alternatives. |

What Are the Instructional Benefits of Using the Multiple Intelligences Planning Model?

The multiple intelligences planning model is a management tool that serves as a guide to label the targeted intelligences for instruction to meet the diverse needs of each student. The learner has a better chance of grasping knowledge and understanding when his or her strongest intelligences are used to learn a standard, skill, concept, or information.

- The targeted intelligences can be labeled in each planned activity.
- Everyone has all intelligences. Everyone can become more intelligent.
- Everyone has at least three or four areas of strengths that can be enhanced and used to learn more. An individual's weaknesses are identified so they can be strengthened.
- The intelligences addressed in activities are labeled, not students.
- The planning model guides teachers to incorporate the learner's strongest intelligences in learning new standards.

Implementing Standards Using the Multiple Intelligences Model

- Plan using the multiple intelligences. To reach more students, use a variety of intelligences in the plan.
- Label each activity addressed in a lesson with a targeted intelligence and one or two supporting intelligences.
- Observe students as they work and interact with others to identify the intelligences they use in daily activities and interactions. Share with students the many ways they are smart.
- Establish learning zones and independent tasks, providing choices around the intelligence targets to reach the learners' diverse needs.
- Plan and use intelligences that are not in your comfort zone if they are conduits to reach the learner. It is natural to use your strong and most comfortable intelligences. Remember, the students' strengths and your strengths may not be the same.

Demystifying the Multiple Intelligences Planning Model

Tell the students that Howard Gardner, a Harvard professor, named eight ways people are intelligent or smart. In the chart (see Figure 6.5), the intelligences are listed with suggested words and phrases you can use to help students understand each one. Adapt our descriptors for your learners as you introduce an intelligence and discuss the many ways students are smart.

Share with students how their strengths can be used to overcome their weaknesses. For example, if they are strong in musical/rhythmic intelligence and have difficulty memorizing facts, they can place them in the form of a jingle, rap, or rhyme and repeat the repetitive pattern until the facts are mastered.

Five-Star
Tips for Using the Multiple Intelligences Planning Model

1. Follow the planning model and meet the needs of more students. Each individual has areas of strength in three or four intelligences.

2. Remember, label strategies and activities, not students. Consciously label the targeted and supporting intelligences when planning activities and strategies.

3. Instructors are human, so they often use their strongest intelligences to teach. Plan activities incorporating the learners' areas of strength.

4. Make learning interesting, challenging, and exciting with multiple intelligences planning. For example, if students are struggling to remember a procedure and they are strong in the bodily/kinesthetic and musical/rhythmic

intelligences, guide them in chanting the information as they perform a simple exercise, such as jumping jacks or clapping hands.

5. Design the plan to incorporate the ways students are grouped to give opportunities for the interpersonal and intrapersonal learners. A teacher is usually dominant in the intrapersonal or interpersonal intelligence. Avoid planning around your preference. Intentionally plan to meet the students' needs or strengths.

Figure 6.5   Multiple Intelligences at Work

Intelligence	Describes someone who is smart in . . .
Verbal/linguistic	Reading Writing Listening/talking Linking information Making connections
Musical/rhythmic	Dancing Playing an instrument Singing/composing Creating poetry, rhymes, or jingles Identifying tonal patterns Developing rhythms and beats Chanting and rapping
Logical/mathematical	Placing thoughts or things in order Discovering and using patterns Using numbers to create and solve problems Using the world of technology Using manipulatives
Bodily/kinesthetic	Moving the body using large or small movements Using eye and hand coordination Making large (gross) or small (fine) body movements
Visual/spatial	Using the mind's eye to see lines, color, and space Designing Building Using graphics and pictures
Naturalist	Knowing about nature Working with nature Exploring areas of science
Intrapersonal	Working alone Being independent Feeling comfortable with one's own thoughts and feelings
Interpersonal	Working successfully with others Socializing with other people

Examples of the Multiple Intelligences Planning Model

Example A: Individual Unit Planning

A teacher follows the planning process presented in the model to design the upcoming unit of study.

Example B: Team Unit Planning

A grade-level team follows the process to plan an upcoming unit of study. Team members brainstorm activities and strategies using the various intelligences. Each teacher assesses his or her students and decides which activities and strategies to incorporate in their personal plans. As the unit progresses, the reference list of brainstormed possibilities is available for new learning opportunities.

Example C: Lesson Plan Analysis

The teacher uses a 2- to 3-week section of previously taught lesson plans and labels the targeted intelligence for each activity and assignment. Each intelligence addressed is listed and tallied as it was used. This procedure identifies omissions, overkills, and intelligences addressed properly to meet students' needs.

THE TRIARCHIC TEAMING MODEL ■

What Is the Triarchic Teaming Model?

Dr. Robert Sternberg's triarchic theory of intelligence emphasizes three ways of thinking to adapt and shape the environment. These successful intelligences are analytical, creative, and practical. He recommends creating a problem-solving team composed of members who are strong in each area. The group can engage each individual's strengths and approach the task from the various perspectives.

What Are the Instructional Benefits of the Triarchic Teaming Model?

- Students become familiar with three ways of being smart, interacting, and communicating in a group.
- The teacher and students identify their strong areas in the triarchic model.
- Each student has a distinct role using an analytical, creative, or practical point of view.
- When students use their strongest areas to think and communicate they are comfortable during the learning process.
- More productive teams are created using this model.

Implementing Standards Using the Triarchic Teaming Model

- Define Sternberg's three ways of thinking so the students understand the attributes for each area. Refer to the chart in Figure 6.6.
- Identify each student's area of strength in group work.
    a. Conduct a student survey to discover each student's area of strength and identify members for a problem-solving team.

    1. Study the words and phrases for Sternberg's theory listed on the chart.

    2. List Sternberg's three intelligence areas. Prioritize these by placing the number 1 next to the intelligence that reflects the best way for you to contribute to a problem-solving team. Select another area that you would use. Place the number 3 beside the area you would use least.

    ____ Analytical

    ____ Creative

    ____ Practical

Figure 6.6   The Triarchic Model Activity

Analytical	Creative	Practical
• Compare • Contrast • Identify the parts • Evaluate each section • Analyze the benefits	• Imagine _____. • Use _____ to invent. • Find a new way to ____. • List your ideas about ____. • Suppose _____.	• Find the most helpful or easiest way to use _____. • Apply _____. • Adapt _____ to intelligence.

Write and discuss reasons for the order of your selection with a partner. Turn in the survey results to the teacher. Use the data to form compatible working teams.

b. Observe each learner making contributions in a group situation to identify individual strengths.

- Place students in groups with at least one representative for each of the analytical, practical, and creative areas.
- Observe the groups working together through several tasks.
- Adjust groups as needed from observation and performance notes.

Demystifying the Triarchic Teaming Model

Explain the meaning of *tri-* and *arch*. Draw three arches. Write one area under each arch to illustrate Sternberg's theory. Define and explain the benefits of each one. Periodically, have students analyze and reflect on their personal and group performance.

**Five-Star
Tips for Using the Triarchic Teaming Model**

1. Know the student's strongest intelligence area for the most effective placement in team or group work.
2. Remember, each student has one strong area to contribute to a team.
3. Plan team activities that engage each learner. A student usually contributes automatically to a group when working through the lens of personal strengths.
4. Create teams with three to six members.
5. Assign a representative of the analytical, practical, and creative areas to each group.

Examples of the Triarchic Teaming Model

Example A: Assigned Problem-Solving Triads

Groups or triads are formed with students who are strong in each of the triarchic areas: analytical, practical, and creative. Each group is assigned a problem to process and solve. The group works through the problem and shares conclusions. Team members make entries in their individual journals, recording their roles and the thinking process used by the triad team.

Example B: Student-Selected Project Teams

The groups form three teams of their favorite role in a team situation:

Team A: Analytical   *Team B: Practical*   *Team C: Creative*

Taking one member from each team forms a triad to complete a project. Students choose their teammates.

Example C: Random Assignment Team

Students complete a survey to identify their individual strengths as team players: analytical, practical, or creative. The results are given to the students. Three areas of the room are labeled by displaying one triarchic intelligence on a large card in each space. Students line up in front of the word that matches their strength. The students in each line number off (e.g., 1, 2, 3, 4, etc.). The 1s form a group, the 2s form a group, and so on. This creates triad teams. The teacher gives each group a problem, project, or cooperative task to complete.

◼ THE ACTIVITY ANALYSIS MODEL

What Is the Activity Analysis Model?

The activity analysis model is a guide to strategically selecting and thoroughly planning an activity for an individual or group of students. The outline presented in the model is designed to serve as a planning guide so the most appropriate activity is selected for each learning experience.

The preassessment data identify students who need to learn a specific standard or skill. The teacher considers each activity that could be used to teach the skill. The lead-in questions and statements can be used to make a quick but in-depth analysis of each step in the decision process to select and organize each activity. This model is a guide to selecting the most effective activity for an individual or group.

What Are the Instructional Benefits of Using the Activity Analysis Model?

The activity analysis model is a guide to making more accurate decisions when selecting instructional activities. In a differentiated classroom, this decision process is more complex, as the teacher plans activities for the needs and strengths of individuals, small groups, or the total class. This model provides a practical and easy-to-use format to assist in each planning session.

- Guides the teacher to select appropriate activities for an individual or specific group of learners.
- Avoid activities that become busywork, assignments that do not teach the needed information or skills, and assigning inappropriate activities.
- Assists the teacher in avoiding use of their favorite activities because they are accessible, familiar, and easy to use. The analysis helps teachers avoid this natural tendency, because the question outline leads to a strategic selection process that provides the most effective learning experiences.
- Solves the dilemma of deciding which standards and skills to identify for instruction and which activity to select for the total class, a specific group, or an individual.
- Serve as a guide in choosing between two or three activities for one time segment.

Demystifying the Activity Analysis Model

Let students know that much of your planning time is used to select the very best activities for the class, individuals, and small groups. Explain that each activity is carefully selected or designed to help them become successful in using the skill or information. Use the following metaphor to guide the discussion:

> *When I am trying to find the right activity for you, it is like selecting a hat for a special occasion. It must match the outfit and be comfortable. In the same way, I find the activity that matches the way you learn and fits the lesson you need so you will be comfortable as you engage in each learning experience.*

Figure 6.7 Planning With the Activity Analysis Model	
WHAT are you going to teach?	• Identify the standards, concepts, skills, or information. • Select the unit or topic. • Select assessment tools to use during and after the activity. The results serve as a guide for instruction.
WHO needs it?	• Use the preassessment data to identify the students who need: ○ A specific segment of instruction ○ More or less instruction ○ To use an extension or enrichment activity ○ To work alone ○ To work with others • Decide how to assess during learning and evaluate progress to identify immediate needs. • Assess at the end of the learning to identify students who have needs that can be addressed in the upcoming plans.
WHEN are you going to teach it?	• Identify the best time to schedule instruction for the activity. • Decide when to teach each part of the lesson. Establish the order for each instructional segment. • Identify the best time to take an individual or small group aside for a special assignment or intervention. • Integrate the new learning in various areas of the curriculum, if possible. • Be aware of the need to revamp or readjust during instruction.
WHERE will the student(s) work productively?	• Identify the best learning scenario for the student using the TAPS acronym. • Identify the best area for the student to work: Learning zone Center Station Lab • Identify the best place for the student to complete the tasks: At a table On a desk In a chair On a rug
HOW will the activity engage the student?	• Decide if the student learns best engaging in a student-focused activity or a teacher-directed activity. • Select the most effective group design for the student: Multiage Knowledge base Ability Interests Random Cooperative team Peer tutoring • Identify the type of assignment: Homework Anchor task Choice board Agenda Contract Project

Implementing Standards Using the Activity Analysis Model

- Identify the activity to teach the standard, concept, or skill.
- Use the suggested questions in the checklist in Figure 6.7 to analyze the activity's effectiveness.
- Strategically decide if this is the best activity to teach, reinforce, or enrich the standards. Can the activity be integrated with other content, seasonal, or real-life events?
- Identify who needs the activity. Keep instructional grouping fluid so students move to an appropriate group for review, intervention, or enrichment.
- Place the activity in the plan, being aware that it may need to be changed or adapted for the learner. Provide time for students to give feedback and explain why an activity was too easy or difficult.

Five-Star
Tips for Using the Activity Analysis Model

1. Dig into the preassessment data to discover who needs the new standard or skill, what content to use, when to teach it, where the students will work productively, and how to teach it.

2. Analyze an activity to see if it is the most effective way for the group or individual to learn, review, or extend knowledge of the information.

3. Remember to differentiate assignments.

4. Realize all students may not be ready to learn the skill at the same time. Some students may waste valuable time completing the activity and would benefit from working on an alternate assignment.

5. Use the checklist in Figure 6.7 when you need to analyze the worthiness of the task as the most valuable opportunity for learning.

Bonus Tip

Be aware of unexpected events and unusual objects that can be molded into the most valuable learning activities or teachable moments. For example, a big snow presents an opportunity for students to learn about friction while riding their sleds. They may be able to watch drivers as they try to control their vehicles on icy roads.

Become a scavenger while shopping and traveling. You may find the most valuable visuals and manipulatives for an activity in unexpected places. Ask business owners for discarded displays, signs, and objects to make an activity more inviting.

Examples of the Activity Analysis Model

Example A: Analyzing an Activity

The teacher uses the checklist on the chart presented in the model to analyze the benefits of an activity. It is selected and considered for an individual group ("who"). It is chosen to teach a specific standard and content information ("what"). The "when," "where," and "how" of the model checklist are applied to analyze the activity. When the analysis process is complete, the right decision can be made for learners.

Example B: Activities for a Student Agenda

The preassessment data reveal that two students ("who") know the upcoming skill. After considering the options as to "what" these students need, the teacher decides learners can expand their knowledge of the skill ("what") using some enrichment activities in an agenda. Student-focused activities are selected because the two students are responsible, self-directed learners ("how"). They work independently and as partners while the remaining students work with the grade-level skill assignment ("when").

The teacher selects activities to engage each learner's strongest intelligences: The first student is strong in the visual/spatial, musical/rhythmic, and interpersonal areas ("how"), so the activities for that student include producing an illustration and creating a rap using the facts. The second student's strongest areas are verbal/linguistic, visual/spatial, and interpersonal. The tasks on this learner's agenda include reading an article related to the skill and designing a graphic organizer for the facts. The students share their work with each other and prepare a short class presentation or display.

The two students choose the most comfortable place to work independently and move to another chosen area to share and prepare their presentation ("where").

Example C: Small-Group Activity

The informal preassessment reveals that three students ("who") have not learned the prerequisite procedures for the upcoming skill ("what"). The teacher knows the students must master these procedures quickly to be successful in the study. Teacher-directed instruction ("how") is planned for these learners while other students are engaged with center activities ("when"). The group is gathered at a table for the intervention ("where"). The teacher reintroduces procedures and guides them through appropriate practice sessions. A choice board ("how") is presented with activities specifically designed for the learners to demonstrate individual mastery of the prerequisite skills.

■   THE STUDENT-DIRECTED LEARNING MODEL

What Is the Student-Directed Learning Model?

The student-directed learning model empowers each learner. The model's goal is to teach each student to be productive while working and learning with a partner, in a group, or independently. The student feels empowered with a sense of control in how to work, takes charge of his or her work, and assumes responsibility for learning.

In a differentiated classroom, students work independently or in groups with little or no adult supervision. When students become self-directed, self-regulated learners, the teacher spends less time giving reminders, repeating directions, keeping students on task, and answering trivial questions.

What Are the Instructional Benefits of the Student-Directed Learning Model?

Responsibilities for learning are turned over to students. The teacher becomes a learning facilitator.

The model develops learners who do the following:

- Know how and where to find resources or assistance
- Become engaged self-initiators
- Are reflective thinkers, knowing how to listen and analyze the ideas of others to make the best decisions
- Occupy their time wisely while completing activities or assignments
- Know how to take responsibility for their own learning

Implementing Standards Using the Student-Directed Learning Model

- Give clear, specific guidelines, the parameters, and a time frame. Use fewer commanding verbs and directives, such as *list, move, sit,* and *write*. Guide learners to make decisions, take control of their actions, and complete tasks.
- Turn over more responsibilities to students so they become self-directed learners who are actively engaged.
- Present motivating options whenever appropriate for assignments, materials, sources, activities, assessment tools, and presentation formats.
- Explain the value and purpose of each activity so students realize its importance in their learning process.

- Adapt the following suggestions to guide learners through a student-directed activity.
  - o Have students use self-questioning techniques such as the following:

    Why do I need to learn this information or skill?

    What can I do to learn this information so I can use it automatically?

    What do I need to complete the task in the allotted time?

    How can I best learn this information?

    Will I be more successful working alone or with a partner?

  - o Check to see that directions, timelines, and rules are understood before students begin the activity.
  - o Give students opportunities to demonstrate their understanding of how the activity helps them learn the standard.
  - o Have students ask questions or complete statements similar to the following for reflection and growth in journals, stations, or group activities:

    I learned _____.
    Which tasks were easy/difficult for me?
    What do I need next?
    Now that I completed this activity, I realize _____.

  - o Provide learners opportunities to model and show their process thinking in small-group discussions.

Demystifying the Student-Directed Learning Model

Use a metaphor similar to the following to introduce the student-directed learning model:

In self-directed learning, the learner is similar to the builder and the student's tasks are similar to the role of the subcontractor, who receives a special assignment and a timeline. For example, the electrician and plumber receive copies of the blueprint with specific directions and a deadline. The different tasks are completed independently. The plumber cannot complete the electrician's work. The electrician cannot complete the plumber's tasks. In the same way, specific tasks are assigned to individuals and groups by the teacher. The directions guide the learner to complete the various tasks independently or with classmates. During these tasks, they work with little assistance.

**Five-Star
Tips for Using the Student-Directed Learning Model**

1. Use assessment data to identify the more effective activity for independent assignment. This task should not bore or frustrate the learner but provide a needed, challenging learning opportunity.

2. Model or demonstrate each addressed standard or skill. Give the student opportunities to practice the task before it becomes an expectation in a student-directed assignment.

3. Remember, this task is designed for a student to perform with little or no adult supervision! Stay in close proximity while you work with other students.

4. When appropriate, assign more than one task using a menu or agenda. This allows the students to work at their own pace, select the task order, and tailor the work to their specific needs.

5. Establish checkpoints or times for reflections and self-assessments.

Examples of the Student-Directed Learning Model

Example A: Homework

A self-directed learner working on homework realizes help is needed, but no adult is available to assist.

The student knows to consider options for assistance, such as the

- Use trial and error
- Revisit notes
- Review the textbook material
- Read highlighted handout notes
- Contact a study buddy

Example B: Class Assignment

A student works on an agenda, special assignment, or project using guidelines, directions, task expectations, and a timeline provided by the teacher. The learner assumes responsibilities for

- Pacing
- Approaches to tasks
- Finding solutions to problems
- Using self-assessment tools
- Correcting

Example C: Studying for a Test

A student is studying for a social studies test and realizes the importance of knowing historical events and dates in the chapter. He knows several memory tools to use, such as rehearsal, graphic organizers, and mnemonic devices. He selects the best strategy to learn the important facts.

■ THE TEACHER-DIRECTED LEARNING MODEL

What Is the Teacher-Directed Learning Model?

The teacher-directed learning model is a structured approach to teaching standards, specific skills, or a procedure for mastery. The teacher becomes the information disseminator. Bruce Joyce and Marsha Weil identify five steps in the approach as orientation, presentation, structured, guided, and independent practice (Carnine, Silbert, Kame'enui, & Tarver, 2009, pp. 370–372).

This instructional method is a common practice in classrooms today because many teachers feel pressured to cover a large amount of material to prepare students for standardized tests. Direct instruction is not *the* way to teach, but it is *one* way.

What Are the Instructional Benefits of Using the Teacher-Directed Learning Model?

This model is most effective when used with individuals or small groups who need to master specific skills or procedures. The students benefit from this approach in the following ways:

- The teacher guides struggling students to master the assigned standards, skill, or concept.
- Lessons are structured, with the teacher presenting and pacing instruction.
- Teacher–student interactions occur during each instructional segment.
- The teacher provides immediate feedback, encourages, assists, reinforces efforts, and gives suggestions for improvement.
- Individuals or groups are led through an introduction and practice sessions with the teacher directing the work. In the second stage of practice, the teacher guides and assists as needed. When students demonstrate knowledge and understanding, they practice in a student-focused setting.

Implementing Standards Using the Teacher-Directed Learning Model

- Use a preassessment to identify students who need to master a specific standard, skill, or procedure.
- Use a lecturette to provide information in a way to make content come alive.
- Give students an overview of the steps they complete to master the skill or procedures.
- Select actively engaging, guided practice activities on the students' level of success.
- Assess, monitor, and adjust to the students' needs in each step.

Demystifying the Teacher-Directed Learning Model

Use a lecturette similar to the following to introduce the teacher-directed learning model:

> *I may work with the total class, with a small group, or with you individually to explain a skill or something you need to know. I will guide you through each step. I will continue to work with you until you can do it by yourself.*

★ ★ ★ ★ ★

Five-Star
Tips for the Teacher-Directed Learning Model

1. Use an orientation that presents the lesson's purpose with a connection to the learner's prior knowledge and experiences.
2. Present new vocabulary words, phrases, and terminology.
3. Teach and explain the new standard, skill, or concept by demonstrating its use with artifacts, illustrations, or models.
4. Provide structured, monitored practice with assistance.
5. Assign guided practice activities the individual can complete successfully and independently.

Examples of the Teacher-Directed Learning Model

Example A: Using Color and Manipulatives

The targeted standard is "using context clues." Some students do not know how to use context clues. The teacher introduces the use of synonyms as one way to unlock word meanings. The student is led through sentences that contain examples. The student is then given small plastic disks to place next to the unknown words and a colored pen to mark the synonyms. The teacher monitors and guides the activity. When the student demonstrates understanding, an assignment or activity is provided as independent practice with the standard.

Example B: Using Demonstrations and Movement

A small group does not know how to measure the perimeter of objects. The teacher introduces the term *perimeter*, discusses practical applications of the skill, and demonstrates how to measure the perimeter of several different shapes. The students measure the perimeter of objects with the teacher's direction and assistance. They receive independent practice activities to find the perimeter of various areas in the room.

Example C: Using Visuals and a Beat

A music student does not know the names of notes on the music staff. The teacher uses a large diagram of a music staff to introduce notes on the lines. A rap is used as a memory strategy to repeat and recall the names of the notes on sight.

THE NESTED ACTIVITY MODEL ▪

What Is the Nested Activity Model?

This model is Heidi Hayes Jacobs's design for integrating curriculum (Chapman, 1993). Since it is a decision-making device for selecting the most appropriate instructional activity, we named it the nested activity model. This planning tool analyzes an activity to see if it is a valuable use of instructional time. There are many standards and skills to teach. This planning tool outlines and highlights all objectives addressed in one activity, such as the standard(s), social skills, multiple intelligences, and thinking skills.

What Are the Instructional Benefits of Using the Nested Activity Model?

The nested activity model is a planning strategy that assists in making the most effective activity choices for a particular time segment. A commonly heard, valid teacher complaint is, "There is never enough time to teach all the required information." The nested activity analyzes the value of a chosen activity.

- The planning tool addresses more than one standard, skill, or intelligence at a time.
- The teacher can analyze the learner's needs and identify categories to address such as academic or social needs.
- The model guides the teacher into deep analysis of the lesson.
- It is a decision-making tool for identifying the most beneficial assignment for a time segment.
- Teachers become consciously effective while designing and making wise activity choices.

Implementing Standards Using the Nested Activity Model

- Realize that the purpose of this model is to analyze an activity selection to make the most accurate curriculum decision for a particular time period.
- Place categories that fit your personal, local, or state requirements in the model form. Some examples are standards, benchmarks, competencies, thinking skills, or social skills.
- Select an activity and analyze it.
- Remember, this model can also be used to compare two activities for a time segment to see which one offers the optimum benefit for a group of learners.
- Keep your nesting notes for reference when making a curriculum decision for this particular activity.

Demystifying the Nested Activity Model

When students are experiencing an activity designed with a nested format, guide them in filling in the grid. This helps learners recognize the many goals, standards, and skills taught during the activity. They realize that many experiences are included in one learning activity.

Demonstrate nesting by placing the word *movie* in the center of a circle. Draw nested circles around it. Fill in related terms such as *stars*, *plot*, *setting*, and *rating criteria*.

★ ★ ★ ★ ★

Five-Star
Tips for Using the Nested Activity Model

1. Use the model as a planning tool to analyze the value of an activity. If the activity does not meet the learner's needs, it is not a wise choice. This analysis eliminates activities that are time wasters and fluff or unimportant experiences. The organizer identifies the most effective use of an activity for a learning segment.

2. Try the following use of the nested activity model: Compare two activities to decide which one is most effective in meeting the current needs of an identified group.

3. Be selective! Differentiate! An activity that meets the needs of one group may not meet the needs of another group.

4. Remember, identify what students learn.

5. Use the data gathered to identify students who will or will not benefit from using the activity.

Examples of the Nested Activity Model in Action

Example A: Original Nested Model

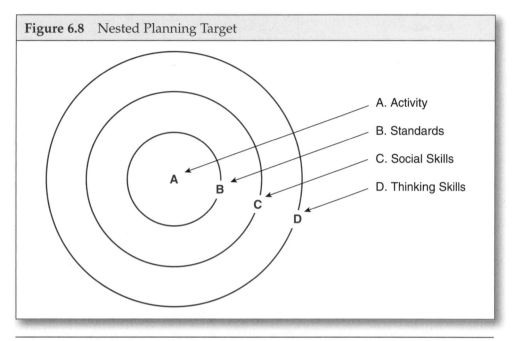

Figure 6.8 Nested Planning Target

A. Activity
B. Standards
C. Social Skills
D. Thinking Skills

Example B: Nested Box Plan

Place the activity in the center of a box.

1. Identify categories to analyze the activity.
2. Draw a nested box for each category. Determine the number of boxes by the number of categories you are exploring.
3. Write each category outside the nested boxes. Draw an arrow from each category to a box.
4. List the items addressed for each category in the corresponding box.

Example C: Adapting the Nested Model to a Chart

1. Identify an activity.
2. For the boxes, choose categories that coordinate with individual needs to address (see Figure 6.10).
3. Analyze each category to be sure it fits the requirements in your school, district, or state.
4. List the standards, skills, concepts, or information the activity teaches in each category. If a category is lacking, add needed information to the plan.
5. If the activity does not benefit this particular group, replace it with one that does.

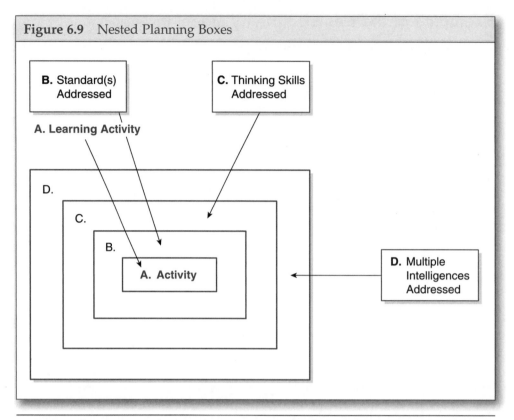

Figure 6.9 Nested Planning Boxes

Figure 6.10 Nested Planning Grid

Activity _____				
Standards, Benchmarks, Competencies	**Objectives or Skills**	**Social Skills**	**Multiple Intelligences**	**Thinking Skills**

THE THREADED MODEL ■

What Is the Threaded Model?

The threaded model is a Heidi Hayes Jacobs planning tool for integrating the curriculum. A specific standard, skill, or concept is identified as the target for instruction because of its importance, misunderstanding, or weakness. The selected target becomes the planning focus in each subject or topic in all curriculum areas.

The threaded model may be used as a planning tool in a self-contained classroom or across grade levels. It may be used by the resource specialist, grade-level colleagues, an inclusion team, a total school, a district, or a state. Each task is designed to develop a weakness into an area of strength. The threaded model gives students opportunities to view the same standard, skill, concept, or information through different lenses in various subjects and situations, and then apply it in various ways.

What Are the Instructional Benefits of Using the Threaded Model?

This model provides opportunities for more than one teacher or subject-area team to address the needs of one or more learners. This organizational planning tool analyzes how and when the targeted standard is presented in each subject or class.

Teachers often feel as though they are alone on an island because of their isolation within four classroom walls. They feel they have to do it all with little or no assistance. The threaded model gives teachers a tool that benefits students when plans are created and carried out to intentionally teach targeted standards and skills.

- In planning sessions, each educator shares ideas, vocabulary, and creative approaches to address the identified standard.
- Teachers work together across grade levels in an elementary school or across subject areas in a middle or high school, making conscious efforts for everyone to address the need.
- More students learn, because the team effort and the major focus are on a targeted area.
- Students see different uses, interpretations, and views of information.
- If students do not fully understand the standard in one lesson presentation or activity, they have more opportunities to take ownership of it.

Implementing Standards Using the Threaded Model

- Identify the learner's weaknesses in working with a standard. Share them with an individual or team who teaches or works with the student(s).
- Plot various ways to address the student's needs in each subject or topic.
- Commit and devote time to address the learner's weakness in the instructional plans so he or she has several opportunities to reach understanding and master it.
- Share your accomplishments with your partner or team. Listen to experiences of team members. Identify the next steps for advancement.
- When the skill is mastered or becomes automatic, use the threaded model to focus on another weak area.

Demystifying the Threaded Model

Debut the threaded model with a discussion of the phrase "threading it through." Adapt the following introduction to the model:

The standards, skills, and information you need to learn will be used in different ways in other subjects or classes. Watch for the threads. By threading a skill through your activities and topics, you have more opportunities to grasp and use the information in many ways.

Five-Star
Tips for Using the Threaded Model

1. Target standards that need more work by analyzing test data, grade-level performance, previous trouble spots, or teacher concerns. This leads to the realization that learners have a specific weak area that must be emphasized because most students did not master it. Concentrated focus on a weak area can develop it into a strong one.

2. Use the threaded model in a self-contained classroom by addressing the same standard in various lessons, activities, and subject areas.

3. Use the threaded model with a team. Each member has a role in improving the identified standard. The team must be committed to changing the targeted weakness into an area of strength.

4. Remember, if a student does not master a skill in one way, plan more opportunities for the individual to understand and master it in other subjects or activities.

5. Survey students to discover their hobbies, fads, and other areas of interest. Connect the targeted learning experiences to the students' interests to intrigue and motivate them to learn the information.

Examples of the Threaded Model

Example A: Threading Across Grade Levels

The assessment results reveal that students need more emphasis on reading and interpreting data with graphs. In most academic areas and on standardized tests, graphs are presented for the reader to interpret the represented information.

Each team identifies ways to address the graphing skill.

Example B: Threading Across Content Areas in a Classroom

1. Analyze test results to identify the weakest standard to target.

2. Thread the targeted need through each contact area during a period of several weeks. This gives students many opportunities to overcome the weak area.

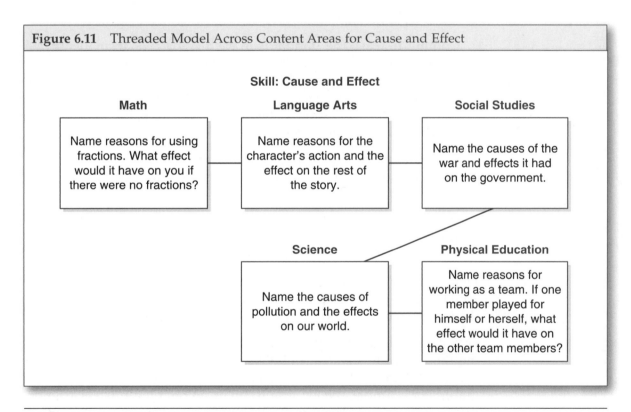

Figure 6.11   Threaded Model Across Content Areas for Cause and Effect

Skill: Cause and Effect

Math

Name reasons for using fractions. What effect would it have on you if there were no fractions?

Language Arts

Name reasons for the character's action and the effect on the rest of the story.

Social Studies

Name the causes of the war and effects it had on the government.

Science

Name the causes of pollution and the effects on our world.

Physical Education

Name reasons for working as a team. If one member played for himself or herself, what effect would it have on the other team members?

Example C: Threading Schoolwide—Using Graphs to Interpret Data

1. Identify the standard information students need to know about using graphs to interpret data.

The teachers' brainstorming session reveals the following:

- Teach graphing by plotting gathered data from the topic area in each classroom
- Give the learner opportunities to use three types of graphs: bar graphs, line graphs, and pie charts
- Demonstrate and teach graphs three ways: human, picture, and symbolic
- Emphasize related terms:

  more than   *less than*   *total*   *compare*   *plot*

- After a graph is complete, stimulate thinking with probing questions and statements such as the following:
  - What does this graph tell or show? How do you know?
  - The graph's data prove _____.
  - The most important information on the graph is _____.
  - I learned _____ from this graph.

2. Commit to teach the standards in each grade-level team identifying "how to use graphs and interpret the data" as a targeted need over a 9-week period. Threading gives each team member responsibilities for teaching the graphing standards and ways to interpret them. The students' skills become stronger because the graphing is emphasized by each teaching team member. Here are some examples:

Prekindergarten: During calendar time each morning during the month, add information to create a weather bar graph. Discuss what the graph tells as the information grows.

Kindergarten: During calendar time each morning, add to a weather bar graph. At the end of the month, students collect all the pictures that symbolize the daily weather and construct a pie chart.

First grade: In a science class, students construct a line graph to compare the growth of two plants over a period of time. Interpret the data the graph reveals at periodic times while plotting the information.

Second grade: During a math study, students create a bar graph recording their favorite ice creams, books, or sports. They make a pie chart using the data. Discuss the differences between a pie chart and a bar graph. For example, the bar graph can be an ongoing process as information is gathered. The pie chart cannot be completed until all information is available.

Third grade: The football team's scores from the previous season are compared on a line graph with this year's scores. The vertical lines on the graph represent the game number. The horizontal lines represent the score of each game.

Fourth grade: The teacher gives an assignment for students to go on a scavenger hunt for a week and collect graphs. Each student brings the collection to a group-sharing session for discussion, interpretation, and discovery. Each group shares their favorite graph with the class and tells how it is used.

Fifth grade: In a graphing station, students interpret the data on graph samples from newspapers, magazines, brochures, and the web. Each learner selects one graph sample, places it in a journal, and writes an interpretation of it. The student signs the explanation. Another student reads the journal entry and adds more data. The teacher checks the explanations for correct or incorrect interpretations.

CONCLUSION ■

Become familiar with the models for planning instruction. They are designed to simplify the difficult task of organizing and managing lessons to teach the standards. Select the most appropriate model to plan effectively for the learners' diverse knowledge backgrounds, interests, and abilities.

It is important to match the right hat to the occasion. Just as the chosen hat enhances an outfit, the selected model is tailored for a student's learning event. Know how each model benefits differentiated teaching and learning, and strategically select one to plan effective instruction!

Figure 6.12 Personal Reflections Using Differentiated Models

1. After reading the chapter, identify a new model to assist you in planning instruction for targeted standards. Adapt the selected model for an upcoming lesson.

2. How does the Adjustable Assignment Model assist you in meeting the differentiated needs of learners when data reveal they are on three knowledge levels related to a standard?

3. How can you adapt the Project Packet on page 208 to guide individual or small groups through each stage of an upcoming, standard-based project? Identify aspects of the project that give learners choices in decision making. Which decisions will you make?

4. Use the list on page 213 to identify three to four of your intelligence strengths. How do your strengths impact planning for your classroom?

5. Set a goal for using one aspect of the activity analysis model discussed on page 218 to improve your instructional planning.

Figure 6.13 Five Activities for a Professional Learning Community (PLC) Study

1. Exploring the Differentiated Planning Models
   a. Have each participant make a foldable booklet with a page for each planning model explored in the chapter. As the group reads and learns about each model, individuals write important facts in the booklet with their plans for adapting and/or using it.
   b. Jigsaw the models by assigning each one to a small group. Provide time for in-depth study, discussion, and application ideas. Present two models in the sessions.

2. Adjustable Assignment Model
   a. Each participant makes a blank grid to plan an adjustable assignment like the one on page 126. Label the columns as follows:

   Level I: Beginning Level   Level II: Approaching Mastery   Level III: High Degree of Mastery

   Note: Participants can work in small groups to fill out the grid, but each individual needs a copy for his or her personal portfolio folder and to use in a future lesson.

   b. Select a targeted standard.
   c. Write the assessment tool(s) to identify where the learners are in their understanding of the targeted standard. The assessment tool identifies the learners' individual knowledge levels for the differentiated assignment.

   Note: Read the five tips for the adjustable assignment model before completing each step.

   d. Begin with the Level II column. Analyze and write the learners' background knowledge. Develop an assignment for students who are at grade level to work with the standard.

Level II: Approaching Mastery (Grade Level)	Have the foundation needed to learn the standard.	Learn the grade-level standard.	Grade-level assignment is on grade level.
Names of Students at This Level	Identify what they know.	Identify what they need next.	Develop an appropriate grade-level assignment.

   e. Ask participants to look at the Level I column and write an activity to meet the needs of this group of students who are on the beginning level of mastery. Remind everyone that this intervention needs to fill in a gap of knowledge.

Level I: Beginning Level	Lack background, so class presentation is exposure.	Need to zap the gaps to build a foundation.	Use intervention to fill in holes in learning or to zap the gaps.
Names of Students at This Level	Identify background.	Write an intervention to teach.	Write assignment to intervene.

f. In Level III, the "beyond mastery" column, write an assignment to challenge these learners. They review the standard information and use it while extending their knowledge using higher-order thinking skills and problem solving.

Level III: High Degree of Mastery	Know the standard, so the information is a review.	How to use or apply the information in the real world.	Challenging task to using the standard using higher-order thinking and problem solving.
Names of Students at This Level	Identify the learners' backgrounds.	Identify what they need next.	Write an assignment.

g. Each member chooses a partner to share the end product and discuss their "aha" moments. Remember, this is not the only way to differentiate, but it is an effective planning tool.

h. Make copies of the completed assignment grids. Place them in a notebook so the school has these assignments for future reference.

3. Multiple Intelligences Model

   a. Follow the step-by-step procedure to plan a unit of study using the multiple intelligences, explained on page 210.
   b. Form energizing partner teams to discuss ways to use a learner's intelligence strengths to teach an identified standard. Share highlights of the discussion with the total group.
   c. Remember, label activities, not students!

4. Threaded Model

   a. Draw a design for the threaded model.

Example: Standard _____

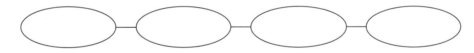

   b. Identify a standard students need to learn.
   c. Select four subject areas or topics to use in teaching the standard.
   d. Write activities in each section to teach the standard.
   e. Share and display the finished products.
   f. Place a star on the activity after you use it in your classroom.

5. Nested Model

   a. Form interest groups.
   b. Turn to the nested model on page 227.
   c. Select an activity or task to analyze its use in the classroom.
   d. Write it in the center circle.
   e. Brainstorm the thinking skills, multiple intelligences, and standards the activity or skill addresses. Select the most beneficial ideas and write them in the appropriate portion of the concentric circles.
   f. Add other areas to analyze as needed.

7

Planning for Standards With Differentiated Instruction

PLANNING IS A COMPLEX, STRATEGIC PROCESS IN the multidimensional features of differentiated instruction. The plan outlines steps for teaching the standards using the most effective strategies and activities for each learner's unique strengths and needs.

When a fire crew comes upon a blazing building, the captain of the fire department carefully charts the crew's course to follow. When the teacher puts on the fire captain's hat, plans are mapped out for students as they learn and master content. Like the fire captain, who assesses each crew member's specific skills and talents, you must learn all there is to learn about the students.

Once the captain knows his crew's strengths, he assigns duties designed around their talents to ensure a safe plan of action. A teacher assigns tasks based on students' strengths and talents, maximizing their learning capacities. It is crucial to design instructional plans with intent or purpose to avoid wasting the learner's time. Each strategy and activity is selected strategically to teach the standards in a way that leads each student to success.

Managing plans for differentiated instruction is a challenging but rewarding process. With this in mind, we designed and selected the following suggestions, techniques, and tips to assist with these multifaceted planning tasks so you work smarter, not harder.

■ WHAT IS PLANNING FOR A DIFFERENTIATED CLASSROOM?

Knowledgeable, successful teachers commit to making a difference in students' lives through planning. The plans are designed for a unit, a semester, or a year by teachers, grade-level colleagues, and/or administrators. Avoid becoming locked into a plan, because it has to be adjusted and revamped to meet the ever-changing needs of individuals and groups.

1. Become familiar with the mandated standards for your subject area and/or grade level.

2. Outline the standards in sequential order.

3. Select meaningful content that presents the best medium for teaching the standard or objective. Keep in mind that subject matter creates the mental links and connections for the learner as the standards, skills, and assessment are woven into the content.

4. Create a logical flow and timeline for introducing each standard with the strategies and activities.

5. List the materials and resources needed, noting items that must be acquired.

Preliminary Planning Tips

All teachers become more proficient as planners when they take time to become familiar with all factors that need to be considered. The following information is necessary to plan strategically for the diverse learners in today's classrooms:

1. **Know your standards.** Use the standards as a navigation guide to destinations in your instructional plans. Students must master the mandated standards to be academically successful.

2. **Know your students.** Focus on individual talents, strengths, and needs. Be aware of their interests and the current fads so you can use them as attention-grabbing hooks or keys to learning. Build on their sense of wonderment and anticipation about what will happen next.

3. **Know your strategies.** Maintain an array of tools and activities to continually challenge and motivate learners. Adapt the strategies to the students' knowledge levels and personal characteristics.

4. **Know your content.** Become thoroughly familiar with the content so it will be easier to select the most relevant and beneficial information. Keep in mind that you do not have to teach or cover all textbook information or content, unless it is mandated. Let it serve as a conduit or channel for activities and strategies. Carefully select content to transmit or convey knowledge and skills to each learner. This gives students meaningful ways to make mental connections to the standards.

5. **Know your resources and materials.** Identify the most effective and appealing materials to reach individuals. You will be able to select the most valuable resources when you know the students' strengths, needs, and interests.

Text Reference Self-Analysis

Where are you with implementing the categories of differentiated instruction? Try the following inventory for a self-analysis. Examine your responses periodically to see growth. Refer to the page numbers in this book for reviews, additions, and management tips for using a new category.

Figure 7.1 Implementing Differentiation

Categories	Page	Not Yet	Some	Often	Usually
Environment	17				
Affective	18				
Physical	31				
Differentiated models	193				
Adjustable assignment model	194				
Curriculum rewinding	196				
Curriculum fast-forwarding	199				
Curriculum compacting	201				
Problem-based model	203				
Project-based model	207				
Multiple intelligences model	210				
Triarchic teaming model	215				
Activity analysis model	218				
Student-directed model	222				
Teacher-directed model	225				
Nested model	227				
Threaded model	231				
Mastery learning model	244				
Grouping strategies	153				
Flexible grouping	155				
Total group	158				
Alone	161				
Partner	165				
Small groups	167				

(Continued)

(Continued)

Categories	Page	Not Yet	Some	Often	Usually
Grouping designs					
Knowledge-base grouping	171				
Interest groups	177				
Ability grouping	179				
Multiage groups	181				
Cooperative groups	183				
Random grouping	185				
Peer tutoring	188				
Instructional strategies	109				
Focus activities	113				
Sponge activities	116				
Anchor activities	118				
Cubing activities	120				
Choice boards	124				
Graphic organizers	129				
Centers, stations, and learning zones	132				
Agendas/menus	137				
Academic contracts	141				
Products	146				
Content activities	243				
Assessment tools					
Self-assessment	58				
Informal assessment	62				
Response cards	65				
Signals	69				
Stand and show	72				
Formal assessment	75				
Pretest/posttest	77				
Effective questioning	79				
Anecdotal records	85				
Surveys	88				
Journals	90				
Portfolios	94				
Grades	98				
Teacher-made tests	101				
Standardized test preparation	104				

TEACHING CONTENT   ■

Teachers usually select content to teach one or more standards. Some districts require teachers to follow a timeline to teach standards using specific content. For example, a math teacher may be required to teach Chapters 3, 4, and 5 during the second 6-week period.

Know your content thoroughly so it will be easier to decide where and when to plug in the standards. When the content is familiar, it is easier to place it in sequence and create links and connections.

Required skills are presented to teachers as standards. District administrators usually give teachers freedom to select the content from approved textbooks and auxiliary materials.

Selecting Content

Use questions similar to the following to guide the content selection process as a conduit to standard mastery.

- Is this content segment essential for the learner?
- Is this content the most valuable way for students to learn the standards?
- Which segments of the information does the learner need? Do I use selective abandonment and eliminate irrelevant content?
- Are the content segments organized to make learning flow sequentially with the standards?
- Do I use this content information next or save it until later?

Always remember, it is not necessary to teach content information because it is in the teacher's guide and supporting materials. Use the textbook and supplementary materials as resources. Select relevant information and the sequence for teaching it.

Selecting Appropriate Materials and Resources

Select resources to meet student needs, coordinate with the content, and enhance learning:

Examples:

- Books to teach the standard on the learners' various reading levels
- Supplementary materials provided by the textbook company, such as books, posters, electronic programs, workbooks, videos, and other technical gadgets
- Internet sources
- Local resources available from civic organizations and businesses
- Auditory books, stories, poems, and songs

■ MASTERY LEARNING

What Is Mastery Learning?

Mastery learning engages the student in activities and practice sessions with one standard or skill until it is learned thoroughly.

The term *mastery* indicates that the student learns the information and is able to use it successfully. The teacher uses assessment data to identify a standard, skill, fact, or concept the student has failed to master. The learner is guided through specific teacher-directed activities that include an introduction, modeling, guided practice, and student-focused assignments until mastery is evident.

A learner at the mastery level is able to explain "inside" thought procedures to tell how the problem was solved. The student is able to respond, "This is the way I got the answer. First I . . . , then I . . . ." In this metacognitive activity, they are required to think about their thinking. Students on the mastery level are ready to move into a higher level of automaticity. Give students opportunities to move beyond the mastery level whenever possible. This is more likely to occur when students make personal links and have opportunities to use the new learning in their own way.

What Are the Instructional Benefits of Mastery Learning?

- A specific goal or level of mastery is identified and introduced to the learner.
- Time is provided for the student to practice using a standard needed as a base for future learning.
- The tasks are within the learners' level of success so they do not become frustrated and give up. When learners master information or a skill, they will not be overwhelmed with future tasks that build on this basic knowledge.
- Students receive constructive feedback so they never feel lost. They become more perseverant as a result.
- Mastery generates intrinsic motivation as the teacher leads students successfully through each step or procedure. The feelings accompanying success usually create a desire to learn more.

Using Standards to Implement Mastery Learning

- Use an assessment to identify the student's current ability or knowledge of the standard.
- Identify an obtainable goal or level of success.
- Give assignments in small chunks or tasks.
- Provide specific, corrective feedback often.
- Celebrate successes when the goal or level of mastery is attained.

Demystifying Mastery Learning

Explain that mastery learning is used so students practice using information or a skill until they take control of it and own it. When this happens, they can use it independently without assistance. Here is a suggested dialogue to use in introducing mastery learning to students:

When you were learning to ride a bicycle, you started with training wheels while someone helped you balance. You then learned to ride by yourself with the special wheels. Later, you mastered riding the bicycle by yourself without extra wheels or assistance.

In the same way, you may receive extra assistance and take special steps to learn some of our standards. When you master something, you understand it and can use it whenever you need it.

Five-Star
Tips for Mastery Learning

1. Analyze the assessment data to identify specific skills, concepts, or information the student must know or master.

2. Select the most efficient, effective procedures or steps to teach the information to the individual learner.

3. Use the students' strengths to improve their weaknesses.

4. Remember the adage, "If you do not use it, you lose it"? Link, spiral, and review so students continue to apply the mastered standard.

5. Assess knowledge before, during, and after learning for strategic planning.

Examples of Mastery Learning

Example A: One Student Needs to Master
Vocabulary or Sight Words

- Seven of the most common sight words are placed on flash cards.
- A sentence, picture, or definition of the word is placed on the back of the card.
- A tutor or peer is assigned to teach the seven words to the student.
- When the seven words are pronounced with the definition, a timer is used to increase speed.
- When the student reaches the mastery goal, the next seven words are presented.

Example B: A Small Group Needs to Master
Steps to Work a Problem

- The steps are presented orally using a visual aid, such as a poster or chart.
- The students echo the teacher as the steps are stated. This continues until the students can state the facts independently and automatically with confidence.
- The teacher provides a practice session in which the students' work is monitored, so immediate feedback and assistance is provided.
- The students receive a short assignment for independent practice so they can demonstrate mastery.
- Students create a rap or dance using the steps to showcase their mastery of the standard.

*Example C: A Student Must Show Mastery of a
Rule and Be Able to Apply It*

- Introduce the rule by showing how it is used and explaining why it is important.
- Demonstrate its use in various examples.
- Monitor and assist the student as he or she applies the rule in independent tasks.
- Ask the student to use his or her preferred learning styles and strongest intelligences to present or display an example of the rule and its use.
- Listen to the student explain his or her step-by-step thinking while applying the rule.

A PLANNING DIALOGUE ■

In this section, a guide is provided for planning before, during, and after a unit of study. Explanations of the steps and questions or statements to address are included to assist as you plan at each stage. Use each management step for lesson preparation to thoroughly plan the curriculum for your differentiated classroom.

Planning Before Teaching the Unit

1. Choose the topic or unit, and then select the standards to address during the study.

Standards are the facts, concepts, and skills students are expected to master in each grade level. These expectations are usually mandated. Textbook companies and local curriculum guides often provide the recommended scope and sequence for presenting the standards. Planning creates the instructional route to reach each learner. Students must master the mandated standards to create foundations for future learning. The teacher relies on professional and personal judgment to select the standard and the most effective time and place to introduce it. Consider questions and statements similar to the following when selecting each standard:

- Identify the standards to target for the learner's knowledge, experiences, and understanding.
- How can the standards be clustered or taught together for efficient use of time and for understanding?
- Which previously taught standards need to spiral into the new learning?
- What facts and skills need to be included in instruction for standard mastery?
- How long will it take to teach the standard so students on all levels learn it?
- List the students who have the background knowledge and skills to understand the new standard. List the students who need to expand their background knowledge and skills to understand the new standard.

2. Preassess the student to identify the knowledge base and interests, and then analyze the data.

A formal or informal preassessment tool reveals the learner's level of experience and knowledge related to the standard. The preassessment is administered prior to the lesson to provide time to analyze the results and customize instructional plans.

This vital planning step leads to selection of the most appropriate strategies and activities for each student to learn the standard. During this phase, use questions similar to the following as a guide:

- What is the most efficient, informative way to preassess students?
- Will an informal preassessment reveal the learner's prior knowledge of the standard?
- What do the assessment results tell me about the learner's level of understanding in relation to the standard?

- Am I asking the right questions or test items in the most appropriate way to identify the needed information?
- Do students understand how assessment results are used in planning?
  - What are the entry points for instruction for each level?
  - What are the learning gaps or needs?
  - Which gaps do I need to zap to help the student learn the required material?
  - Which students have common needs?
- How can the learner's strengths be engaged to overcome his or her weaknesses? Refer to the learner's strengths and needs recorded on a grid or chart.
- What is the learner's level of mastery? (See page 231 for more information on levels of mastery.)

___ Beginning   ___ Approaching mastery   ___ High degree of mastery

    ("Rewinding")   ("Grade level")   ("Fast-forwarding")

3. Select the content, materials, and resources that most effectively teach the standards.

Content is the subject matter or information selected to teach the standards, skills, and concepts. The majority of content material is presented from textbooks or computer programs. Remember, just because the information is in the adopted textbook does not mean it is necessarily the best material to teach the standard. If it is boring, confusing, or frustrating to you, it will be even worse for the learners. In this planning step, rely on your professional expertise and reasoning to select the content to use in presenting the standards and skills.

Consider resources not included in the supplementary materials. Students, parents, and community members often have information that can enhance specific lessons. Whenever appropriate, encourage the learners to teach the class or a small group using their materials.

Use the following questions to guide your selection of content, materials, and resources:

- Which segment of information will be used to teach the standard?
- What part of the content should be emphasized to assist the learner in making links and connections to the information?
- Are other resources available? If so, list them.
- What parts of the content material do not address the standards and can be omitted?
- Does the content information present the standard or skill in a way that develops understanding?

4. Identify the flexible grouping designs.

Crucial decisions are involved in creating the instructional grouping designs. The recorded results of the preassessment data are analyzed to design the most effective grouping scenarios for instruction. The acronym TAPS (T = Total group, A = Alone, P = Partner, and S = Small group) is recommended as a guide to make grouping decisions in a differentiated classroom.

Use the following questions to guide planning for flexible grouping.

- What information is needed by the total group?

  ___ Introductions and wrap-ups

  ___ Lecturettes and discussions

  ___ Directions and guidelines

  ___ Review of rules, rituals, or routines

  ___ Reminders for independent and group work

  ___ Summative evaluations

- Which students need independent instruction or assignments?

  ___ Reteaching/rewinding

  ___ Review

  ___ Practice or reinforcement

  ___ Enrichment/fast-forwarding

  ___ Compacting

- How will students be grouped to learn the standard?

  ___ Knowledge level

  ___ Interest

  ___ Ability

  ___ Peer to peer

  ___ Random

  ___ Cooperative learning

  ___ Project teams

- When do students need to

  Work alone? _____

  With a partner? _____

  With a small group? _____

- What criteria will I use to effectively move a student to another group?

5. Brainstorm a quantity of activities for each individual or group to produce quality plans.

The next step involves identifying and listing the best activities to teach the standard for individuals and/or groups. Consider all possibilities. This is a reference list for future ideas that can grow as you discover meaningful activities in professional material and sharing sessions with colleagues. Choose quality activities from the list to meet the differentiated needs of groups and individual students. Consider questions similar to the following to analyze your selection of activities:

- Will the activities and strategies teach the standard and the content information in the most effective way?
- Do I have challenging activities to motivate learners at the different levels of entry points?
- Does the content information present the standard or skill in a way that develops understanding for each learner?
- Do the activities address the students' varied learning styles, modalities, and intelligences?
- Do I have the most effective strategies and activities to make my plan?

Laying Out the Plan

1. Strategically select instructional strategies and activities for a quality plan.

Select strategies and activities to activate or set the learner's mental wheels in motion. This occurs when a student connects the new standard to prior knowledge and experiences. Activation is maintained with interesting and intriguing activities.

Carefully select the strategies to transfer the learning. In this fundamental step, instruction is designed for the student to take ownership of the new standard so it can be used independently.

Become familiar with an array of instructional strategies to teach each standard on the student's level of need. Maintain a collection of techniques and approaches that continually challenge and motivate learners. Consider questions similar to the following in the selection process:

- How will I debut the new standard or skill in a way that captures and focuses the learner's attention?
- Which activity will create a connection from the new standard or skill to prior knowledge or experiences?
- What is the best strategy to make the learning personally meaningful and understandable?
- How will the student be actively engaged in learning?
- How can students use their learning preferences or strongest intelligences to learn the new information?

2. Study and assess the plan to be sure the most beneficial approaches are in place for each student.

Use the following questions as a guide to assess the plan:

- Does the strategy or activity use the best technique to teach the standard?
- Will the student have opportunities to build on prior knowledge and experiences?
- Do the activities promote transfer of the information?

- Will the new learning foster mental links and connections?
- Does the plan use the individual's strengths?

Planning During and After Teaching the Unit Information

1. Teach the information.

Teaching is the process of guiding students to understand new standards so they can be mastered and used with automaticity. It is important to remember in this phenomenal process that the student's brain is being wired or programmed during each experience.

- How will students know the purposes or objectives of the lesson?
- Which strategy will hook the learners into yearning to work with the new standard?
- Can students sense my enthusiasm and genuine desire for them to learn?
- Are new vocabulary words and phrases clear and easy to understand?
- Do students have an opportunity to demonstrate an understanding of the directions?

2. Use flexible grouping and assess changes to meet needs.

In a differentiated classroom, teaching takes place in total groups as well as in individual and small-group activities. The grouping process is fluid, because learners moved often from one group to another due to growth, misplacement, or a diagnosed need. Here are some questions to consider during instruction:

- Are the groups moving toward or fulfilling the set goals? How?
- Which grouping scenario is the most beneficial for completing this assigned task?
- How are the groups getting along socially? Why or why not?
- Which students will benefit from remaining in the group? Which learners need to change to a new group? Why?
- How can I assist a learner in adjusting to a new group?

3. Assess during learning.

It is essential to assess during learning to keep students on track in each lesson. Everyone needs to understand the value of ongoing assessment. Individuals, partners, and small groups can use assessment tools during learning to self-monitor and make corrections. Ask yourself the following questions to guide assessment during learning:

- What does each student know?
- What is each student doing to demonstrate that he or she is learning?
- How will I stay aware of the student's needs during the lesson or assignment?

___ Observations   ___ Checkpoints   ___ Self-checks

___ Appropriate questions   ___ Anecdotal records   ___ Notes

- Which actions will become a recorded grade?
- How will individual needs be addressed during learning?

4. Readjust instructional strategies and activities for learners.

- Does the student need to review information or skills?
- Which learning gaps need to be filled for the student to learn the grade-level information?
- What learning gaps require an intervention?
- Is the student ready to move to a more challenging activity?
- Do I need to bring a group of students together for reteaching, an academic contract, or a separate assignment?

5. Assess after learning to develop new plans.

Assessment is a never-ending process. The results of the assessment after learning are addressed in the upcoming lesson design. Use questions and statements similar to the following to guide development of new plans:

- What assessment tools will be used?
- Which parts of the lesson can the learner self-assess to see mistakes and make corrections?
- The students who mastered the standard or skill are _____. The students who need more opportunities for learning are _____.
- Is each student able to use the new information independently?
- The segments of the lesson needing a review or identified for reteaching are _____.

■ A PLANNING GRID FOR DIFFERENTIATED INSTRUCTION

The following planning tool is designed to teach standards in differentiated instruction. Use the grid to plan a successful unit of learning. This initial planning is a guide to working smarter earlier so students work harder and eagerly on tasks strategically selected for their individual needs.

Remember, assessment drives curriculum plans.

Figure 7.2   Differentiated Instruction Planning Grid

Unit topic _____ Date from _____ through _____

I. What will you teach?

   As a result of this unit, the students will learn:

Standard	Content	Skills	Concepts

II. Preassessment tool(s) _____   **Date_____**

Analysis of Preassessment Data

   A. Total Group Needs

   B. Small-Group Needs

   Level 1: Readiness (identified needs to develop background knowledge)
      What do they know?
      What do they need next?

   Level 2: Approaching mastery (on grade level)
      What do they know?
      What do they need next?

   Level 3: High degree of mastery (knows most of the standard information, concepts, and skills)
      What do they know?
      What do they need next?

   C. Individual Needs

Student's Name	Knows	Needs	Level (1, 2, or 3)
1.			
2.			

(Continued)

(Continued)

III. Content to Be Taught

To total group

To small group

To student

Selected Content		
Level 1	**Level 2**	**Level 3**
1.		
2.		

IV. Resource Selection

Total Group

Resources
1. 2. 3.

Small Group

Group	Resources to Use
Level 1	
Level 2	
Level 3	

Individual

Student's Name	Resources to Use
1.	
2.	

Individual Assignments

Total Group Plan

Assignment	Time	Multiple Intelligences Addressed	Groups TAPS/ Type	Materials	Assessment Tools
1. 2. 3.					

Differentiated Small-Group Plan

Group	Assignment	Time	Multiple Intelligences Addressed	Groups TAPS/ Type	Materials	Assessment Tools
Level 1						
Level 2						
Level 3						

Independent Assignment

Student	Assignment	Time	Multiple Intelligences Addressed	Groups TAPS/ Type	Materials	Assessment Tools
1.						
2.						

V. Evaluation: Summative Analysis Report and Reflections

   A. End-of-Unit Assessment(s)

   1.

   2.

Total Group on Grade-Level Evaluation Analysis	
Mastered	
Needs Next	

   B. Individual Needs
   C. Comments: Things to Remember and Reflections

Student's Name	Mastered	Needs Next
1.		
2.		

■ PROACTIVE PLANNING: CREATING A TROUBLESHOOTER'S GUIDE

Proactive planning supplies you with tools to provide seamless instruction to teach identified standards. A troubleshooter's guide identifies predicted, instructional dilemmas that may be encountered. Suggestions are provided as solutions for each situation.

Complete your troubleshooter's guide for planning during the first few weeks. Use information derived from an analysis of cumulative records, as well as conferences with the student, parents, and other teachers. Observe, observe, observe. Fill in the blanks with the name of the individual or group. Customize the following form for your students, and adapt it to the learner's needs throughout the year.

Figure 7.3   Trouble Shooting Guide to Planning

Projected Trouble Spots	Possible Solutions

_____ rarely ever has materials for class.	• Post a list of materials needed for class on the outside of the classroom door: "Materials for class today!"
	• Establish routines. For example:
	  Each day you need ____.
	  Every Wednesday you need ___.
	• Occasionally, verbally reward those who have their materials.
	• Do not allow a student to use this as an excuse to get out of class.
	• Provide extra materials.

_____ is easily distracted.	• Assign the student a spot that has the fewest distractions. • Use proximity and reminders. • Create buy-in with high-interest assignments! • Use a timer. • Say, "If you complete ___, you can ___."
_____ needs more time to complete the work.	• Give specific, verbal praise for being on task and for work completed. • Do not assign too many tasks at one time. • Model expectations. • Use a timer. Challenge the student to complete the work before the bell rings. • Break tasks into small segments or shorter time frames.

Projected Trouble Spots	Possible Solutions
_____ knows an upcoming standard.	• Give the student an exemption, and move to another topic. • Challenge the student to apply the information in a unique way related to the standard. • Prepare an academic contract for a research project. • Let the student design a new game related to the standard. • Complete a web search and present learned information to the class.
_____ has trouble following directions.	• Give the directions in smaller chunks. • Provide the learner time to explain the directions to someone. • Use the student's favorite method to demonstrate procedures. • Assign a personal consulting partner. • Vary the style used in giving the directions: written, oral, or both.

■ ADDRESSING DIVERSE CULTURES IN TODAY'S CLASSROOM

Remember!

- Children develop language by interacting with others. The more verbal interactions the learner has with people who use English, the faster the student will learn it.
- Oral language develops before writing or reading.
- Daily involvement in activities promotes language skills in reading, writing, speaking, and listening. Active engagement with classmates allows a student to learn a new language and leads to academic success.
- Students often experience confusion and combine the languages.
- Always honor the student's culture and language.

★ ★ ★ ★ ★

Five-Star
Tips for Addressing Diversity

- Label the learner's environment. Post signs and directions to assist the student.
- Survey family members to identify the student's customs and cultural background.
- Encourage family members and the learner to share information about their native customs, language, and background with the class.
- Use flexible grouping scenarios to promote peer interaction.
- During the transition from their native language to English, allow students to mix the languages or express themselves in their own language to show what they know. Often, the student knows more than is evident because of the language barrier.

Questions to Ask Yourself About Diversity

- Do I keep a foreign-language dictionary handy and available for students and for me?
- Am I providing directions each learner understands?
- Am I infusing literacy experiences to reflect a variety of cultures?
- Do I research and learn about the cultures and heritages of my class members?
- How can I honor each learner's special days or holidays?
- What aspects of the student's cultural background do I need to explore?
- Am I providing ample opportunities for the student to become English proficient?

INTRODUCING A DIFFERENTIATED   ■
OBSERVATION TOOL

Use the following observation form (Figure 7.4) as a guide to assess differentiation in action before, during, or after implementation. Adapt it to meet the needs of your school or classroom. This observation tool is designed to be used by

Peer-to-peer coaches   Mentors Administrators Curriculum specialists

Supervisors   Teachers   Professional developers

Figure 7.4   The Differentiated Classroom Observation Form

Teacher _____   Grade Level/Subject Area _____

Observer _____   Date_____

Physical Environment

Evidence Indicators	Often seen	Sometimes occurs	Little or no evidence
1. Presents an inviting, relaxed environment for learning			
2. Provides comfortable desks and work areas			
3. Provides space for academic and personal items			
4. Is designed for quick and easy groupings of tables and chairs			
5. Is arranged for teacher and student movement during work sessions			
6. Provides work areas for small groups			
7. Showcases current learning through student displays and artifacts			

Feedback

Strengths
Recommendations

(Continued)

(Continued)

Teacher Behaviors

Evidence Indicators	Often seen	Sometimes occurs	Little or no evidence
1. Works with total groups, individuals, and small groups			
2. Moves appropriately among students to monitor engagement.			
3. Uses a variety of appropriate ongoing assessment tools			
4. Applies assessment information to guide instruction			
5. Addresses academic, emotional, social, and physical needs of students			
6. Provides time for students to actively process information			
7. Gives specific feedback to individuals and/or small groups			
8. Exhibits excitement and enthusiasm for the standard			

Feedback

Strengths

Recommendations

Materials and Resources

Evidence Indicators	Often seen	Sometimes occurs	Little or no evidence
1. Are available in appropriate levels			
2. Are accessible to students			
3. Support the standards			
4. Are age appropriate			
5. Are up-to-date			
6. Has adequate supplies			
7. Uses appropriate equipment			
8. Include a variety of manipulatives			

Feedback

Strengths	
Recommendations	

Instructional Strategies

Evidence Indicators	Often seen	Sometimes occurs	Little or no evidence
1. Uses assessment tools before, during, and after learning			
2. Uses varied strategies			
3. Meets the diverse needs of learners			
4. Plans with flexible grouping			
5. Presents with varied strategies and activities			
6. Uses centers and/or stations			
7. Engages students with projects and/or problem-solving activities			
8. Presents students with choices in learning activities			

Feedback

Strengths	
Recommendations	

(Continued)

(Continued)

Standards-Based Teaching Instruction

Evidence Indicators	Often seen	Sometimes occurs	Little or no evidence
1. Standards are the foundation for instruction.			
2. The level of each learner's knowledge base is identified through assessment to determine starting points.			
3. Standards are posted in a visible place so students know the lesson's purpose.			
4. The practice of chunking standards is used appropriately.			
5. Standards are taught in various ways, using differentiated instructional strategies.			
6. Learners actively engage in assignments to learn the standard.			
7. Students engaged problem solvers and decision makers while applying new information for personal use and understanding.			
8. Standards are revisited through other areas, units, topics, and lessons so students retain and continue to use them and learn.			
9. Response to intervention is appropriate.			

Feedback

Strengths	
Recommendations	

Example A: Pass Response

Each selected indicator from the various differentiated observation tools (Figure 7.4) is placed on a separate large piece of paper. The faculty members sit at tables in small interest groups. Each group is given one numbered subtopic from the observation form. The group brainstorms the attributes, characteristics, and ideas included in an ideal differentiated classroom. A recorder writes individual responses on the large paper. The session leader gives a signal for the groups to pass the papers to a nearby group. They read the posted responses and add their brainstorming ideas. Continue to rotate the papers until they are filled. Post the large sheets around the room, and provide time for the groups to take a gallery walk. This offers teachers and administrators new insights and interpretations of each expectation. The responses deepen an observer's understanding of the aspects of differentiation to identify when conducting a classroom visitation.

Example B: Self-Assessment of Differentiated Instruction

Give each teacher a copy of the observation form (Figure 7.4) for a personalized self-assessment of implementing differentiated instruction. Ask participants to fill in each section and then meet with a partner, department, grade-level group, team, or interest group to compare and discuss their notes. After the sharing session, individuals set short-term improvement goals.

Example C: Carousel Gala

The Carousel Gala (Figure 7.5) is an effective activity for a professional development session. The data gathered show which areas of differentiated instruction are being implemented, viewed, and interpreted by the group. The following examples present various ways to use this grid:

1. Select the items from the observation form that are appropriate for the group's stage of implementation or interest.

2. Place each selected statement or question for Figure 7.5 on the top of a sheet of chart paper or large wipe-off board. Place these items around the room to create a carousel.

3. Groups of three to five are assigned to each statement or question.

4. The group reads the question or statement. A recorder lists the shared individual responses.

5. After the group presents some answers, the session leader gives a signal for each group to move to the next poster in the carousel. The group reads the question and responses from the previous group. The recorder adds new brainstormed responses from individual group members. This procedure continues until all posters are filled.

The following directions may be used as a culminating activity for the Carousel Gala.

1. The participants move to the next chart and take it back to their table.

2. Each group reads and compiles the recorded information and adds new ideas to the original list.

3. The group comes to consensus on two or three of the most important items to improve differentiated instruction.

4. A spokesperson in each group shares highlights from that group's chart and discussions with the total group.

Figure 7.5 Carousel Gala			
How do you differentiate curriculum?			
1. Name your favorite preassessment tools for students. *Informal Formal*	2. List effective assessment tools to use during the learning. *Informal Formal*	3. List useful, evaluative tools to use at the end of the learning. *Informal Formal*	4. How do you get to know your students?
5. Brainstorm components of an effective learning environment.	6. How and when do you use flexible grouping?	7. Name ways to move students into groups.	8. How do you challenge gifted students?
9. List tips for using a variety of assignments to meet individual needs.	10. List various activities for independent work assignments.	11. Provide tips for using academic contracts.	12. Brainstorm effective ways to provide choice.
13. What do you need to remember when assigning projects?	14. How do you motivate students to learn?	15. How do you teach students to become independent thinkers?	16. How will differentiated instruction help you with curriculum mapping?

THE ADMINISTRATOR'S SUPPORT ■ ROLE FOR IMPLEMENTING DIFFERENTIATED INSTRUCTION

1. Remember, change happens gradually.

- Become familiar with all aspects of differentiated instruction so your knowledge base is accurate. For example, one myth related to differentiation is that the teacher must have groups throughout the class period. Group instruction is *one* way, not the only way, to implement differentiated instruction.
- Differentiate professional development to guide teachers on their paths to differentiation. Each teacher is unique in professional knowledge, experience, and interest in implementing this philosophy.
- Realize that educators often go through a state of dissonance when asked to abandon teaching beliefs and replace them with new approaches. In this state, they have a tendency to cling to familiar, successful practices as they become aware of their need to change.
- Teachers readily embrace a new program or strategy when they see the value in its effectiveness and are convinced it is better than "their way."
- Everyone is differentiating to some extent without realizing it. Start by "tweaking" the effective strategies and/or activities, and then add new ones. Help teachers see and celebrate their current approaches to differentiation. Guide them to see that they don't have to change every aspect of instruction.

2. Provide support.

- Make newsletters and morning announcements highlighting teacher successes.
- Present highlights and kudos for teachers who are implementing differentiation in their classrooms. Give specific praise statements from the observation.
- Encourage teachers to submit their classroom success stories in newsletter articles, morning announcements, or "stardom time" during faculty meetings.
- Submit happenings, articles, and pictures to the local, state, and national newspapers and education journals.
- During morning announcements, let students showcase their learning.
- Spotlight a teacher! Select a DI Teacher of the Month and showcase the ways he or she is addressing differentiated instruction to meet the learners' needs.
- Encourage parents, local business people, and community members to attend events showcasing differentiation.
- Have students share their portfolios with parents and peers.
- Schedule sharing times for teachers to brag about professional growth, a new activity, or a funny story.

- Compile lists of improvements made by individual teachers, grade-level teams, subject-area teams, or pod partners. When teachers share their plans and strategies to benefit learners, they become a stronger professional learning community.
- Provide time for group sharing at faculty, professional development, and/or grade-level meetings.
- Place signs around the school promoting and reflecting student success.
- Display and showcase artifacts representing the information students are learning. Place the artifact displays in classrooms, hallways, media centers, and other common areas.
- Host a "Sharing Party." Teachers yearn to learn new ideas.
- Host an expert breakfast so everyone can share what is working and not working. Remind teachers to address problems that can be solved. Focusing on problems that cannot be solved zaps energy, kills momentum, and wastes time.

3. Conduct classroom visits.

- When engaged in a pop-in visit during a lesson, leave a sticky note stating how you saw differentiated instruction being practiced.
- Walk into every classroom every day so students and teachers see you. It is important to be visible and to speak to each staff member.
- Remember, when giving suggestions for improvement, discuss aspects of instruction you saw working well before and after you identify a weakness or need.
- As you tour the school, identify spots alive with creativity as a result of outstanding teaching. Give specific praise and positive feedback to the teacher.
- Create a school scavenger hunt. Form teams to go on the hunt at a faculty meeting. Assign several things from notes made on your tour, and ask the teachers to locate them in the school. They identify the place the item or display is located and note ways to use the generated ideas to promote student learning in their classrooms. Call on individuals to share highlights from the scavenger hunt. Celebrate the discoveries!

4. Provide quality professional development opportunities.

Such opportunities might include the following:

- Strategic planning to teach standards
- Curriculum mapping
- Professional learning communities
- Planning with subject and grade-level teams
- Ongoing training sessions in faculty meetings, workshops, in-services, and retreats

5. Be a catalyst for differentiation.

- Plan professional interactions strategically using the most effective tools.
- Believe you can make a difference for learners and the staff each day.
- Tweak or adapt your leadership strategies for the unique needs of learners and staff.
- Believe in the philosophy that all students CAN learn.
- Share your success with colleagues in addressing differentiated strategies.

Figure 7.6 Personal Reflections for Putting It All Together

1. Complete Figure 7.1, the self-analysis chart on page 229. Check the appropriate boxes to indicate your implementation level for each category. Analyze the results. Use the results to set self-improvement goals. Revisit the chart often, and watch your differentiated instruction implementation growth.

2. How do you plan for mastery learning of a standard?

3. Identify an area of differentiated instruction to improve. Ask a peer or coach to use the checklist while observing your lesson. Request constructive feedback in a formal discussion or conference.

4. Hide a tape recorder in the room. Record yourself while teaching. Analyze your needs and strengths. Target two to three areas for improvement.

5. Develop a lesson plan by following the step-by-step plan for designing the differentiated lesson on page 000.

Figure 7.7 Five Activities for a Performance Learning Community (PLC) Study

1. Carousel Gala
   a. Make a copy of the grid in Figure 7.5 for each member of the study team.
   b. Follow the plan presented for the activity on page 249.
   c. Ask a volunteer to compile the teams' ideas and distribute a copy to each participant for classroom use.

2. Observations and Conferences
   a. Have members individually study Figure 7.4 and identify an area for improvement.
   b. Complete the pass response activity outlined on page 249 to collect team members' ideas and suggestions for improving differentiated instruction.
   c. Form partner teams with members who selected similar areas for improvement.
   d. Partners discuss each observation entry related to their growth needs.

(Continued)

(Continued)

    e. A time is scheduled for partners to take turns observing and teaching a lesson. Each one takes notes during the lesson. Afterward, they have a conference to share feedback and make constructive suggestions for improvement.

    f. During the next PLC session, partners share highlights from their observation and conference experiences. They discuss the role of partner work in the professional growth process.

3. Planning Grid for Differentiated Instruction

    a. Have each participant bring a copy of a lesson plan to a study session. Allow time for members to analyze the segments included and identify the segments omitted.

    b. Ask each member to identify improvement goals for future implementation.

    c. Have interest teams or partners develop lesson plans following the step-by-step procedure.

    d. Tell the groups to discuss each step as it is addressed.

4. Great and Getting Greater!

    a. Ask class members to individually brainstorm the growth statements made during the study.

    b. Have each participant explain how the improvements are evident in his or her teaching.

    c. Create a class list of the professional growth statements.

    d. Have the class repeat the following phrase in unison:
       "We are great and getting greater!"

5. Sharing Blast

    a. Ask individual members to share students' work including displays, PowerPoint presentations, posters, artifacts and portfolio entries that represent the study's impact on teaching and learning.

    b. Share "aha" moments and highlights from the PLC study.

    c. Celebrate learning!

THE KEY TO PLANNING AND ORGANIZING STANDARD-BASED INSTRUCTION: DIFFERENTIATE! ■

The following acrostic provides a way to view the key components of differentiated instruction. Grade-level teams or interest groups can create personalized acrostics to describe their differentiated classrooms.

Determine the standards and concepts to teach.

Identify student needs with strong assessment tools before, during, and after learning.

Formulate lesson plans to link the targeted standards with individual needs.

Find effective strategies and activities to teach the information.

Engage students in activities employing their interests and ways they learn.

Relate learning to the students' worlds.

Encourage risk taking with wise choices.

Nurture the social and emotional aspects of students.

Target the learners' needs with flexible grouping designs.

Ignite each student's desire to learn.

Adjust assignments to match the learner's abilities, knowledge levels, and interests.

Tailor lessons for the standards with active, customized learning activities.

Entice and ignite lifelong learning!

CONCLUSION ■

Prepare to chart your course by assessing the strengths and weaknesses of your crew, and use their talents in meaningful, intriguing ways. Teach standards by using innovative, challenging assignments to motivate learners. Remember, a key to learning is engagement. Develop a quality differentiated classroom to nurture and support individuals in their learning adventure, and you will have a happy, productive crew!

OUR HATS ARE OFF TO YOU!

References and Suggested Readings

Achieve, Inc. (2010, August). *Aligning assessments with the Common Core State Standards.* Retrieved from http://www.ode.state.or.us/wma/teachlearn/commoncore/ccssassessments.pdf

Barkley, S. (2005). *Wow! Adding pizzazz to teaching and learning.* Allentown, PA: Performance Learning Systems.

Beattie, J., Jordan, L., & Algozinne, R. (2007). *Making inclusion work: Effective practices for all teachers.* Thousand Oaks, CA: Corwin.

Carnine, D. W., Silbert, J., Kame'enui, E. J., & Tarver, S. G. (2009, April 5). *Direct instruction reading* (5th ed.). Upper Saddle River, NJ: Pearson.

Chapman, C. (1993). *If the shoe fits.* Thousand Oaks, CA: Corwin.

Chapman, C., & King, R. (2009a). *Differentiated instructional strategies for writing in the content areas* (2nd ed.). Thousand Oaks, CA: Corwin.

Chapman, C., & King, R. (2009b). *Test success in the brain-compatible classroom* (2nd ed.). Thousand Oaks, CA: Corwin.

Chapman, C., & King, R. (2012). *Differentiated assessment strategies: One size doesn't fit all* (2nd ed.). Thousand, CA: Corwin.

Chapman, C., & Vagle, N. (2011). *Motivating students: 25 strategies to light the fire of engagement.* Bloomington, IN: Solution Tree Press.

Conley, D. T. (2003). *Understanding university success: A report from standards for success.* Eugene, OR: Center for Educational Policy Research.

DuFour, R., & Mattos, M. (2013). How do principals really improve schools? *Educational Leadership, 70*(7), 37.

Dunkle, C. A. (2012). *Leading the Common Core State Standards: From common sense to common practice.* Thousand Oaks, CA: Corwin.

Frey, N. E., & Frey, D. B. (2010). *Enhancing RTI: How to ensure success with effective classroom instruction and intervention.* Alexandria, VA: Association for Supervision and Curriculum Development.

Gardner, H. (2006). *Multiple intelligences: New horizons in theory and practice.* New York: Perseus Books Group.

Goleman, D., Kaufman, P., & Ray, M. (1993). *The creative spirit.* New York: Plume.

Gregory, G., & Chapman, C. (2012). *Differentiated instructional strategies: One size doesn't fit all* (3rd ed.). Thousand Oaks, CA: Corwin.

Hayes Jacobs, H. (Ed.). (2010). *Curriculum 21: Essential education for a changing world.* Alexandria, VA: Association for Supervision and Curriculum Development.

Haynes, J. (2007). *Getting started with English language learners: How educators can meet the challenge.* Alexandria, VA: Association for Supervision and Curriculum Development.

McTighe, J., & Wiggins, G. (2013). *Essential questions: Opening doors to student understanding.* Alexandria, VA: Association for Supervision and Curriculum Development.

National Center on Response to Intervention. (2012). *Essential components of RTI: A closer look at Response to Intervention.* Retrieved from http://www.rti4success.org/pdf/rtiessentialcomponents_042710.pdf

National Governors Association and Council of Chief State School Officers. (2010). *Common Core State Standards Initiative: Preparing America's students for college and career.* Retrieved from http://www.corestandards.org/

Partnership for Assessment of Readiness for College and Careers. (2010, June). *The Partnership for Assessment of Readiness for College and Careers (PARCC) application for the Race to the Top comprehensive assessment systems competition.* Retrieved from http://www.fldoe.org/parcc/pdf/apprtcasc.pdf

Schmoker, M. (2011). *Focus: Elevating the essentials to radically improve student learning.* Alexandria, VA: Association for Supervision and Curriculum Development.

Silver, H. F., Dewing, T., & Perini, M. (2012). *The core six: Essential strategies to achieving excellence with the common core.* Alexandria, VA: Association for Supervision and Curriculum Development.

Sousa, D. (2011). *How the brain learns* (4th ed.). Thousand Oaks, CA: Corwin.

Sternberg, R., & Grigorenko, E. (2007). *Teaching for successful intelligences: To increase student learning and achievement* (2nd ed.). Thousand Oaks, CA: Corwin.

Sylwester, R. (2007). *The adolescent brain: Reaching for autonomy.* Thousand Oaks, CA: Corwin.

Tomlinson, C. A., & Imbeau, M. B. (2010). *Leading and managing a differentiated classroom.* Alexandria, VA: Association of Supervision and Curriculum Development.

Tomlinson, C. A., & McTighe, J. (2006). *Integrating differentiated instruction and understanding by design.* Alexandria, VA: Association for Supervision and Curriculum Development.

U.S. Department of Education. (2010, March). *A blueprint for reform: The reauthorization of the Elementary and Secondary Education Act.* Washington, DC: Author.

Vaughn, S. (2011). *Response to Intervention in reading for English language learners.* Retrieved from http://www.rtinetwork.org/learn/diversity/englishlanguagelearners

Index